FIRST LOVES ARE FOREVER

(My True-Life Fairy Tale)

Brett Berson

Copyright © 2016 Brett Berson

Hardcover ISBN: 978-1-63491-182-5
Paperback ISBN: 978-1-63491-183-2

All rights reserved. No part of this publication may be reproduced, stored in a retrieval system, or transmitted in any form or by any means, electronic, mechanical, recording or otherwise, without the prior written permission of the author.

Published by BookLocker.com, Inc., Bradenton, Florida.

Printed on acid-free paper.

BookLocker.com, Inc.
2016

First Edition

Cover Photograph by Jeff Urquhart

Dedication

There's only one person to whom this book can be dedicated. She knows who she is, and, dear reader, so will you.

Foreword

Our story begins like every fairytale: "Once upon a time, long ago and far away…" And, we hope, it will end like every fairytale: "…and they lived happily ever after." In between are excitement, and passion, and wonder, like every love story. So what's special about me and Alana? Boy meets girl, boy loses girl, boy gets girl…It was the best of times; it was the worst of times…Haven't we heard it all before, in every iteration possible? But what makes this story different and unique is that it is entirely real and accurate: a modern-day romance that is as miraculous as a novel, too fantastic to believe, but all true nonetheless. I still pinch myself and wonder if I'm sleeping. But so far I haven't woken up. I hope I never will. So here's a story that will strain your credulity. But again—believe it or not—it's all true. It's a story for lovers and dreamers and believers, who wish to believe sometimes dreams do come true…

PART I

Chapter 1

April 26

It began like every other ordinary Monday. As usual I slept poorly. As usual my alarm was set for 5:30. As usual I got out of bed at 5:15. I did what I do every morning...I took a quick shower, had a cup of coffee, pulled on my nondescript surgical scrubs, and drove to my office in the dawn of a late April south Florida morning. It was already hot and humid by 6:30, when I got out of my car. The A/C is automatically turned off all weekend in the office building, so it's usually stifling inside and even hard to breathe. I'm always the first person in the parking lot, the first person in the building, the first person in the office, the first person to log on, and the first person to turn on the lights and greet the staff. It was a Monday morning like any other.

And the day started like all others. Effie, the receptionist, came in at 7 and prepared the front desk for the first patient, who arrived at 7:30 for an 8 o'clock appointment. Fanny, my medical assistant, showed up at 7:59, a little rushed and harried, as usual. Yvonne, the office manager, came in shortly after 8, as usual. The usual parade of patients rolled in, with the usual list of ailments, the usual complaints and requests for meds, or forms, or disability, and always looking for sympathy. After twenty-three years, I've calculated that I've seen close to 250,000 patients. By now they are a faceless and nameless stream, never-ending, continuously flowing by with barely a ripple. The beginning and the end are nowhere to be seen. I stand on the bank, watching this mass of humanity floating by, barely disturbing the flow, barely touched by those I've pledged to help, heal, save. The innocence, optimism, idealism of the long-ago medical student had given way under a lifetime of boredom and emptiness and disappointment. I was too numb even to wonder how it had come to this, or why, or where to go from there? The silence was deafening, and the ennui crushing. I think my public face appeared normal, even interested. Internally was a hollowness that was bottomless, infinite, seemingly eternal.

So it was just another day like any other. Or so it seemed…and then something happened, not with a bang but with a whisper; not even a whisper, but the faintest hint of a shift in the wind, a barely perceptible but undeniable disturbance in the ether causing an unfamiliar imbalance in the forces that defined my universe; call it what you will, but something had happened, something that, without warning, would slowly gather steam and momentum until it rocked my world and changed my life forever. I never saw it coming.

Chapter 2

"...keep your cast dry, elevate for pain and swelling, and come back in a week. If you have any problems before then, give me a call. We'll check the X-rays then, and see if you're ready for therapy."

I came back into my office to dictate my note, sat down at my desk, and opened the patient's electronic medical record. Ever since we went "paperless," I spend more time dealing with my computer than with my patients—electronic medical records, voice-recognition dictation, digital X-rays that appear on my desktop screen. Our zeal to become more efficient through technology has distanced me from my patients. I may be more efficient as a record-keeper but am less connected; the therapeutic touch has been replaced by high-tech wizardry, sophisticated scans and techniques that are full of promise, devoid of good old-fashioned hearing and feeling and caring. My dad was a general practitioner who spent thirty-five years in a two-room office with one nurse and, without any tools but his hands and his heart, he took better care of generations of patients than anyone I knew. His soul and saintliness were powerful therapies indeed! He was an amazing role model—as a dad, as a doctor, and as a human being. I always tried to be a physician in his image.

So I finished my note, and quickly scanned through my emails before moving on to my next patient. I saw the usual: general notices from various hospital staff offices; online credit card and bank statements; Word of the Day...and one from "Alana," subject "old friend." I had only known one Alana in my life, and so long ago that it couldn't have been the same person! Who could this "Alana" be?

I was glad for any excuse to stay at my desk a few extra minutes. So I opened the email and read the following:

"Hi Brett,

"I was looking on the ACS website and found your profile. It made me start to wonder how you are doing and what life is like for you in Florida.

"I am practicing breast surgery on Long Island. I am married and have a 17 year old son. Mom lives across the street from me and my dad passed away 2 years ago at age 89.

"How is your practice? Your life? Your family?

"I am going to my 25th medical college reunion in NYC on 5/22. I can't believe it has been that long since I graduated.

"Hope you and your family are well.

"Love, Alana"

I went off to see my next patient with a curious excitement I hadn't felt in many years. After all this time…Alana…What's up with *this*? I couldn't wait to get back to my desk. The longest journey begins with the first step, and little did I know that I had already taken mine.

Chapter 3

I went through the motions with Jesus Ramirez, an injured worker with back pain. He spoke little English, I speak no Spanish, and so a translator was present, who must have been new at this because she didn't get the basics of interpreting. She kept talking while I was speaking (rather than waiting until I paused), so it took not just twice as long but four times as long (and wondering about Alana made it feel like ten times as long!) Eventually—probably no longer than five minutes later, but which felt like an eternity—I sat down again at my desk to re-read the email. How could this be? Alana? *Alana*??!!!! The familiar office walls began to recede and shimmer a little (just like a dream sequence in a movie). I remembered a young girl named Alana from the distant past, from so long ago it felt like a previous lifetime. "Al" was my first serious girlfriend, whom I had met when I was eighteen and had last seen almost thirty years before. I knew immediately that I would be writing back. But what was she expecting, and what could she possibly want with me after all these years? My heart was racing, and I had no idea what to write. But I started typing, and surprised myself ...

"What a very nice surprise to hear from you! It has been a long time but I have thought of you often and fondly over these many years. You sound well, and I hope you're enjoying your surgical practice after all it took to get there. I graduated from medical school 32 years ago! I've been a doctor for longer than I haven't been a doctor!! Somehow the years really have flown by.

"After finishing my orthopaedic residency I went to San Diego for a fellowship in Joint Replacement surgery. It was a good time for me to be leaving NYC because my father, who always took proper care of himself, developed metastatic pancreatic cancer and died within 3 months of being diagnosed at age 68. That was in July 1987, and I was glad to get away and head west. I still think of, and miss, him every day. My mother is still alive and lives in your old stomping grounds at North Shore Towers. She is now 87, and, unfortunately, suffering from Alzheimer's disease. She still knows who I am, but I dread the day when I call or see her, and she doesn't recognize me. I'm sure that day isn't too far off. But she is physically healthy, has no pain, and is happy as a clam. So at least she is not suffering at all, which is a blessing.

"I'm sorry to hear about your Dad. I still remember when he and your Mom went to Cleveland for his kidney surgery. Apparently it worked wonders if he lived to 89! And I'm glad your Mom is alive, I hope well, and living near you. Please give her my regards.

"I moved from San Diego to South Florida in 1995 when managed care came in with a vengeance and California was going bust (which it still is). I loved living in San Diego, but it became impossible to make a living there as a physician. My whole group of 4 guys all left, along with an exodus of hundreds of others because the economy was so poor. Things have been somewhat better in South Florida although we're all feeling the crunch, and, I'm sorry to say, it will only get worse with the new healthcare reforms.

"I have a 26 year old daughter who has been the love of my life. She graduated from the University of Florida with a degree in Elementary Education, got a Masters from U. of P., and is now getting a second Masters in Library Science from Pratt. So she remains on the payroll (still largely mine) but may get a job someday. Her fiancé and I are hoping! She lives in Manhattan, and I try to get to see her whenever possible.

"I have patients waiting so I will sign off for now. Thank you so much for writing. It's been nice, if only for a few minutes, to get back in touch with that 18-year old boy who spent New Year's Eve with you, Eddie, and Dale 40 years ago! To be perfectly honest, you're the one old flame that never went out, and I still carry deep feelings for you.

"All my very best wishes to you and yours.
"Love,
Brett"

I hesitated for a brief moment, then pressed "Send" and got up to see my next patient.

Chapter 4

The rest of the day passed in a blur—Alana! Why did she write to me? After all these years! What could she want? Why now? It seemed like a different lifetime when I had known Alana, so long ago, "in my salad days when I was green in judgment," as Shakespeare said. I had buried that part of my life, but I could still remember what she was like, what I was like back then. Alana! We met on a blind date one New Year's Eve, set up and double-dating with her cousin and my best friend. We had a whirlwind romance that lasted two and a half years, a lifetime when you're eighteen. I wondered if I would hear back from her. Was I too forward by telling her I still had "deep feelings"? What the hell…If she weren't open to that, why would she have written? She must still have some feelings, or else why would she reach out?…What was her agenda?

I couldn't stop thinking about her…After so long…it seemed surreal…Was I dreaming?

I went about my business, seeing one patient after another. After all these years, I could almost function on autopilot. There may be 1000 possible musculoskeletal diagnoses patients present with, but 90 percent are one of the ten most common ones. Medical knowledge supposedly doubles every five years, but common things are common, and most of my patients fell in the very middle of the bell-shaped curve. Although I tried to read orthopaedics nearly every day and stay up-to-date with the literature, the more I read, the more I realized that major discoveries are few and far between, and, despite the popular media, very little has changed regarding most orthopaedic problems in the past twenty-five years. So I continued to smile, appear engaged, nod my head, ask the right questions, dictate the right notes, fill out the right paperwork—when, all the time, I was "long ago and far away," wondering if some major phase-shift were about to occur in my life. *At this late (st)age?*

FIRST LOVES ARE FOREVER

My life had been so steady for so long—not particularly good, not particularly bad, just very steady. I had given up on finding true happiness and the "meaning of life" long ago. My marriage was not what I had hoped for (whose is?), and I had grown to accept an okay life, considering the alternatives. I had a healthy, grown daughter, I was healthy, my practice was successful, and there were no major disasters in the past or in the foreseeable future. I never really liked risky adventures, roller coasters and the like...so I was accepting, if not satisfied, content, or fulfilled. I thought that all my life's "dramas" were behind me, and my life would simply play itself out with the script that had been already written and finalized. My job was merely to show up.

My marriage had been one of those that probably should never have happened. I got married at the wrong time and for the wrong reasons, and, not surprisingly, things didn't work out. It is amazing that it lasted so long, twenty-five years—a combination of refusal to accept failure, refusal to face divorce, a focus on work, the love of my daughter, and belief in the sanctity of the nuclear family. Divorce was certainly not alien to me—most of my friends had been divorced at least once. But divorce was foreign to my family. No one in my family was divorced— not one person. They weren't necessarily happily married, but they never chose divorce. My father was a staunch believer that everything was genetic—*everything*, including behavior, beliefs, etc. He was way ahead of his time in that respect. I always knew he was very bright, but in this belief he was a true pioneer. I grew up in an age when psychotherapy was coming into its own as a science, and more available to the everyman, not just the neurotic Hollywood celebrities and crazed rock stars. The average middle-aged suburban housewife was allowed the luxury of emotional problems, post-partum depression, panic attacks, anxiety disorders, and the like. And the various popular psychotherapeutic/psychoanalytic theories of that time claimed validation and justification by endorsing nurture over nature as the pivotal determinant of one's personality and psychopathology. But my dad didn't believe that. Years of treating generations of patients lent him wisdom and insight into human behavior that few others possess. He believed that, by and large, our destiny is determined the moment sperm meets egg, and everything after is just manifestation of that chemistry.

I grew up believing the popular mythology that one's upbringing influences, if not determines, one's development. But as I've gotten older, I have come around to my dad's way of thinking, and perhaps even to a greater extent than he. Certainly physical qualities are genetic. Most mental attributes, including intelligence, are genetic. And I even believe that most emotional and personality elements are genetic. How else to explain the ease and aplomb with which some people navigate through one divorce after another, without missing a beat, while others, including myself, stay married despite all reason and logic dictating failure? There must be a "divorce gene" somewhere on the human genome, but it was missing on mine because I was absolutely stuck in my marriage. I wasn't afraid of divorce, of the process, of the cost…I wasn't afraid of being alone…and there were certainly very few positives keeping me in the marriage. But year after year I stayed married, not because I had any hope that things would improve, but because divorce was not for me, regardless of the consequences of a failed marriage. I had been a true romantic in my youth, and felt that finding love was undoubtedly the Holy Grail of human existence. As years went by, I had to face the fact that I would never drink from that intoxicating cup. Because of my aversion to divorce, I rarely indulged the fantasy of "What if…?" But every now and then I would look off into the distance, and the haunting voice of "I could have been a contender!" would suddenly permeate my insulation and defenses, and a deep sense of sorrow and emptiness would momentarily strike, until I could regain my balance and composure.

Over the years I learned how to survive in my marriage—how to accentuate the positives, and essentially ignore the negatives. My work was satisfying and interesting so I threw myself into my practice of orthopaedic surgery as much as I could. But my greatest love was my daughter. Jennifer was my wife's child from a previous marriage, and I had fallen in love more with Jenn as a toddler than I had with her mom.

Then, just when things seemed to be going smoothly and as well as could be expected, the unthinkable and unimaginable happened, and everything suddenly went haywire.

Chapter 5

I finished seeing my last patient around 6 p.m., took care of some last-minute business, and couldn't stop thinking of Alana. I was about to log off my desktop and head home when I saw another email "re: old friend"! This one was much longer, and I was very surprised. I didn't know if I'd hear back from her at all, and certainly didn't expect such a rapid response. One question was answered: Alana had more than just a passing curiosity.

"Dear Brett:
"Thank you for taking the time to fill me in on what you have been doing for the past 32 years. I am sorry to learn that your father died at such a young age. It must have been devastating for you and your family. How are your siblings? Do you keep in close contact with them?

"Where is Plantation, Florida? Is it unbearably hot in the summer?

"My son is interested in looking at U Florida in Gainesville because it has a good business program, but very difficult to get in from out of state. He has no interest in medicine and that is fine with me. I don't know if business is a good choice either but he is still young and may stumble upon an interesting field in college. My cousin Karen (Dale's sister) is a dean of the medical school at U of Va. It is a magnificent school and I would love for my son to go there but he is not in the top 5% of his class.

"I live about 25 minutes from your mother. It would be wonderful to see you when you come to visit.

"Let's try to keep in touch.
"Love, Alana"

I sat for a few minutes and re-read the email a few times, trying to figure it out. I was looking for a hidden meaning, something between the lines. She has a son preparing to go to college. She's writing to an old boyfriend. She wrote earlier that she is married, but clearly something isn't going well and she's looking for something. "It would be wonderful to see you when you come to visit," she had written. Is it *me* she's looking for?

I needed to think about this before replying. I wasn't sure if I *should* reply, but I knew I would. I had never cheated on my wife, despite twenty-five years of an unhappy, unsatisfying marriage. I had had opportunities, and temptations, but wouldn't consider an affair unless I was prepared for the consequences and ready for a divorce. I'd never been willing to consider it.

But there was only one Alana in my life. And as I drove the twenty miles from my office to my home, I kept rubbing the eyes of my hindsight, trying to wipe away the dust and cobwebs and improve my focus. I pulled into the garage and spent an extra minute in the car, bringing myself back to current reality, before going in. I knew what to expect inside, and wasn't sure if I was ready for this unexpected development, and the potential minefield ahead. But I knew that great rewards usually result from taking great risks. I was certainly ready for some great rewards!

I switched to auto-pilot when I got home, going through the daily, routine motions that comprised my so-called "activities of daily living": bringing the empty garbage cans up from the foot of the driveway, picking up the newspaper from its usual spot in the front bushes, bringing in the mail.

As usual, my wife Sharon had already eaten dinner and was sitting on the couch watching TV. My standard black poodle was lying next to her, heard me come in, and stood up looking at the back door. When I came in, Shanee jumped off the couch and came over to me, her tail wagging, her pink tongue moving as she panted.

"Hi, girl," I said, putting out my hand for her to lick. "What a good girl you are!" Sharon never looked up or said anything. She always seemed angry, ostensibly because I worked long hours although I doubt that was the real reason. I did work long and hard, but likely because I was so unhappy at home. I would so much rather have enjoyed some down time, but that was never my experience. When I was off from work, on weekends and holidays, Sharon still didn't seem happy. She never wanted to do anything or go anywhere. She had very particular eating habits, and wouldn't eat out very often, and only in one of two restaurants near the house. Although I made more than enough money to support a comfortable lifestyle, she was frugal as could be, and always acted as though she were doing me a favor by "saving your money." I never wanted to save more than I had to. My father and both his brothers had died at age sixty-eight. I hoped that would not be my fate, but I knew that life is short, and my "longevity gene" may be shorter than most. I was caught in an impossible situation, and knew that I could never make Sharon happy, no matter what I did. She inherited the "unhappiness gene" from her mother, who was certifiably miserable and generously showered her misery on everyone around her. She inherited the "entitlement gene" from her father, and, once married, she felt that she was entitled to be taken care of with little to no input or obligation on her part. Sadly, I was stuck, paralyzed, without any traction to get out of this marriage. Had I joined Thoreau's "mass of men leading lives of quiet desperation"? My God, I hoped not, but realized that I probably had.

Until now...maybe this was the push that I needed to get off the dime and overcome my marital inertia?

I came over and said hello to Sharon. She looked up and said, "Hi," and murmured "How was your day?" in a disinterested tone. "Fine," I said, "and yours?" "Okay," she replied.

And with those nine words our conversation for the day was essentially over. I went into the bedroom to change and shower. I looked through the day's mail—the usual bills, bank statements, an expected invitation to a wedding of a friend of my daughter Jennifer's scheduled for the following month, and the requisite throwaway ads and magazines. By the time I was finished, Sharon had warmed up my dinner, put it on the table, and returned to the couch. I sat down to eat dinner alone, as I did most nights. But this night, unlike most, I didn't feel resentful or unappreciated. In fact, I was glad not to have to make small talk, which I had to do all day every day at work. Besides Jennifer, Sharon and I seemed to have less and less in common as the years went by. It's amazing how little we had to say to each other. I'm reminded of the old joke, "What's the longest sentence in the English language?" Sadly the answer is simply, "I do." My sentence so far had been twenty-five-years-to-life.

But on this night I was grateful to be left alone. I smiled inside and amused myself by rhetorically posing the famous "Four Questions" of Passover: "Why is this night different from all other nights?" But I modified the traditional biblical answers with my own spin, apropos to that day's events:

On all other nights I sit alone at the table wondering how it has come to this? But on this night, I have other, far more pleasant thoughts in mind.

On all other nights I sit alone at the table, planning my office and surgery schedule for the next day; but on this night I am a million miles away.

On all other nights I sit alone at the table exhausted, with little to look forward to but getting up tomorrow morning and doing it all over again; but on this night I allow myself the guilty pleasure of recalling happier days from my youth, when any dream seemed possible and my life's potential was limitless.

On all other nights I feel old and tired; but on this night I feel young and full of life.

The Passover Seder celebrates the Jewish exodus from Egypt, leaving behind a life of slavery for a new life of freedom, self-determination, and an uncertain future, but one filled with hope and promise. Perhaps I too was about to embark on such a journey, not knowing what lay ahead but glad to escape from what lay behind, regardless of the risks and uncertainties. I slowly ate my rotisserie chicken (precooked at the local supermarket, but not bad nonetheless) as I enjoyed my little fantasy.

My heart was pounding, my thoughts were racing, and I felt excited…feelings that seemed vaguely familiar from a distant past. I was busy thinking of the events of my day, and of what I was going to write to Alana the next day. I slept unusually well that night, and awoke to the dawn of the first day of the rest of my life.

Chapter 6

April 27

"Dear Alana:

"Tuesday is my OR day. Until recently I still took ER call and did quite a bit of trauma work. But working nights and weekends, rounding at different hospitals, and still trying to maintain a daily office schedule is hectic, to say the least, so my practice has become primarily elective general orthopaedics, adult reconstructive surgery, etc.—mostly sports medicine now, knee and shoulder arthroscopies, occasional fractures, basic hand and elbow procedures. I did find the ER and the big cases exciting, but the sacrifices are enormous, and I think I've done my fair share. I very much respect and admire the work that you do. It must be extremely challenging and difficult to work with cancer patients on a daily basis; but the rewards must be equally huge. Every day, countless times, you are the central person at the crossroads of someone's life. Your work has an enormous effect, both on your patients and their entire "community" (family, friends, etc.). You have the opportunity to really make a difference over and over and over. That's a special place to be, and a very special job. You should be very very proud of yourself and your work. I salute you!

"My father's death had a profound impact on me. You didn't know my parents as well as I knew yours. My father was a very special man—the most ethical and decent man I ever met, truly dedicated to his work and his patients, honest, and, above all, kind. His very sudden passing left a huge void in my world. I still tear up a bit when I think of him.

"My older brother still lives in DC. He practiced pulmonary medicine for many years, but the financial strain of medical malpractice eventually took its toll and drove him out of clinical practice. He, too, was a great clinician—great pedigree (Brown, Harvard, the NIH), also a very caring and loving person. The fact that he had to give up taking care of patients speaks volumes about the failure of our healthcare system. He's now doing administrative work for the government (Medicare). He enjoys it, but there's something special about medical practice that he will always miss.

"My sister became an attorney, lives in Westchester, and has FIVE DAUGHTERS!!! She is well, and, obviously, very busy.

"Unfortunately I never did have a very close relationship with my siblings, and still don't. I don't know why, exactly. My brother left for college when he was 16, and never really spent much time coming back home. My sister had her own issues. They're both well, although we're estranged.

"My brother has 2 adult children—a son and daughter. Neither one has any interest in medicine, and he never pushed them in that direction. My daughter, likewise, never thought of being a doctor, and I'm not sorry about that either. Medicine is very different today than it was when we first entered the field, and it will be even more different for the next generation, and, sadly, not better.

"Fortunately I do enjoy what I do and taking care of patients. My Dad said, "Do what you love and you'll never work a day in your life!" He was right. But Julius Erving ("Dr. J") said, "Being a professional is doing the things you love to do, even on the days when you don't feel like doing it." He's right, too.

"Plantation, Florida is in western Fort Lauderdale, about 10 miles from the ocean. It *is* unbearably hot in the summer, but I never really liked the cold weather, so it seems a good compromise for me. The University of Florida is a terrific school. My daughter spent almost 5 years there, so I spent a lot of time in Gainesville. The school itself has become a world class university—very strong academically with excellent graduate schools (Medicine, Dentistry, Law, Veterinary, Business, etc). And it's also a very fun campus to be on. I'm not sure how fanatic you are about sports (having a teenage son you're probably nearly as fanatic as I am), but UF has terrific sports teams and great college spirit. I went with my daughter to both BCS championships, the NCAA championship, and have seen many a game at "the Swamp." Nothing wrong with having some fun while you're getting a great education.

"Hope you're having a good day.
"Love,
Brett"

It was 4 p.m. when I pressed "Send". It was hard to believe that only one day had passed since my last email. Already I was thinking ahead, waiting to hear from Alana, *wanting to hear from Alana!!* For the first time in so long, I was looking forward to something, and dared hope that I really had something to look forward to. I felt the faintest warmth of long-forgotten, buried, smoldering embers within my chest, my gut, my privates. These feelings were vaguely familiar, but so distant in memory and experience as to be almost unrecognizable. I, who usually felt so cool, calm, collected, controlled, in charge, now sensed that pleasant flutter of excitement and anticipation of something exciting and unknown, though I was afraid to unleash my imagination and let myself dream, or even hope. I had spent so long shutting myself down! Could I, should I, dare I consider a new life? The prospect of the unexpected and unknown was so much more appealing and exciting than terrifying. I surprised myself by this reaction. But I had those feelings nonetheless, and they were real. There was no doubt in my mind that, if Alana wanted to take the next step, I would be right there beside her, if not ahead of her. I had no idea those feelings were so present and alive in me, so ready to be awoken and resurrected. I was uncharacteristically drunk and giddy at this entire fantasy. I had attended college in the 1960s, when stepping through the "doors of perception" via hallucinogenics was part of the rite of passage. In a strange way, I felt the same now, that same slight buzz and tingle that heralded the onset of an LSD "trip". We used to laugh at those grinning idiots who claimed to be high on life. But I felt like that—I was high on Alana, or at least the prospect of Alana, or of rebirth and renewal, or maybe of being young again and having another chance, of going back to the future. It was too impossible to consider; it was too delicious not to. I thought I was dreaming. And all those feelings had been awoken and rekindled by two simple emails.

Clearly there was so much going on beneath the surface. And I wasn't completely blind to the disproportionate, extreme reaction. I just decided to go with it, and see where it led, rather than squash it. What did I have to lose? I reasoned. I knew it was all a mind game at that point, not a threat to anybody really, certainly not cheating or deceiving anyone. I didn't feel an ounce of guilt—what had I done wrong?? I decided to enjoy the moment, whatever it meant, and however long it lasted, hoping for more.

Chapter 7

I went home that evening, wondering if Alana would read my email and respond right away. She had written twice the day before. Certainly she would sense my willingness, eagerness, to follow her lead. After all, she had started this. How could she not be anxious to know my level of interest? Maybe she was feeling the same excitement I was…maybe more!! What a wonderful conceit!!

So I repeated the same nightly ritual when I entered my house—a brief hello to Sharon, a lick from Shanee, dinner by myself—but somehow it was different this time. I was lost in imagination, though I barely knew *what* to imagine. Truthfully, I barely remembered Alana at that time. I had spent so much time and energy looking ahead that I really hadn't looked back to remember what all the fuss was about. Nobody wants to be disappointed, and I'm no different. So I tried not to obsess over what had been, what might have been, what might yet be. I tried to behave as "normally" as possible, though there was certainly nothing normal or routine about what I was experiencing inside. I wasn't concerned that Sharon would sense something was up; I don't think she paid enough attention to my actions, attitudes, or moods, to notice anything different. But I did check my email repeatedly, which was assuredly unusual for me. I was so certain that Alana would write back. I was already composing my next email in my head, ready to send it off as soon as I heard from her. Who knows what she would write this time? Maybe something more personal? Maybe something inviting, intriguing, exciting?? Maybe a third email is like a third date—a time to make a statement and bring things to the next level? I grew up a hopeless romantic and was becoming a hopeful romantic. Maybe my time had come??!!

But my inbox remained empty, no matter how many times I checked and rebooted the computer. Finally, it was time for bed, though I did check right before I crawled in, shortly thereafter when I couldn't sleep, and again in the middle of the night. But I awoke after a restless night, tired, a little disappointed, but anxious to start a new day and hopefully continue my fantastic new adventure. I was sure that I would find something waiting for me, and, for the first time I could remember, I actually looked forward to getting up and going, and the new possibilities that may await.

Chapter 8

April 28 – May 1

    Wednesday is almost everybody's hardest day of the week, mine included. The past weekend is receding in memory; the upcoming weekend is still *so far away*!! And it seems like Friday will never come. That Wednesday was no exception. Despite—or maybe *because of*—my new-found excitement, the hours crept by unbearably slowly. Of course I checked my emails every five minutes. But there was nothing to be found. I didn't get it! What could have happened?? Was my last email delivered? Was there a glitch with the computer?? Did I say something I shouldn't have??? I reread the previous four emails (is that all there were??) a hundred times, until the words were burned into my consciousness. Even as I was seeing patients, making diagnoses, palpating, reviewing X-rays, dictating notes, writing orders…on and on and on…the same routine of the past twenty-five years…I was experiencing something different. I barely knew what I was doing, other than checking for a new message from Alana.

    But nothing new came. I rebooted, checked my sent mail, deleted mail and spam mail—but saw no new message from Alana. I went home confused, upset, and anxious; still checking and waiting…and waiting…and waiting…

    It was the same thing again in the a.m., and p.m., and a.m., and p.m., and a.m., and p.m.…It was over, before it even had begun. I felt like such a jerk, a desperate pathetic loser…what was I thinking? After all these years…never again…never again…

Chapter 9

May 2

"Dear Brett:

"Sorry for not responding in a more timely fashion. It definitely is more difficult doing emergency work after age 50. I stopped doing general surgery in 1996. I was forced to take ER call for another 18 months despite my protestations that it was not good medicine (or medicolegally appropriate) to render care for general surgical problems when I was not practicing the specialty on a daily basis. The surgical department just wanted another name to put on the schedule to lighten the load for the other general surgeons. Since I limited my practice to just breast surgery, the 'guys' have been less than friendly. The funny part is that breast surgery pays terribly; but it is a lifestyle that I can deal with. My husband is a vascular surgeon and when my son was a baby it was not unusual that we would both be called out in the middle of the night, and I left my son at home with a third-world nanny who slept in the basement! I realized that the situation was nuts and I had to be available for my son.

"Unfortunately the amount of paperwork and busy nonsense work that comes with the territory makes the practice just a job. If the reimbursement was good it would be much easier to deal with the nonmedical side of practice.

"My apologies for complaining. On a lighter note, the weather in New York was almost summer-like yesterday—89 degrees! Long Island is a great place to be in the Spring/Summer…the flowers are now blooming and everything is green.

"Do you come up to NY to visit your Mom? Please let me know if you do; I will make myself available.

"First loves are always special. I cannot remember why we broke up, do you? I too will always have a special place in my heart for you.

"BTW—I Googled you and found your practice Website in Florida. What happened to that thick dark beard (hippie-like) you used to have?? I loved that beard! Ever think of growing it back (lol)?

"Make it a great Sunday!

"Love, Alana"

Chapter 10

May 2

I usually scheduled a half-day clinic session on Saturdays, to make room for those patients who worked Monday-Friday and would otherwise have to take time off from their jobs to see me. My schedule was always jam-packed, but I enjoyed the Saturday sessions more than any others. Even though I was in the same office setting doing the same work, Saturdays still had a different vibe, a weekend mind-set for the patients, the staff, and for me. The Saturday patients were appreciative that the office was open for them; therefore they were more pleasant and less demanding, even if they had to wait longer to be seen because of the crowd. Things seemed less rushed and harried than the craziness, chaos, and frantic pace during the week. I even had considered having hours on Sunday to accommodate the overflow. Imagine how grateful those patients would have been! But even a worker bee like me needed some downtime, so I spent Sundays at home (a different kind of torture from being at work).

At least on Sundays I could sleep in, and I took full advantage of that, rarely stirring before 10, enjoying the luxury of arising slowly, at my own pace, allowing time to stand still, at least for a while. I wished the day were entirely mine, to relax and recharge. I wished spending the day with my significant other was enjoyable and fulfilling. Unfortunately, that was not the case. Sharon seemed to resent me even more on Sundays. My day of rest was her chance to demand my undivided attention, to have her due (with no "lame excuses" from me that work was calling). Invariably, I had a list of chores for my Sundays off, tasks and errands that Sharon could easily have accomplished, but saved up for me. I suppose this tactic was her way of feeling important in the marriage, in control, relevant. How much nicer it would have been to spend the day relaxing and luxuriating at home, away from the grind of work. But she had different ideas, so Sunday was *also* a workday for me, but with a different master, whom I could never seem to satisfy. At least during the week I felt rewarded and gratified by my relationships with my colleagues, staff, and patients. Not so much on Sunday. But after a while you can get used to almost anything, both things you put up with and things you do without. Such was my experience.

Needless to say, Sunday, May 2, was a different kind of Sunday. Alana's email said so much to me, both answering and asking questions I couldn't wait to think about and respond to. My inner fantasy life was expanding exponentially. My Big Bang was happening, and my universe evolving. My private face and my public face were never so disjointed. The incongruity should have been maddening; instead it was exciting and delightful.

I admit that I was disappointed that Alana had no recollection of why we broke up. That was a seminal event in my life, something that to this day I'll never forget. But perhaps it was good that she didn't remember? Maybe I had done something that had driven her away? If so, I'm glad she had no bad memories.

But the rest of the email was a homerun for me. She heard me and my naked feelings (that I had been reluctant and hesitant to bare), and responded positively. "First loves are always special"! How great was that?!! I guess I felt the same way. She had a "special place in her heart" for me! Honestly I thought that she had forgotten about me…that she didn't care and I was a childhood fling that was over and done with. I felt like I'd been waiting nearly forty years to hear those words. "I will make myself available," she had written. She wanted to see me!! *A grand slam!!* She had Googled me, was curious about how I looked and, despite my being thirty years older, was still interested! *How great is that??!!!*

Wow, we're on our way, I thought. *Where this road will lead, I have no idea*. But I did have hopes. If a dream is a wish the heart makes, I had dreams.

Chapter 11

May 2 (continued)

"Dear Alana,
"I am so sorry (and surprised) to hear of your dissatisfaction with your surgical practice. I had an entirely different image of what you were doing and feeling. My practice, too, has become very heavy in paperwork. I do a lot of workers compensation work, which is form-filled and tedious. Too often attorneys are involved and it becomes more med-legal than medical, which I don't like. But the work at least pays fairly well, to offset some of the nausea of working with attorneys. Sometimes the extraneous noise distracts from what we really do, which is take care of sick patients who need us. I try to stay on track, and remember what our mission is, and not be overwhelmed by the crap that goes along with it. My dad was a great role model who kept his priorities in order. Every now and again I stop, take a deep breath, and force myself to remember that despite all the technology and paperwork it still comes down to me and a patient, sitting in a room, looking at each other, connecting and figuring it out together; that interaction is what makes it all worthwhile for me.
"BTW—I Googled you also this morning. In all honesty, you look exactly the same... as beautiful as ever (no kidding!) I guess you learned that no-aging trick from your mom!! (be sure to tell her I said that! lol)
"As far as "why did we split up?" I do remember, perhaps *too* well. If you have a few minutes come join me in my memory banks for a trip back in time:

"It was the summer of 1972. You and I had been together for about 2 ½ years. I had just finished my junior year at Yale, and you your freshman year at Connecticut College. I was probably the only college kid who hated summer vacation because it was the one time when I couldn't see you for an extended period. I was crazy head-over-heels in love with you. I drove you up to Camp Waziyatah where you were going to spend the summer as a counselor. We spent a few great days there (before the campers arrived), then I drove to Connecticut to spend my last season doing summer stock theatre at the Ivoryton Playhouse. Previous summers apart we wrote often and resumed our love affair in September where we had left off in June. But not this time. After a few weeks your letters became shorter, less frequent, colder than usual. We finally spoke on the phone, and you told me the words that every guy in love dreads hearing, "I think we should see other people." Apparently the fencing instructor (Zoltan?) was interested in you, and vice-versa. You felt smothered by me and our relationship, and you wanted guiltless freedom to have a relationship with him. I never blamed you or hated you (maybe a little)—how could I? You were a beautiful 18 year old who wanted to explore and experience life! Of course you were entitled. But of course I was crushed. The letters stopped. I hoped that when the summer ended we would have a wonderful reconciliation and an even better year ahead! But I was wrong. When we both came home at the end of the summer, Zoltan came home with you for a few days, and you showed him your hometown. He sat at your dinner table, in my seat, and broke bread with you and your parents. When he left, we did get together. I still remember that day, and the movies we went to see…but you clearly had no interest in continuing our relationship at that time. So we went our separate ways, and I spent my senior year at college crying on Dave Black's (my roommate's) shoulder, still hoping that we would get together again in a meaningful way. Our paths crossed a few times that year—we went to Betsy's wedding, where you spent the whole evening flirting with Randy while I was silently crying in the corner; coincidentally we ran into each other over Christmas break at Eddie's house, but you were distant and still not interested. Later that year you had a photography project for a class, and you drove to New Haven to photograph me as your nude model. We made love, and I was so hopeful…but again not to be. After I graduated I desperately tried one more time-- we went to see "Grease" on Broadway and then out for dinner. But you were lost to me by then, and I knew it. I had to move forward without you, which I did, but I never really moved on. Although I was too young to have considered a marriage proposal, I still never pictured my life without you, and over the years have always wondered what if?..I've carried a torch for you for 40 years!! That must belong in the Guinness Book of World Records!!!! I guess I've never gotten over you.

"Please don't misunderstand me. None of the above is meant to make you feel bad or guilty or whatever. You asked, so I answered, honestly. I've always worn my heart on my sleeve, perhaps to my detriment. I see no reason not to be completely honest with you now. When I did my Psych rotation at Misericordia Hospital, I had an attending whose mantra was, 'Have your feelings; don't let your feelings have you.' Well, these are my feelings.
"Write back when you can.
"Love,
Brett"

Chapter 12

May 2 (continued)

    The rest of the day I was in a trance. After I sent that email to Alana I was lost in a dream, and the butterflies were in full flight! I hadn't really thought about that break-up consciously for so long, and the visceral pain was buried, along with my dad's death and my daughter's broken engagement, as the most traumatic times of my life. As I wrote the email, I relived that pain, and nearly started crying, but had to hold back my tears with Sharon around. I was surprised myself to see how emotional I became, and at the depth and intensity of those feelings from so long ago. I had lived a whole life since then—other relationships, medical school, post-doctoral residency training, marriage, a daughter, moving to San Diego, starting one, two, three medical practices, moving to Florida…So much water under the bridge. And yet here I was, twenty-one years old again, broken-hearted and confused. Proust's "madeleine" was no more acute in recalling his past than Alana's email was in recalling mine. I strained to remember as much as I could about her, what we had had together, what had happened between us, what happened after we broke up. It was foggy but crystal clear, removed but so present, fantasy prepared with a reality reduction. Once again I was dependent on cyberspace to connect and move forward (or not). I had no idea how Alana would react. I had never discussed that time or those feelings with anyone. Perhaps it would be too much for her? Perhaps that had been the problem in the past that led to our break-up? Perhaps *I* was too much (too passionate, too romantic, too sentimental, too intense) for her? Perhaps *that* had led to our break-up? I really didn't know but felt sure I would find out. I was no longer twenty-one years old, nor she eighteen. Am I an idealist and a romantic? Yes I am, because I never had the courage to believe in nothing; I believed in love and passion and magic: something bigger and better than little old me. I wouldn't have it any other way. People truly in love are far greater than the sum of their parts, and I was all in and fully immersed myself in that, wanted to be part of that, and couldn't imagine living and being any other way, despite the pain and heartache that unrequited love may bring. That is my DNA, who I am, who I ever was and always would be, like it or not, no matter how painful or difficult, no matter what obstacles and trials such a philosophy held in store. I had no choice but to be that person, with that faith and consciousness. I would be true to myself.

I was quite sure that she would respond, and in an honest (perhaps brutally honest?) way. I had some vague recollection that's who *she* was—straightforward, no sugar-coating, saying it like it is. I felt that the next email would be very telling. After my last email, the feelings I had, the pain I had gone through, still very raw, how could she not respond with her own feelings, feelings from yesteryear, feelings from yesterday? I couldn't wait to hear from her…I was scared to death to hear from her…

I heard nothing for the rest of Sunday. Monday would be a brand new day, filled with infinite possibilities, a day never even been used yet! I wondered with increasing trepidation what it would bring.

Chapter 13

May 3

    I barely slept at all last night. I'm not sure what I expected to hear from Alana, and imagined every possible scenario, from no response to a declaration of long-lost love, regret at what had happened, desire to reconnect and renew. I tried not to be too hopeful, but that was futile. I stared at the ceiling while Sharon slept soundly next to me, unaware that her life too was on the brink. I slipped out of the bedroom to check my emails several times, admonishing myself to be patient and realistic and wait until the morning, but knowing that love and hope are never that. I wondered if Alana too were awake, staring at her ceiling, recalling her "first love"? I had so many questions begging for answers, none of which were forthcoming as the hours crept by. I looked at the clock every few minutes, wanting to drift off, knowing how tired I would be in the morning, but full of nervous energy that could not be denied. Suppose Alana responded favorably, warmly, lovingly? Suppose she too was ready to begin a new chapter in our lives together? Was I prepared to take the steps necessary, make the changes required, to see her, test my feelings, and possibly start a new life? I knew it was way premature to even imagine such a scenario, but I couldn't help it. Should I, or even could I, end this right now before it went any further? Change is hard; divorce is so traumatic (or so I'd heard). Was I prepared to start down this road? I finally got up, even earlier than usual, showered, dressed, and left for work in the still darkness.

Chapter 14

May 3

    The roads were empty, the parking lot at work deserted, the office quiet. In a way I enjoyed experiencing the office this way, so peaceful for now, knowing that in a few hours it would be manic with patients overflowing the waiting room, four doctors and twenty staff hustling and bustling to contain, entertain, and attend to the madding crowd. I've always felt that the sounds of a time and place defined the activity best. In the hospital, for example, the sounds of the ICU are distinctive and unique, more so than any other element—the rhythmic pulsing and whooshing of the respirators breathing life into the inert flesh waiting to be reawakened by some miracle of God or man; the constant, maddening alarms from the monitors, signaling that something was awry (or more often just a technical glitch corrected, never soon enough, by the nursing staff); the monotonous moans and groans from the patients, each different and characteristic, denoting to the trained ear the vocalist and his condition better than any monitor or machine; the popping of syringes, opening of medicine cabinets, hushed voices of the staff talking amongst themselves or softly with the patients. These sounds become burned into a resident's memory, like an old song one never forgets and responds to from the gut.
    The office in action had different, but no less distinctive, sounds: the requisite satellite radio in the background (my choice was always Sinatra and the American Songbook—peaceful, familiar, predictable, so unlike everything else that was transpiring in the middle of the work day); the tinny, much-less-pleasant blare of the TVs in the waiting room, usually set to a cable news station, though few people were watching or listening; the multiple voices conducting business as usual; computers humming; phones ringing; cell phones ring toning. The decibel level would rise and fall in lockstep with the schedule:

pianissimo at daybreak when the first patients straggled in to be met by the staff, all tired and sleepy-eyed; *forte* in mid-late morning as the a.m. crowd was at its heaviest and most boisterous; *mezzo-piano* at noon, as the remaining morning patients were being seen, and the staff rotated out for lunch; *fortissimo* at mid-day with the afternoon schedule full and emergency "add-ons" overcrowding an already overcrowded ledger; and finally *diminuendo* as the last few patients were being seen and the sun was setting. A symphony of cacophony from start to finish, to be played over and over (with slight variations) from one day to the next. Clearly the peace and quiet of the early morning was my favorite time.

I had gotten into the habit of having a morning grounding circle with the staff prior to registering the first patient. I got the idea from my daughter, who had taught in a Quaker school. The concept of everyone sitting together in a circle and sharing thoughts and feelings to start the day was very appealing to me. If it worked for kindergarteners, why not with grown-ups? The idea of bonding, remembering that we were a team, re-establishing our connection with each other, and recalling our group "mission statement" (to take care of every patient as though he/she were family) kept us focused, centered, and on track. It's so easy to get lost in the business that we forget why we're doing what we're doing, why we chose this noble profession in the first place, that it's never about us but always about the patients. Sometimes we sang familiar songs to start the day smiling, positive, and enthusiastic (not easy at 7:45 a.m.). But it was a worthwhile initiative. If this type of team-building activity worked for Toyota plants assembling cars, how much more important for a medical staff reassembling lives? Attendance was optional, and sometimes it was just me and Jorge (my X-ray technician and the best employee I've ever had the pleasure and privilege of working with); those days we just had a morning "line" but it was always good for me, a good way to start my day, regain my focus, and pull out the positive energy I would need to get through. Despite my encouragement, however, none of my seven partners ever participated…their loss.

On this particular day, the early morning quiet was soothing and stabilizing, in contradistinction to the tumult I was feeling within. Everything was in its place, as usual; the staff appeared mostly on time; the morning circle proceeded as planned (an excellent turnout!). We completed by singing (with surprising enthusiasm, or maybe that was just me?) "Rise and Shine and Give God Your Glory, Glory," a very uplifting tune that seemed appropriate for a day with unknown potential.

We all arose, the staff walked to their respective stations, and I headed for my office to log-on and check my email.

Chapter 15

"Dear Brett,

"I just received your email. What a way to start the week! I must be demented. I don't even remember your driving me up to Maine. What a memory you have!!

"The character you describe sounds like a real witch! I am so sorry for having caused you all that pain.

"Anyway I feel so bad now about having hurt you so deeply. I can't recall the details you describe except that we separated and went our separate ways. I'm so sorry.

"Stay in touch. I hope you're happy. I'd like to hear from you when you have time to write. Even better would be a phone call (my cell is 555-264-9770).

"Love,
Alana"

Chapter 16

May 3 (continued)

Of course I was happy to receive Alana's email and that she wanted to "stay in touch." I never understood why we broke up, and she provided no explanation or illumination. Could her parents have thought we were too serious at too young an age, and steered her away from me? I had always gotten along so well with them and felt right at home in her parents' house; I thought they felt equally comfortable with me. Of course there was the time that her mom found a used condom in the wastebasket in Alana's bedroom. She wasn't too happy about that! But time went by and I was sure she was over it.

I certainly spent a lot of time there and ate more meals at her mother's table than at mine. I remembered Alana's parents very well. Her mom was a strikingly beautiful woman in her forties, sophisticated, bright, always well-dressed, well-appointed, well-spoken (well-*everything!*). She worked as a radiology/lab technician in a general practitioner's office, and thought doctors were practically gods among men. A successful TV show of the time, *Marcus Welby, MD*, glorified the life and work of the family doctor, hardly believable in retrospect but wildly popular and accepted back then. Doctors were the culture heroes of the day, and Gladys truly believed that doctors could do no wrong. The MD degree conferred an air of respectability in her eyes. The fact that my father, brother, and uncle were all doctors was very appealing to her. The fact that I was hesitant to follow in their footsteps perplexed and frustrated her. In any event, she made it her mission to convert me, and spared no opportunity to extol the great virtues of medicine as a profession, the high regard and respect doctors commanded, let alone the financial rewards that accompanied all the rest. In her mind, if one could become a doctor, one did—no questions asked. There was no comparable career. I, on the other hand, didn't share her enthusiasm at the time.

In any event, the idea that Milton and Gladys were somehow guilty of causing our break-up made no sense to me. Why would they do that? It seemed to me that I was a damn good catch, a *Jewish* mother's dream son-in-law. I wasn't conceited or obnoxious about it, but certainly didn't feel like a loser, or someone a mother would warn her daughter to stay away from. I just didn't get it. And Alana should have been strong enough to stand up for herself, and follow her heart if it led to me. I always thought that Alana was very young, inexperienced, and wanted to test the waters—*that's* why we broke up. But maybe there was more to it than that. Even after we separated I continued to stop by her parents' house (when I knew she wouldn't be there), to eat at their table, to maintain a relationship, always hoping for some information about Alana, perhaps some knowledge about her social and romantic life, hoping for an opening and a right time to reconnect with her. But none was forthcoming. Gladys never talked much about Alana except to say that she was fine. She never mentioned that Alana ever asked about me, or might be available and interested in seeing me again. I concluded that things were over and done with, and Alana no longer cared or had any interest in "us." It was a bitter pill to swallow. I never pushed too hard, because I remained too vulnerable to risk even more hurt and rejection. I gradually and painfully accepted that Alana had easily and cheerfully moved on. Gladys always seemed happy to see me, interested in my life, hospitable and very friendly, but never an ally in my pursuit of her daughter. Perhaps I should have seen the light then, but never did.

So where to go from here? I knew I would respond to Alana's email, but was not sure what to say. For some reason, I didn't feel ready to call. Somehow that would put this new relationship into a whole different place, and I wasn't sure I was ready to go there yet. And after all these years, with all these rekindled and confusing feelings, I might find myself tongue-tied. It would be harder to interpret her meaning over the phone and respond appropriately than it would in an email. So no phone call for now. But what to write…?

Chapter 17

May 4

"Dear Al,

"Please don't misunderstand me. I am not blaming you for what happened 40+ years ago, and I am sorry if you interpreted my last email that way. Of course I was hurt, and hurt deeply, being rejected by the woman (girl) I was in love with. But I guess that's me being me—romantic, optimistic, idealistic, and unrealistic in expecting a 15 year old girl to commit herself to someone for life! How ridiculous is that? But the heart wants what the heart wants, and my heart wanted you. I get that you were too young and needed to spread your wings and fly (away from me); but that explanation and understanding, while making perfectly good sense, doesn't make it hurt any less. Puppy love may be the purest love of all—innocent, all trusting, full of hope, with no expectation of failure. Too bad life happens and we learn "life's lessons".

"But I didn't mean to hurt or upset you in any way. You were never a witch in my eyes. I still remember the Alana and Brett of 40 years ago, the way I felt, the ebullience, effervescence, and fire of youth and first love. I admit that I have been bathing in and relishing those memories for the past few days. It's been great!

"Perhaps you've already figured out (duh!) from my emails that my life hasn't worked out the way I had hoped. I always assumed that I would find the girl of my dreams (besides you), marry her, and live happily ever after. Man plans and God laughs, and unfortunately things didn't happen for me that way. I married the wrong person at the wrong time for the wrong reasons, knew I made a mistake even as I was walking down the aisle, but have always believed in marriage vows, so stayed and "took the high road" rather than leaving and abandoning Jennifer. Now Jenn is an adult, engaged to be married, and lives in New York. I am proud of how well she turned out, and I can say without conceit that I played no small role in that. I'm not so proud of how my life turned out, and the choices I made. But I gave my daughter a stable home environment, and that I feel very good about.

"Anyway I'm sorry if I'm depressing you. I hope you've been more successful in creating and managing your own personal and family portfolio. I remember you as a wonderful and special person who deserves to have that kind of life.

"Write back when you can. I look forward to your emails and hearing about you and your story.

"Love,
Brett"

Chapter 18

May 5

A day had passed and there had been no response from Alana. As things became more and more personal, with more and more intimate sharing, I wondered where we were going with this new "beginning"? I had never signed up for Facebook, MySpace, or other social media websites, because I never really wanted to hear from most people in my past, and did not want to feel obliged to "friend" people, stay up to date with their postings, or respond on a regular basis. Friends and acquaintances from previous lifetimes in New York and California were in my rearview mirror, and I didn't stay in touch with them. It was a new experience for me to reconnect with an old friend.

Yet, having said that, I always liked the idea of life being a series of big rings that somehow circle around and reconnect. The symmetry of that, the completion and closure, lent a certain stability, identity, and eternity to life's experiences. I had never felt that until now.

I recalled a movie I'd seen called *Peggy Sue Got Married*, which espoused the "burrito theory of life." Burritos are tortillas that circle around and whose ends touch, completely enclosing the contents within. That idea always seemed very appealing to me (I don't know why); but here I was living The Burrito Theory. My life had circled around to reconnect with an earlier time. I remembered Alana and *us* but I also remembered the *me* of so many years ago. I was reconnecting not only with Alana but with myself of days gone by, when life was so much simpler, and easier, full of hope and promise. I enjoyed that reconnection and experiencing myself and the feelings I had as a teenager. It was the strangest sensation, but so interesting. I always felt that we age physically and emotionally in entirely different ways. Our physical aging process is chronological and linear: one day leads to the next, we became older one step at a time, with each step throughout our lives approximately the same. Barring illness or accident, the difference between forty and forty-one is similar to the difference between sixty and sixty-one, insofar as our organs and physical well-being are concerned. But we age mentally and emotionally in an entirely different way, by quantum leaps, through stages. At age sixty I cannot possibly relate to the way I felt physically and the tasks and activities I could perform at age eighteen. *But* at age sixty I can still entirely relate (not just remember) to how I felt emotionally at age eighteen—the same hopes, and dreams, and desires, and heartfelt passions. Pictures I have of myself at age eighteen show a young man with a full beard, an amazingly full head of black hair, and no wrinkles. My picture today looks nothing like the original. But emotionally I can still resonate with the feelings I had at age eighteen, especially when inspired to do so by a distinct memory. That is the emotional feeling I still had when thinking about Alana. It was a time long gone by, but a time that still felt like yesterday. Whatever it was—chemical or otherwise—I liked it and wanted to savor that feeling and inhale that aroma for as long as I could. *How will it feel tomorrow, or next week, or six months from now?* I wondered. I had no idea, but couldn't wait to find out.

In the midst of this musing, I realized that day was Sharon's birthday. So sad that I hadn't remembered, and felt nothing. And so telling…

Chapter 19

May 6

"Dear Brett,

"I'm sorry to hear that things didn't work out for you the way you had planned. My story is somewhat different but with a lot of similarities. Like you and your daughter, my son Pierce is the apple of my eye and the light of my life. I was almost 38 when he was born, and it has been a wild ride. As far as my marriage is concerned, I met my husband during residency. We both went to the same medical school, but never dated until we were interns at St. Vincent's Hospital. One thing led to another, we began living together, and got married when we were both third year residents. I don't have to tell you how crazy residency is. General surgery at St. Vincent's was extremely taxing—a lot of trauma, up night after night, exhausted most of the time, eating, sleeping, working, and little time for anything else (barely time for eating or sleeping!) Maybe that's not the best time to meet someone and get married. But Martin and I seemed to get along well, although we always had issues, even back then. I always seemed to be the one who had to take charge—planning vacations, arranging our social calendar (whatever little there was), paying bills, etc. We both did the same residency with the same responsibilities, but somehow the burden always fell on me to take care of business. And nothing has changed after 22 years.

"I'm not sure I was ever sure either that Martin was the one. I felt my biologic clock ticking and rolled the dice. In the beginning things were OK. After finishing residency Martin did a fellowship in Vascular Surgery at Montefiore and I entered a General Surgery group practice on Long Island. When he finished his fellowship Martin was clueless about what to do so he joined me in my office and started a solo practice. With time we figured out how to live together and made it work. We became successful professionally, bought a house, made friends, and raised Pierce. We both still work at the same hospital, live five minutes away from the hospital and the office, have offices across the hall from each other, and our professional and personal lives are intertwined.

"A few years ago I caught Martin cheating on me. It was a complete surprise and he handled it like he always does, avoiding confrontation, self-loathing, indecisive, and insensitive. Pierce was just fourteen then, idolized his father, and was crushed when Martin up and moved out without warning or talking. We got into therapy, and things were better for a while. We learned to communicate better, but I could never get over it and trust him. A few months ago I caught him at it again. He hasn't moved out but things are tense and I have a hard time seeing him every day and pretending things are the same, because they're not. I haven't made any decisions or plans about what to do. For now I'm taking it just one day at a time.

"I'm sorry if I'm depressing *you*!!

"Pierce is a junior in high school. He's an athlete and plays lacrosse and football. We'll be looking at colleges soon. He still has another year at home, and I don't want to traumatize him again. We'll see what happens.

"Got to go. Patients are waiting. Write when you can.

"Love,
Alana"

Chapter 20

May 6 (continued)

"Dear Al,

"Once upon a time, long ago and far away, in the estates within the kingdom of Jamaica, lived a young prince. As young princes do, he spent his time frolicking with his friends and fellow princes, whiling away his days with sport and camaraderie, with nary a thought about his future or focus.

"One day his good friend, the Earl of Schechter, told him of a beautiful young princess who lived in the nearby kingdom of Holliswood. Our young prince was intrigued by his colleague's description and sought to meet this young damsel. Once a proper assignation had been arranged, the two met on the eve of the New Year at the Gardens of Madison Square, chaperoned by the Earl and his Lady, Dale of the Village of Parkway. The young prince was smitten immediately, and fell hopelessly in love with the princess.

"Time passed, and the two young lovers became closer still, nearly inseparable, hearts intertwined as one. The prince knew that he had found his lady fair, and that the Fates had been kind and generous to him. He was very happy.

"Until one day he was struck without warning by an arrow that pierced his heart. His passion and energy and hope were suddenly sapped from his very essence, and he fell into a deep sleep, lost to the world, lost in this abrupt and unforeseen vacuum of emptiness and loneliness and despair. His world grew cold and grey and silent. Despite all the efforts of his comrades, he could not be aroused, and the kingdom mourned and the angels wept at his pitiful plight.

"Years passed, and the prince remained asleep and oblivious to the world around him. Until one day Cupid came to call. The princess was still a maiden, curious about the state of her beloved. In her own agony she sent another arrow that awakened the prince, and rekindled his spirit. He warmed to the memory of her, and came to life once again. His own deep fog gradually lifted, and his love, his life returned. Out of the depths arose a new star that would light the firmament and right the wrongs.

"Kismet had come."

Chapter 21

May 6 (continued)

I'm not sure why I chose to write a fairytale instead of picking up the phone and calling. I was surprised by Alana's story. She was such a beautiful girl. I always thought of her as a natural-born winner, one of the lucky ones who got what she wanted when she wanted. After our breakup I thought she had moved on, found what (who) she was looking for (obviously not me), and was happily married to one very lucky guy. In my naiveté (and the poignant memories of rejection and longing) I couldn't fathom someone cheating on her. That seemed incomprehensible. I always assumed that she would be the rejecter, not the rejectee, the heartbreaker not the heartbroken. Perhaps I should have felt a touch of redemption at her being on the receiving end of this torment (as I had been), and her suffering the shock and confusion and feeling that her world was crashing down around her (as I had). But I felt none of that. Schadenfreude has never been for me (except in a few rare instances when someone hurt my daughter). This was a decidedly unexpected turn of events.

Not knowing exactly what to say, but not wanting to wait very long and break the chain of communication, I chose the allegory. There was no ambiguity about the characters or the message. Yet it didn't commit me to anything, it bought a little time, and it allowed Al the chance to consider her own situation and options, including my place in her life, and to respond. So far we had been sharing some very personal thoughts and feelings, but very little about our feelings for each other, and where this might lead. If she were as curious about me as I was about her, and if a future together was even a consideration, we were approaching a fork in the road. As Yogi Berra famously said, "When you come to a fork in the road, take it." And I knew we'd have to "take it," although which path to take remained a mystery.

So I continued about my daily chores, waiting for Alana's response, knowing that we were about to embark on a dangerous journey. But staying where I was seemed increasingly less of an option for me. And Alana, too, miraculously, may have been at the same place. Given where we were, professionally, socially, and geographically, and not having seen each other for nearly forty years, moving forward together would require a great leap of faith. Either we'd fly together or crash and burn separately. Great rewards require great risks. Were we ready?

Chapter 22

May 7

Five o'clock in the morning. An expectedly restless night. Sharon slept straight through, but I was up hourly checking my email. Nothing yet. I tried to convince myself that Alana was busy, taking care of patients, doing surgery, attending to her son, etc. Maybe she hadn't even had time to check her emails. But these excuses didn't assuage my excitement and anxiety. If she blew me off again and wasn't interested, I had lost little but a week of pleasant fantasizing. Or had I? Somehow the feelings that were awakened—feelings of love and longing and missing, not necessarily of her but of that part of my life—would still be alive after she was gone. Even if she didn't give me a different life, she had shown me the possibility of a different life, and that wouldn't be as easy to get over and forget. Would I be able to retreat into and reassume the same numbing shell I had occupied for the past twenty years? Or would my exposure to these strong, long-buried feelings leave me more dissatisfied than ever with my marriage and life? Like the chained inhabitants of Plato's cave, could I ever be the same once I had seen the light of a new reality? All these crazy thoughts raced through my mind as I lay wide awake in bed. I felt that I had spent so much time in my fantasy world that I had already left Sharon and Florida behind me. If there had been any doubt about which path to take, there was no doubt any longer. Now if only Alana were on board!!

Six o'clock: leaving the house and on my way to work. Sun rising, 80 degrees already, another day full of patients. Yet I was strangely insulated from that world. I had but one thing on my mind, and couldn't wait to get to the office and check my emails. It might be a very long day…

Seven o'clock: Office dark and quiet, alone at my desk, logging on to my computer…

"Dear Brett,
"This is getting nuts already. We need to talk. I'll be in the office all day. Please call around 5 if you can. You have my cell (555-264-9770), or you can call the back line (555-583-1414).
"Talk to you later.
Alana"

Before I knew it, it was 5 p.m.: the moment of truth. You can't steal second base if you're afraid to take your foot off first. Here goes nothin'…

Chapter 23

May 7

"Hello, Alana?"

"Yes, speaking."

"Hi. Guess who?"

"Hi, Brett. I don't know anyone else with a 305 area code, so I guess it's you".

"Yes. Well, it's good to finally hear your voice after all these years. I'm sorry I haven't called sooner, but this whole thing is a new experience for me and I've been hesitant to start something I wasn't sure I could finish."

"Well, what do you think you started?"

"I don't know exactly, but it feels like we started something…at least, that's the way it feels inside to me. Are you free now to talk awhile?"

"Yeah, I'm done with patients, just finishing up a few charts and phone calls, but that can wait. Everyone else has left for the day."

"Well, I think we have a lot to talk about, at least from what I've gathered from your emails. I wish we could talk in person. I've never liked the phone for anything personal—it's too *im*personal. I actually like letters or emails a lot better."

"Well, I'd like to see you too. Do you have any trips planned to New York, to see your mother or your daughter, or anything?"

"Actually, I'm going to a wedding in New York at the end of May, Memorial Day weekend, a friend of my daughter's. I have a dog who I hate to kennel. So I'll be driving with her, and we'll stay at my daughter's apartment in Manhattan. I'm coming up on Thursday, the rehearsal dinner is Friday night in New Jersey, the wedding is Saturday night, and I'm driving back on Sunday."

"That doesn't leave much time. I usually do surgeries Friday morning, but I can keep my schedule free if you can get out to see me. It's only about an hour's drive from Manhattan."

"Well, it might be difficult to find an excuse to leave Sharon and Jennifer, but let me see what I can come up with."

"Please do. Y'know, that reminds me—I have a dog, too, a big yellow lab named Rex. I was thinking of you the other day because Rex has a serious orthopaedic problem. Maybe you can give me some advice?"

"OK, be happy to."

"He had bad hips, underwent hip-replacement surgeries, and his sciatic nerve was cut in the second surgery, so he's totally unable to use his back leg now. He drags it around, and it's so sad and pathetic. I have to lift and carry him outside to do his business, and he weighs 120 pounds, so it isn't easy."

"Okay, do you have X-rays you can send me?"

"Yes, as a matter of fact I do. I'll mail them to you."

"Send them to my office, obviously. Write "Personal" on the front to be sure they get to me."

"Okay. Will do. I'll send them tomorrow, overnight delivery. Maybe you can look at them and we'll talk again on Monday?"

"Okay, no problem."

"And maybe you can find a reason to visit? I think we have a lot to talk about."

"Yes, you're right. I'll see what I can do."

"Okay. Well, it's getting late, and I still have to finish up. Have a good weekend and I'll talk to you soon."

"Okay. Bye."

"Bye."

(Click)

And so it began: Phase 2. I was nervous about the call but it went as well as could be expected. Short and sweet. She was friendly, sounded exactly the same as I remembered her, interested in seeing me and carrying on whatever it is we're doing. It was a little awkward, but not bad. Food for thought. Now, how could I get to see her? It seemed like we were moving in the right direction.

My thoughts ran like this: But I really don't know anything about Alana. She's undoubtedly not the same girl I remember from 1972. Times change, people change, life happens. And she almost killed me back then! What am I thinking, and what am I doing? I've been so caught up in this dream that I haven't really thought about anything but undoing the past, and "making it right" (whatever that means). The sudden gush of emotion that has been flooding and drowning me these past ten days can't be genuine, at least not in the sense that it's based on reality. It's been a really long time, but I guess I was so hurt by what happened in the past that I still have a tremendous well of deep feelings that have rushed to the surface, feelings that I suppressed all these years but never resolved or jettisoned. I've been contacted by other girlfriends from the past, but never pursued a connection and never thought twice about them. The idea of "getting back together" with other previous lovers never occurred to me, despite my unhappiness and dissatisfaction with my marriage.

But this time is so different. The idea of *not* reconnecting with Alana hasn't occurred to me. I can't imagine not pursuing this to its inevitable conclusion, whatever that is and wherever that takes me. When I stop, take three deep breaths, and try to view it objectively (as though I were advising a friend about what to do in a similar situation), the whole thing seems insane! Who does this? And how can it ever work out? If it didn't work out forty years ago, when I had the luxury of being young and foolish, why should it work out now, when I no longer have that luxury?? Stop the world, I want to get off!!

But that's my head speaking. My heart says, "Stop the world I want to get on!!" I want another chance, another chance with Alana, another chance to be the Brett who loved life and couldn't wait for tomorrow. Where is *that* guy? Maybe here's my time machine, a chance to have a "do over." George Eliot famously said: "It's never too late to be what you might have been." Maybe my time has come!

In Judaism the concept of sin is very different from Christian doctrine. Jews don't consider a sin to be a terrible crime against God or man, but rather a mis-step, a loss of guidance and proper direction, losing one's way on the highway of life. Maybe that's what happened to me and Alana? A sin in that sense—we lost our way, veered off track, took a wrong turn; and now maybe we're back on the right path. Maybe this was meant to be—God's true plan!! I'm all in.

Chapter 24

May 8 - 9

The weekend crawled by as I continued to visualize what it would be like to see Alana after all this time, and how things might play out. They say that the best way to know how your wife will age is to look at her mother, and I remembered Al's mom being a very attractive mature woman. The last time I had seen Gladys was when she attended my wedding, and she was about the same age then as Alana was now. When I got home I pulled out my wedding album, and there was Gladys, all dolled up and made up, and still quite a looker. I expected Alana to age the same way.

So my next challenge was to strategize a plausible excuse for leaving Sharon and Jennifer for a few hours to meet with Alana. Just as I felt about the first phone call, I knew the first face-to-face meeting would be major in terms of deciding (for both of us) whether or not there was a future for us. Suppose Alana looked young and beautiful to me but to her I looked aged and unattractive? Would it be one and done? As hopeful and optimistic as I think I am, I've also always been a worst-case scenario person, hoping for the best but preparing for the worst. In surgery I always considered the worst possible things that could happen during a case, the most extreme complications and unexpected problems, and tried to prepare for them in the event they occurred. If I were ready to tackle the worst of the worst, I would have no problem if things went normally well as expected. So I did the same with Alana, and tried to anticipate an absolute catastrophe, and how to react. Suppose she was disappointed when she saw me, expecting me to look like the twenty-one-year-old kid I was when she last saw me? Would that be the end? Would I be crushed? Would I be able to have a nice, cordial conversation with her, be pleasant and courteous, shake her hand and walk away with my head held high? I would hope so, but maybe not. Maybe all the feelings from the past would return, and I'd have to spend another year getting over it, this time with no one to cry to, and not much of a future to look forward to. No matter how much I thought about it, I realized that no matter how hard I tried to devise a script for every possibility, I wouldn't know until we met how I would feel or what would be the appropriate thing to say. I would have to trust my instincts and let spontaneity rule the day. I really had no other choice, as anxiety-provoking as that was, but to march into battle unarmed and unprepared. Really not my style…

But first I had to make it to Square One, so I started to lay the groundwork for a first meeting. I began to plant seeds, dropping hints at home that I might need to take a trip to Long Island that Friday we were in New York. I considered using a visit to my mother as an excuse, but then Sharon might offer to come with me, and it would be awkward and suspicious to discourage that. A "business meeting" would be a lot safer, with no reason for her to accompany me; so that would be my plan. And I sketched out a strategy for making that happen.

Time seemed to be slowing down and speeding up at the same time. My reality of going to work, coming home at night, and following my normal routine was increasingly tedious; but my inner life was moving at warp speed. May 28 became the target date, Long Island the destination, the course of events to be finalized, the outcome unknown. The only thing certain was my growing commitment to finding out more and my heady excitement at the prospect of seeing Alana again.

Chapter 25

May 10

7 a.m.:"Dear Alana,

"It was great speaking with you on Friday. I'm glad you pushed me to call, and sorry for my initial reluctance. I hope you had a good weekend. The weather in Florida has been typically hot and muggy for this time of year, sometimes unbearable to be outside. I'd like to talk to you later if you're free. My office hours are essentially non-stop from 8-6, but I can make a time to talk that's convenient for you. Just let me know.

"FYI—the last 2 weeks (is that all it's been?) since we've been communicating have been very provocative and stimulating for me. I never thought that I'd hear from you again, be in contact or speak with you. I thought that you had stopped thinking or caring about me long ago. I sense an interest, curiosity, even excitement on your part, too (please correct me if I'm wrong). I hope we can continue this journey and explore its possibilities.

"Looking forward to hearing from you, and speaking to you, soon.
"Love,
Brett"

9 a.m.:

"Dear Brett,

"I too have been thinking about you all weekend, and would like to keep thinking and talking. I never stopped caring about you. I'm not sure why I chose to look you up and reach out to you after all these years. Maybe it was simple curiosity; maybe it was more than that. I'm not as deep a thinker as you, and don't see the "big picture" as you do. But whatever the reason, I'm glad we're in touch now and would like to know more about you, your life, your hopes and dreams. I find myself withdrawing more and more from my husband and marriage, although haven't confronted him or made any demands or decisions. The first time he cheated and I found out, I gave him an ultimatum and eventually he chose to stay and I to try again. This time I'm not as forgiving or open to yet another chance. It was hard enough to stay together before; now that boat may have sailed.

"I'm not afraid to be divorced or alone. But I am afraid what a divorce would do to my son. He was so young the first time and it was so devastating. Seeing his heart getting broken made the situation so much worse, and I'm sure that was a major part of my reconciliation with Martin. Now he's not much older, still my baby, still immature, still very sensitive and fragile in his own way. He tries to put on airs of being macho and strong and independent, but seeing his father move out again would be devastating to him. My hesitancy about pulling the trigger and forcing the issue is no doubt largely influenced by my desire to protect Pierce. He's my #1 priority, by far the most important thing in my life, and I'll do anything for his sake. I just don't know how much longer I can continue this charade of a happy marriage, or sleep in the same bed with Martin without going a little crazy myself. I'm in therapy again, with the same therapist I saw during the last infidelity. I'm not sure if therapy helps but I need someone to vent to. My life with Martin is so enmeshed in my community and professional life that I haven't felt comfortable sharing my personal issues with anyone. At least I can talk to the therapist.

"Anyway let's talk later. I usually take lunch around noon, and finish sometime around 5. I'll make time to talk then.

"Have a quiet day.

"Love,

Alana"

So, despite having patients waiting, I called Al at noon, and she was free. We spoke for nearly an hour, mostly discussing mundane things, our work, schedules, things we had done over the weekend. We talked about our families (whom we both knew from the past) and began to introduce the names of our friends and other parts of our daily lives. The conversation became smoother, easier, and more natural until it was past time to hang up. My staff was surprised by my closing myself in my office in the middle of the day, but respected my closed door, assuming it was something important or I wouldn't have taken time out of my schedule. And they were right; it *was* something important, more than they (or I) could possibly know. We said goodbye with "Speak to you later," knowing that we would speak again soon. The afternoon went quickly, and promptly at 5 p.m. I called again, anxious to talk some more, as was she. This time we spoke for nearly two hours, and we hung up knowing there would be more of the same tomorrow. The ice had been broken and it was full steam ahead.

Chapter 26

May 11 -15

The following day I called Al at 8:45, knowing that she started seeing patients at 9. She answered immediately, expecting my call even though we hadn't arranged any set time to speak again. We spoke briefly then, again at noon, and again at 6. Instead of being awkward it was easy, free-flowing conversation. We talked about anything and everything, from our lives back in the seventies, mutual friends we had had back then, through an overview of what we had been doing since. We had both followed long and winding roads, and we were both hungry to share our experiences, the good and the bad, the triumphs and the failures, the highs and the lows. Not being much of a phone person, I was surprised how easy it was to talk with Alana, like we had been doing this forever. We thought the same way, experienced and reacted to things the same way, even anticipated each other's thoughts. I had never fallen out of love with Alana, but I found myself falling in love all over again, with this "stranger" who didn't seem to be a stranger at all. But was it real or was it Memorex? Were my feelings truly for Alana, or were they about the past, the pain, the hurt, the desire for closure and renewal, the boredom and despair of a failed marriage, etc? Could I trust my feelings? And what about hers?

We also continued to email several times daily:

"Dear Brett,
"Another day at the salt mines. I find it increasingly difficult to get through my day, waiting to talk to you and hear from you. I feel like a teenage girl again, and feel anxious between our calls. I live from one call to the next, hating to hang up, counting the minutes until our next conversation. Do you feel the same? You say that you still love me, but is it the me of today or the memories of me that you love?

I guess only time will tell. But I can't wait! I really hope that you can work something out to see me when you come to NY. I'm hoping and counting the days.

"Love,
Al"

"Dear Al,
"See you on the 28th.
"Love,
Brett"

"Dear Brett,
"The 28th? For real?"

"Dear Al,
"Yes, for real. Let me know where and when and I'll be there. Can't wait to see you at last and continue this conversation in person. It's time."

"Dear Brett,
"Yes, I agree. I'll arrange my schedule and give you details. Maybe I should reserve a hotel room? Is that too forward and inappropriate?"

"Dear Al,
"No, not at all. A hotel room would be perfect, someplace we can have some privacy, sit and talk without staff or patients or life to intrude. I promise to be a gentleman."

And so the days passed with increasing excitement and anticipation. Our worlds, so separate and distant, were on a collision course. I wrote often and passionately, sent romantic e-cards, and indulged my fantasies. My heart and sense of romance, frozen for so long, was beginning to thaw. Maybe I could yet be a contender?

I left the office late Tuesday evening before leaving for NYC (*and Alana*) the next morning. I finished my tasks, office notes, and last-minute phone calls. I sent one last email to Alana, straight from the heart and yesteryear into the future:

A Love Poem for My Girl

Yours is a smile that lights up a room;
Mine is a laugh that drives away gloom.

Yours is a face that brings back my past;
Mine is a love that always will last.

Yours is a soul that's honest and true;
Mine is a heart that beats, "I love you…"

Yours is a mind that's searching and keen;
Mine is a sense of someone supreme.

Yours is a touch that I long to feel;
Mine is a passion that's ever so real.

Yours is a spirit that stirs my desire;
Mine is a fervor that never will tire.

Yours is a life that's meant to enjoy;
Mine is the essence of feelings of joy.

Yours is a beauty of highest degree;
Ours is a story always meant to be…

Chapter 27

May 26

Over the past ten days my focus had been on getting to New York and to Alana, without Sharon (or Jennifer) suspecting anything. Jennifer was engaged (to a wonderful guy) and her wedding was scheduled for July 24. She had previously suffered an awful traumatic last-minute broken engagement, and one thing I would *not* allow to happen would be ruining her wedding because of my new-found relationship with Alana. I remember going to my high school senior prom with a girl with whom I had already broken up (and we weren't the only ones there in that situation!). It was very unpleasant and that was peanuts compared to what *this* would have been like. I've had friends who separated shortly before their daughter's wedding, and the wedding had been a fiasco. Instead of a joyous occasion there was anger, discomfort, even fist-fights in the bathroom before, during, and after the ceremony. The family and group pictures were a travesty in and of themselves. I vowed not to do that to Jennifer. After the wedding I could accept it if my infidelity became apparent (though certainly not my choice and something I would do my best to avoid). But definitely not *before* the wedding!

I knew in my gut how important those next forty-eight hours would be. Of course I didn't know where the road would take me. Was I on the highway to paradise? Or was this my personal "second star on the right and straight on till morning": a one-way ticket to Neverland, that mythical place with a bright, shining, hopeful exterior concealing a dark underbelly of untold misadventures? I figured it was likely somewhere in between, a yellow brick road leading to a magical place of dreams, though there might be hidden dangers and challenges along the way. *Those* I was prepared to deal with.

I loaded the car with our suitcases, put Shanee in the back seat in her usual appointed spot, and headed north on I-95. I had made this drive many times before when visiting Jennifer, first Gainesville and the University of Florida, then to Philadelphia where she attended graduate school, and later to Manhattan. Shanee was a great traveler, quiet and comfortable in the back, always sleeping, lying quietly, or sometimes sitting up and watching the scenery go by. Staying in a pet-friendly hotel was more of a challenge since she had an inexplicable fear of elevators. No matter what strategy or ruse I employed, I could not get her into an elevator. So I had to carry her up the stairs in my arms (she weighed eighty pounds) to the room, and hope that she didn't need to go outside during the night. Otherwise, she was a sound sleeper and never a problem.

Spending nineteen hours in a car with Sharon would be another story. The silence was generally deafening, so I always kept the radio playing. Ironically, the first song I heard as I left the house was "Working My Way Back to you, Babe" by The Four Seasons. So apropos. I smiled inside.

I always stopped overnight in Fayetteville, North Carolina, the midway point between Fort Lauderdale and New York. After checking in (and carrying Shanee up two flights of stairs), I needed an excuse to get out of the room alone to speak with Alana. Sharon fell asleep so I took Shanee with me (back down the two flights of stairs), and took a walk along the country road outside the motel. As I walked Shanee I called Al and we had a long talk, about everything under the sun. I told her my feelings—that we were rapidly approaching a crossroads—and asked if she knew what she wanted to do? We had spent a month writing, talking, reliving, fantasizing, pretending—but now our worlds of pure fantasy were dissipating, and reality was upon us. Was she ready for that? Did she know what she wanted, or didn't want, could handle, or couldn't? I felt certain by then that I was ready—if our meeting went the way I hoped and thought it would—to make the move, to turn my life upside-down, to start anew with her. Maybe I was absurdly innocent and naïve to have reached that decision without having even seen her or touched her again? Maybe so, but I felt certain that I had found the right path. Alana seemed ready also. Timing is everything, and the Fates seemed to be on our side. We would find out soon enough (but *not* soon enough, as far as I was concerned).

Chapter 28

May 27

We left Fayetteville in the early morning, drove past Richmond, DC, Baltimore, Philadelphia, and got to New York by 6 p.m.. My daughter was waiting for us; we unloaded Shanee and the car, and went out for dinner. My daughter lived on the 23rd floor, and there was no way I could carry Shanee up that far; so I picked her up on the ground floor, walked into the elevator with her in my arms, and, despite her whining and squirming, held onto her until we got to the right floor. Then I lowered her to the ground and went to my daughter's apartment.

Jennifer was expectedly happy to see us. She was very excited about the upcoming wedding, and spent the whole evening discussing her plans, her dress, the venue, the band, the play list, Steve (my son-in-law to be), his friends, the guest list, and all the things that go along with it. I was glad to have all the distractions so that neither she nor Sharon would notice that far-away look in my eyes as I nervously anticipated the next day's events. I tried to stay focused on the conversation, but with some difficulty. But Sharon and Jennifer were so involved with the planning and details that they didn't seem to notice my distance and preoccupation.

After dinner we went back to the apartment, and Shanee was sleeping comfortably on Jennifer's bed. I truly loved that dog. She was a wonderful companion to me, always seemingly happy, happy to see me, happy to be at home or walking with me, a pick-me-up when I was down, and truly my best friend.

Shanee needed to go out before bedtime so I repeated the routine of carrying her down in the elevator, and walking her to Madison Square Park, a small piece of greenery in the middle of lower Manhattan. There was an enclosed dog-run there, where I could let her off her leash to run and mingle with other dogs. While I sat on a nearby bench in the early spring evening I called Alana. I wasn't sure if she'd be free, but she was, and we spoke for a few minutes, both knowing that tomorrow was a special day. Without acknowledging or voicing it directly, we also both knew that the events of the past month, as uplifting and encouraging as they were, would all unravel if tomorrow were less than we expected (and I, for one, expected a lot). Al had made reservations at a hotel not too far from where she lived, and would meet me there at 10 a.m. I noted the name and address, and told her how happy I was that we would finally have a chance to spend some time together. She said she felt the same way, and we would talk again in the morning when I was on my way. "See you tomorrow," I said; those became the happiest words in my lexicon for the next few months.

I walked back to Jennifer's apartment with Shanee, with a strange peace and serenity now competing and cohabiting with the baseline anxiety that had become my status quo for the past month.

At the apartment everything was quiet and seemingly normal. I went to bed, but couldn't drift off. Sharon was sleeping soundly, and in the middle of the night I got up and left the guest bedroom to lie down on the living room couch. In a strange way I almost felt like I would be cheating on Alana by sleeping next to Sharon that night, and I was not going to tarnish or diminish the next day's experience in any way. If Sharon realized I wasn't there and asked why, I would say that she was snoring and that kept me awake. The truth, of course, was that my dreams of yesterday and tomorrow would not be denied.

Chapter 29

May 28

At 5 a.m., I was still not sleeping, so I got up and made a cup of coffee. The sun was just coming up over the East River and skyline, and it was a beautiful dawn. I didn't allow myself too much time to daydream, though, and I showered and dressed before anyone else arose.

At 6 a.m., I was still the only one awake. I took Shanee downstairs for a walk, for her sake and mine, and then returned as Jennifer was coming out of her room. She assumed that I had gotten up to take care of Shanee so didn't ask any questions. She was off that day and had some chores lined up to do with Sharon. By 7 she was out of the shower and sat down with me for breakfast. I was too nervous to eat so I just had another cup of coffee while she prepared an English muffin for herself. I was a little (*a lot*) paranoid and watching her very carefully to detect if she suspected anything was awry. But she seemed perfectly normal.

By 8 a.m., Jennifer was drying her hair. Sharon was still not up. I took my briefcase (for my "business meeting"), kissed Jenn good-bye, and went downstairs. Once I got into my car I called Alana:

"Good morning, Al. It's a beautiful day in the neighborhood!" (I was almost singing I was so excited.)

"Good morning to you! You're certainly in a good mood."

"Yes I am, and for good reason. I'm on my way."

"Great! Me, too. I have to get Pierce off to school, and then I'm leaving. Can't wait to see you."

"Ditto. I'll call when I get there and you can tell me which room you're in."

"Sounds good. See you soon."

With that brief conversation I set my navigation system, pulled out of the parking garage onto East 30th Street and headed for the FDR Drive, and my future. I could barely contain my excitement.

I spent the next hour or so in moderate rush-hour traffic. Most of the traffic was going into Manhattan at that hour, and I was leaving Manhattan, so it wasn't too bad. Having grown up on the Island and lived in Manhattan, I knew the roads pretty well, and didn't have to focus too much on the directions. But rush-hour traffic, even light-moderate, is still challenging and one thing I didn't need was an accident, even a minor fender-bender that would seriously disrupt my plans. So I was extra careful, hands at ten and two, used turn signals whenever changing lanes, watched the speed limit, kept an eye out for cop cars, and drove very defensively—basically driving the way one should all the time, but most people (including myself) don't. Once out of Manhattan the traffic lightened and I eased into a comfortable 60 mph in the center lane of the Expressway. I wanted everything to be perfect. I knew Alana was a big fan of Starbucks, so I wanted to find a Starbucks near the hotel and bring her a cup of her favorite coffee. I wanted to find a florist and bring her a red rose. I wanted her to open the door, see the rose and me at the same time, and melt in my arms. Of course, I knew that was over-the-top fantasy, but at least I wanted to do my very best to stack the deck in my favor.

Unfortunately I could find neither a Starbucks nor a florist, so, rather than risk being late, I went to the hotel and called. Alana immediately answered and said, "I'm in Room 222. Just come on up." So I did. As I stood before the door, I thought back over all the years and all the history we had. I had had other relationships, including a long marriage and a child; I had been through so much, with all the schooling and medical/surgical training, my dad's death, leaving New York for California, my fellowship and life in San Diego, my move to Florida and my life and practice there. Yet Alana was the defining relationship of my life. Dante had his Beatrice; Romeo had his Juliet; and I had had my Alana. What would I find on the other side of this door? Who would be there, and how would I feel? Were my feelings real or just based on a fantasized memory of a time long ago? Now the rubber would meet the road.

So I knocked on the door and waited nervously for what seemed like hours, but which was actually only seconds. I heard footsteps from inside the room, the door handle turning, and the door opening. I prepared to step inside, not knowing what to expect, but excited, cautiously optimistic, hopefully romantic, and knowing that something important was about to happen. All systems go...

PART II

Chapter 1

December 31, 1969

"So tell me about Dale's cousin, Alana," I said to Eddie as I climbed into the front seat of his dark brown Buick Skylark. Eddie had been my best friend since junior high, and we had known each other from the time we were four or five years old. He was a few months younger than I, and we initially had become close during summer camp. Our parents both owned summer bungalows in a small community in White Meadow Lake, New Jersey, about thirty-five miles west of New York City. He was always in the "younger" camp group but hung around with me and my friends. When you're pre-teens, a few months in age can make a big difference, but Ed's parents, Nat and Paulette, were friends of my parents, and we lived a block and a half away from each other both in White Meadow and in Queens, New York, so we gravitated towards each other until we were inseparable. Jamaica, New York was a bedroom community, upper middle-class, Caucasian and largely Jewish. Overall, I enjoyed a relatively carefree childhood, with my biggest responsibility being tomorrow's homework and next week's school quiz.

It's great having a best friend growing up. My brother, although only two years my senior, always seemed to be much older and in a different world. Because of the "SP" (special progress) programs so prevalent in the 1960s, he was four grades ahead of me academically, and never in the same school I attended. When I was in elementary school he was in junior high; when I was in junior high he was in high school; when I was in high school he had already left for college. So, for better or for worse, we never really connected, had similar interests, friends, etc. I was more of an athlete, he more of a student. I was more gregarious, he more of a loner. He went off to Brown University at age sixteen and never really returned home again. He knew what he wanted career-wise from a very early age, and planned to follow in my father's footsteps and become a doctor. So he applied, and was accepted, into the medical science program at Brown, which was a very labor- and time-intensive program, including summer courses every year, and little vacation. Six years at Brown gave him a bachelor's degree and Master's in Medical Science, and a direct conduit into Harvard University Medical School. He followed that with a residency in Boston at a prestigious Harvard-affiliated hospital, then two years at the National Institute of Health for fellowship training in pulmonary medicine. He graduated and was ready to enter medical practice when I was just finishing college. He knew exactly where he was going, and I, by and large, was taking my time, "searching for myself" as the saying went back then, and looking for a purpose and direction. In any event we were close in age but light years apart in personality and spirit. To this day, we have never been close, and I regret the lost opportunity to bond with my older brother.

My sister certainly deserves mention. Much younger than me (by seven years), she was always the baby of the family, and more of a negative than a positive in my life. Although I didn't appreciate it at the time, I could have been the poster-child for the classic middle child syndrome. There is something unique about a middle child who is the same sex as the oldest, but with a younger opposite-gender sibling. My older brother got all the attention (and pressures) of the first child—burdened with the expectations of successful parents, and expected to be all Dad and Mom dreamed of. When I came along, it was same-old, same-old, and my parents had been there, done that, so my appearance and experience didn't quite have the same excitement as my brother's. Everything he did was new and first-time; everything I did seemed to be a repetition of his, a second go-round. I resented all the focus and excitement he got, so acted out to make my presence known, but not all that successfully. I learned to occupy and satisfy myself, which turned out to be a good thing as I grew older: I never was a needy kid, and never became a needy adult.

When my sister came along, she (the first daughter) stole center stage again, and I remained in the shadows. My sister had a very troubled childhood (diagnosed as Oedipal Complex by a Freudian therapist whom she treated with) and sucked all the oxygen out of the household. She developed a nervous "tic" which drove my dad crazy. Various psychiatrists started her on medications to control her symptoms, and the possible side effects of these drugs (of which my dad, a physician, was all too aware) made him even more worried as he closely observed his daughter. In a counter-intuitive, paradoxical way, the side effects of the meds mimicked the symptoms the meds were supposed to control. So were the tics real or were they side effects? Who knew? But I know who worried, day and night. And that would be my dad. Life in the Berson household was pretty tense during my "formative years."

So despite having a nuclear family of five, I never felt very satisfied, nurtured, or complete at home. Luckily, I had Eddie, who lived so nearby in a time and place when a young boy could walk alone two blocks without the fear of abduction or impending doom that parents now face. In truth, through my early teenage years, I grew up in Eddie's house more than in my own. His parents were salt-of-the-earth, terrific people, and he had younger twin sisters who became my close friends as well. Interestingly, his sisters eventually became high school classmates of Alana, and the various universes of my childhood merged and overlapped (coincidence or karma?). Everything always seemed so relaxed at Eddie's house. His parents weren't uptight about their kids; they had a beautiful collie named Misty who was as much a part of the family as any of them; everyone did their own thing without the weight of worry and anxiety that was ever-present in my house. Eddie rarely came over to visit me because it just wasn't as much fun. My sister was always an issue, with all the focus on giving her room and space, not setting her off (worsening her tics, etc), and she was clearly the dictator, to my and my parents' detriment. My brother was lucky to get the hell out of Dodge before things got too crazy. I wish he had been there longer to share some of the burden with me. But instead I felt very alone at home. I did all I could to support my parents, a strange role reversal for an adolescent. I instinctively and subconsciously empathized with their plight, and wanted to help and be the "good son." But sadly they never thanked me or told me they appreciated my efforts or sacrifice. That would have made it a lot easier for me. So I escaped, too, although only down the block, but it was still another world, and one that I badly needed. I'm forever in Eddie's debt, as well as his family's. They saved my childhood. Even after my parents sold the bungalow in White Meadow, I continued to spend parts of my summers there with Ed and his family. I knew all the other teens and remained part of that community.

I'll never forget one summer, with Ed's dad driving in New Jersey on Route 3, there was a terrible thunderstorm, and the car hit an oil slick. The car started rotating, and all I remember are the headlights glaring off the rain on the windshield as the car spun out of control. I later learned that we jumped the divider, were narrowly missed by a diesel tanker, and instead were struck by two cars coming from the opposite direction. Miraculously, none of us was seriously hurt: Nat had a broken rib, Paulette a splenic contusion from the seat belt, and my knee was banged up a little from being tossed around (no back seat seatbelts in those days). Nat and Paulette were taken to the hospital for observation, and Ed and I went home by cab after stopping by the junkyard where the (totaled) car had been towed to clean out the trunk. Had we been hit by the tanker a few seconds earlier, none of us would have survived to tell the tale. It was really a miracle; Ed and I never forgot that night and the lives we were given. Narrowly averting disaster collectively can bring people together, and after that fateful night we were bonded as never before.

Eddie and I went through all the adventures of pre- and post-pubescent adolescence together. We went to high school parties and double-dated; we took Driver's Education together, and went out driving the minute we passed our driver's tests. I remember coming home from the DMV with my first driver's license—what an exhilarating feeling!! Having never driven alone before, never driven in inclement weather, or after dark, or on the highway, all of a sudden we had licenses, and off we went in my mother's Chrysler Valiant 100, in the rain, at night, on the highway—surely a recipe for disaster. At 100 horsepower, the car was barely more than a powered lawnmower; otherwise we surely would have killed ourselves, and I never would have gotten to tell this story. We had the luxury of being young and foolish, and I guess God was looking over us because we survived that night, and other typical teenage craziness. We spent Friday nights at Hillcrest Jewish Center teenage Shabbat services, and Saturdays we were in two bowling leagues together.

Eddie and I went to different high schools but graduated at the same time, and went off to college. In retrospect, we should have tried harder to attend the same university. But what did we know—we were just kids facing youth's great adventures. I went to Yale, to major in pre-med studies, and Eddie to Cornell to learn to be a vet. Those plans went by the wayside pretty quickly, and by the end of the first semester Eddie was an accounting major and I decided to leave school. I had worked so hard in high school I was burned out at eighteen! I felt ready to retire before I'd even gotten started, so I needed some time away from academia. For the first time I had the opportunity to question my direction, and wondered if medicine was really right for me. Coming from a family of physicians (my uncle, my father, my brother), it seemed like the natural, if not the only, thing to do. But maybe it wasn't? And I needed a break to recharge my batteries, consider my options, and have some down-time. My academic schedule that first semester was hardcore—introduction to everything, with an emphasis on a science track leading to medical school. I think it was Inorganic Chemistry that finally did me in. The course was so confusing that I (who had never gotten a grade below B), received a "16" on the first test. I was devastated! The fact that it was above the class average was little consolation. It seems that life is a series of climbing ladders: when we finally make it to the top of one, we move on to the next level and start off at the bottom all over again. I was riding high as a senior in high school, felt like king of the world the summer after my senior year, then revisited the depths as a freshman in college. I wasn't prepared for that, nor the prospect of four more intense years. It's been said that there's no heavier burden than a great potential. And I was feeling it.

So I mustered up all the courage I could and told my parents I wanted to take a leave of absence from school, nearly unheard of in those days, and especially in my family of overachievers. My dad was surprisingly understanding (my mom, not so much). Little did I know what awaited me...

* * *

So I returned home for Christmas break, feeling pretty low about life in general. For the first time I felt adrift, with no anchor, traction, or direction. Pre-med suddenly seemed a lot less glamorous than it was cracked up to be—I didn't like the classes, or the students, and felt no excitement about the prospect of being a doctor. Don't get me wrong: my dad was a terrific physician, a general practitioner who was as honest and ethical as they come. Atticus Finch from *To Kill a Mockingbird* was the fictional character who most embodied the qualities of Aaron Berson. My dad's favorite historical character was Moses: a brave leader, with a strong moral compass, courageous and willing to tend to his flock and lead by example. Dad was a doctor in the days when people came to their family doctor the way they would come to their clergy. Practicing in Richmond Hill, New York, a largely Italian neighborhood, Dad was in many ways on the same level as the local priest: a figure respected and loved in the community, someone to whom people would come for advice and spiritual support, for treatment for the soul as much as for the body. Oftentimes parishioners were too afraid of Father Colonna to come to him with their problems. But Dad was a gentle soul, and they could always count on a sensitive, receptive ear no matter what the issue.

Dad's office was a small but very homey place—nothing stark or sterile about it—on the corner down the block from where we lived when I was born. It was a "railroad apartment," one long hall with a series of small rooms jutting off the corridor. There was an outside entrance for the patients, and an inside entrance for Dad and his "staff"—one nurse who worked with him for his entire thirty-five-year-practice life! Joann first came to work for my father fresh out of nursing school—a very little girl who actually looked younger than her age. At nineteen, with an associate degree in nursing, she looked more like Dad's daughter than his nurse. The waiting room had the expected *Life* magazines, which never got thrown away but only aged with time, and always a policeman's cap prominently displayed on the coat rack, even though there was no policeman in the office. That cap was the entire security system, and there was never a problem. The patients were salt-of-the-earth, God-fearing folk who respected their doctor, and their local cop on the beat. I enjoyed going to the office with Dad and hanging out in his "lab," a small room with the same microscope my father had used in medical school, a small centrifuge to spin down blood samples, some urine test strips, and a few basic chemicals to stain slides and do "Gram" stains. He also had a simple X-ray machine (we joked that it was salvaged from Roentgen's scrap heap), no more than an old cathode-ray tube and some plates with which he took basic radiographs and did some "barium swallows." All in all, it was as bare-bones an operation as one could imagine, yet somehow the medical care given was exceptional. Dad treated with his heart as much as with his head and hands, and anyone who treats patients knows that patient care is all about caring for the patient; compassion and concern are the most valuable commodities a doctor can possess. And Dad had enough heart for his whole community.

My dad was highly intelligent, keen, and insightful, with an intellectual curiosity that led him to study history, philosophy, literature, and all things academic. He and my mom met when they were adolescents (introduced by my dad's best friend, who just so happened to be my mom's brother), and their love story lasted fifty years. My grandparents came from Eastern Europe, sent to the U.S. on their own as teenagers to find a better life in the States. They spoke no English, had no prospects, but were taken in by the Jewish immigrant community in Brooklyn and found their way. My parents were first-generation Americans who grew up in poverty during the Depression and knew that the key to realizing the American Dream was hard work. Women were largely second-class citizens at the time, relegated to stay-at-home-mom status, and neither of my grandmothers was gainfully employed. Both my grandfathers worked in the garment district, common employment for Jewish immigrants of the day, and provided for their family with the little they had.

My mom went to Barnard College and became a social worker and a government employee during World War II, while my dad's dream was to become a physician. His intellect and work ethic carried the day. Despite the generally-negative and anti-Semitic sentiments of the zeitgeist, my dad was committed to his dream. Notwithstanding high academic achievement at City College, he wasn't accepted to medical school, but he never gave up. He secured a position doing research at the Museum of Natural History in Manhattan, and amazingly pioneered the studies that illuminated the chemical basis for animal behavior. Had he stayed at the museum, he likely would have risen to curator of the department (the position held by his supervisor, Lester Aronson). But my dad was committed to being a doctor, eventually was accepted to medical school, and the rest is history. Interestingly, my mom's brother (who was their "Eddie"), another member of their Jewish intelligentsia, also struggled to achieve acceptance to medical school. He was rejected four years running. Eventually he too became a doctor and medical scientist, concentrating on research to cure his mother's diabetes, which eventually led to his work earning a Nobel Prize in medicine. The lesson here? Hard work and dedication pay off.

But despite his heady intellect, my dad was practical too, and in his infinite wisdom he told me the three things in human life that are most important:

1) Always be honest and you'll never go wrong;
2) Be your own boss, if at all possible;
3) Live within twenty minutes of where you work.

Wiser words were never spoken, and I tried to follow his guidance in all matters.

To return to our story, needless to say my parents were disappointed at my decision to leave school. What made matters worse was that the Vietnam War was escalating and the U.S. had an active draft program, to which I was subject without a college/academic deferment. Everybody had advice for me—go back to school, go to Canada, seek conscientious objector status, etc. I wasn't sure what to do, but I did know I didn't want to go to war. Even Inorganic Chemistry seemed better than that!! I'd figure it out as time went by.

So New Year's Eve 1969 was a strange time for me. I had no idea where I was or where I was going. I wasn't ready to go back to New Haven, but didn't know what else to do. I didn't even have plans for New Year's. So when Eddie (who was home from Cornell) said, "Let's double-date. I have four tickets for the Rangers at Madison Square Garden. I can set you up with Dale's cousin, Alana," I thought, *Why not?* I knew and liked Dale, but didn't know her cousin. I certainly had nothing better to do. Staying home with my parents, with their tone of disapproving concern, was not the way to ring in the New Year. So it was a date, a blind-date, with Alana. Dale was cute, so I was cautiously optimistic. And Eddie wouldn't let me down. The set-up for your best friend is fraught with peril. So much can go wrong. But what the hell; it was just one night, right? Not exactly…

Chapter 2

"So tell me about Dale's cousin," I asked again. "Tell me about Alana."

"She's beautiful," Eddie said.

"Really? Then why is she free on New Year's Eve?"

"Her parents are going out with Dale's. So instead of them staying at Dale's house, they're okay with Alana going out with us. Don't worry, you'll like her. And her parents like that you go to Yale."

Alana was younger than us, fifteen at the time, in 11th grade. Somehow that seemed young to me, who was all of eighteen. High school seemed *so long* ago, and she was only a junior. But it was only one night, right?

So we showed up at Dale's home, a two-story townhouse in Queens. Dale and her sister Karen, Alana, and both sets of parents were already there. I was a little nervous, but had few expectations and so few worries. At worst, I would see a Rangers game at the Garden with my best friend—how bad could that be? At best? I didn't even think of that. I was in such a funk with my school situation and the uncertainties of my immediate, as well as distant, future I really wasn't thinking of much else.

Eddie had been dating Dale off and on during his senior year in high school, so he knew everyone there. He and I did most things together (especially after we got our driver's licenses and grabbed every opportunity to get behind the wheel and explore our new-found freedom), including visiting Dale and her folks, raiding their fridge when we didn't have dinner there, even going out to movies with the family. They had become part of our extended family. In many ways I was closer to my various extended families than I was to my own nuclear family, so I really enjoyed the company and camaraderie. Eddie was extremely likable and friendly, and I benefited by being virtually an appendage, connected at the hip. Eddie had also met Alana's parents, although I never had. So he felt very much at home when we walked into Dale's house, and, as was his practice, he went right to the fridge to see what were the leftovers of the day. I wasn't quite that uninhibited, although I felt free accepting whatever was offered.

Dale's folks, Nat and Ruth, were hard-working, middle-class solid citizens. Nat worked in a shoe store nearby, and Ruth did secretarial work. They were plain in a way, but honest, unassuming, and very good people, as reflected in the harmony of the home and the quality children they begat. Dale's older sister was always the goody-two-shoes, a well-disciplined, respectful young lady, a straight-A student who never gave her parents a day of trouble, and always got along with everyone. She was the type of daughter every parent wished they had and would be proud to call their own. Karen was several years Dale's senior and already deep into her college and pre-med career by then. A very bright academic and professional future could be predicted and awaited her, as she ultimately became dean at a world-class medical school, a pioneer in telemedicine (with a campus building named in her honor), and even got to meet the Queen of England later in her career.

Dale, on the other hand, like so many second children, was much more of a rebel. She followed her instincts, whether they pleased her parents or not. It must have been tough being the younger sister of such a "practically perfect in every way" older sibling. Don't get me wrong—Dale was a great girl, full of life, and spirit, always quick to laugh and seize the *joie de vivre* that others may have missed. Every day was a new adventure, a new opportunity to make a new friend and enjoy a new experience. Dale and Alana were as inseparable as Eddie and I. Their parents were close so they spent a lot of family time together growing up. Their uncle Len owned a summer camp in Maine, and they spent many summers together as campers, creating mischief and having adventures at Camp Waziyatah. They shared a close connection borne of their common upbringing.

As I mentioned, I found Dale very attractive, physically and otherwise. But she was my best friend's girlfriend, so she was certainly off-limits. There are some lines you don't cross, and that was certainly one of them. I always felt that Eddie never treated Dale as well as he should have, that he didn't appreciate her, and that I did. She should have been my girlfriend! But she wasn't, so I had to be content being the third wheel during a lot of my senior year. Eddie and Dale stayed in touch when he went off to Cornell, and it was natural for him to spend New Year's Eve with her when he came home for Christmas break. And it was natural for me to be with them. I didn't have a steady girlfriend at the time, so it was a perfect set-up. But I had no idea how strangely the evening would evolve, or what would follow.

So I was in a pretty good mood when we pulled up to Dale's house. Eddie knocked on the front door, Karen opened it, and I was glad to see her. As usual, she had a big, bright smile and I felt welcome and comfortable immediately. I was very much at-home and familiar with Karen and at Dale's house. And as I looked over her left shoulder I saw a new face, which I knew was Alana. I must say that my first impression was that Eddie was right—Alana was beautiful!! She had shoulder-length blonde hair, and a radiant smile that lit up the room. She must have been a little nervous too, because she hung back a bit, sneaking peeks at the door while pretending to be in deep conversation with Dale. But as soon as Eddie walked in (and headed straight for the fridge instead of straight for Dale!), Alana was left alone as Dale headed for Eddie.

I kissed Karen on the cheek and wished her Happy New Year, but couldn't take my eyes off Alana! Wow! The more I looked, the more I felt drawn to her. There's a dream sequence in *West Side Story* when Tony first sees Maria across a room. Suddenly the ambient noise and conversation recede, everything becomes blurry except for the two of them. I actually had that feeling. The iconic enchanted evening when one sees a stranger across a crowded room and falls in love seemed to be happening to me. And, of course, when I least expected it. My life was at its nadir, and I was feeling so low until that moment, and then, as corny as it sounds, my heart skipped a beat and I felt an adrenaline rush I hadn't experienced in a long time.

But before I met Alana I needed to say my hellos to Dale, Nat, Ruth, and, most important of all, make the requisite introduction and positive first impression on Alana's parents. Gladys and Milton became very important people in my life, and to this day I remember our first meeting. Milton was sitting on the couch talking to Nat, but was very aware of my entrance, as every father of a teenage daughter should be. Gladys was standing with Ruth, smoking a cigarette, with a cocktail in her hand. She was striking in appearance, a center of attention by design, and appreciating every bit of it. She had jet-black hair, was very slender, wore stiletto heels, and a beautiful cocktail dress. "Dressed to kill" may have been a term invented for Gladys. She was quite made up, and wore very flashy jewelry, bling before there was a word for bling. There was nothing subtle or understated about Gladys. Everything about her was over the top. In high school I had always been popular with parents. Why not? I was clean cut, studious, academically at the top of my class, with aspirations of becoming a doctor like my dad. I was "going places," and parents of girls I dated always thought I'd be a good catch. When I went off to college I decided to change my image somewhat. The day of high school graduation was the last day I shaved, and by the time I went off to New Haven I had a very thick and bushy black beard. I let my hair grow long, and, in retrospect, looked pretty wild, much like most of my freshman classmates. That was the look back then, Castro-esque by design at a time when it was cool to be a rebel with a cause. However the Yale legacy must have overwhelmed the Manson look, because both Milton and Gladys seemed very friendly. In retrospect I'm not sure I would have trusted my fifteen-year-old daughter with someone who looked like I did back then, but whatever...

Dale was wrapped around Eddie, so I headed right for Gladys. I instinctively knew that the way to Alana was through her mom, and I needed to make a good first impression. So I walked up to her, extended my hand, and said, "Hello, I'm Brett Berson. So nice to meet you."

As people go, Alana's dad Milton was 180 degrees apart from Gladys. If opposites attract, I understand their connection. While Gladys was flashy and glamorous, slightly coquettish, Milton was quiet and unpretentious. He wore an open- collar, button-down shirt and slacks, and no jewelry other than a plain, gold wedding band, his college ring, and a Seiko watch. His hair was thinning, black, and parted on the side, and he was clean-shaven, though with a swarthy appearance. He could've had a great beard if he had wanted to, I thought. He had the slightly stooped-over posture of so many middle-aged Jewish men, which made him appear a bit shorter than he actually was, and in a way it made him look as though he were carrying the weight of the world on his shoulders. His eyebrows were bushy and his eyes black. His face had few wrinkles, and there was a certain twinkle in his eye, which hinted at a hidden lighter side that belied the almost stern exterior. He arose from the couch and came over to greet me with a firm handshake. He looked me right in the eyes as he said simply, "Hello, Brett. I see you've met the Queen of Sheba," as he tilted his head towards Gladys and smiled. There was a gentle sarcasm in his voice, which I would hear many more times as I grew to know them both better.

"What are your plans for this evening?"

"We have tickets to see the Rangers at the Garden, and then we'll be going out for dinner," I said. I had no particular plans for the evening, honorable or otherwise, so had no reason to seem disingenuous, and Gladys and Milton both seemed comfortable trusting their daughter with me. Such had been my experience with other parents, so it seemed perfectly natural to me as well. The truth is that I just wanted to have some fun, see a hockey game, and move on to 1970. My intentions were honorable in that regard.

"How are you getting to the game?" Milton asked.

"We're driving to Kew-Gardens, and then taking the subway from there. We'll probably come back to Queens after the game, and have dinner at Jahn's on Queens Boulevard."

"Sounds good. We're just going to a friend's house for the evening so we'll be nearby and won't be out late," Milton said.

"Tell me, Brett," interjected Gladys. "How do you know Eddie?"

"Ed's my oldest friend. And I've known Dale since last year," I answered, wondering if I was being paranoid or if there were some undercurrent of suspicion in Gladys' question?

At that slightly awkward moment, Ruth walked over and said, "Milt, Gladys, I see you've met Brett."

"Yes, and he seems like a very nice boy. Brett, have you met Alana yet?" Gladys asked.

"Actually no, but I'd like to."

"Al, come here please. This is Eddie's friend, Brett," Gladys motioned, and Alana came over. There was some more small-talk but I can only remember seeing Alana for the first time up-close. I do believe in love at first sight for a certain lucky few, and I fell and fell hard. I stood for a few minutes with what must have been a really goofy grin on my face; for the first time in months I felt really excited. Timing is everything, and it was *so* the right time for me. I needed to feel good about something, and here was something totally unexpected and potentially really special. An hour before I had been down in the dumps, with nothing to look forward to, but now I felt it was a new day. The weight of the past few months seemed to be lifting. I felt great!

Shortly thereafter we gathered our coats, scarves, and gloves, and left for the city. I sat next to Alana in the back seat. Eddie was his usual garrulous self, and he and Dale seemed very comfortable together. They were chatting away and laughing, and kept us all engaged in the conversation, so there was little time for me and Alana to face the sometimes-awkward silences of a first date. I had intended just to spend an evening with my friends with no other agenda; but now I did begin thinking that I should spend some energy to impress this new girl and try to get to know her better, even lay some groundwork for another date? I had nothing else going for me then, so this was perfect.

The New York subway system is legendary for many things, even falling in love. How many times have there been scenes of a man running to catch a train, only to have the doors close before he can get on, and he stands helplessly on the platform as the object of his affection pulls away?. Or that momentary glance through the window of a train barreling down the tracks which signals first love, and the beginning of a search to find the beloved? My personal favorite "train love scene" has to do with the way Bogart describes waiting for Ingrid

Bergman in *Casablanca* as they are about to leave occupied Paris. He waited and waited but she never showed up, and he describes the sudden shock of realization and somewhat comical (though not really) look on his face as though someone had just punched him in the gut. How powerful!

So my first subway ride with Alana was one of falling in love. The platforms and trains were packed, it being New Year's Eve. We stood, holding onto the hand rails, squeezed together in the crowded cars. I remember feeling very hot and flushed—maybe because I was wearing a winter coat in the hot, stuffed subway car, but maybe for other reasons, too. It was too noisy to talk, so we just stood next to each other, swaying with the train and the crowd, waiting to reach Penn Station. Somehow Eddie was able to talk above the crowd, and he didn't miss a beat. His generally good mood was contagious.

When we finally reached our stop, we poured out of the train with the throng, and walked up the stairs into the cool, refreshing night air. I tried to walk next to Alana, but didn't feel comfortable holding her hand yet. We were also both wearing gloves; but I always found it especially romantic seeing couples with gloved hand in gloved hand. Walking in Manhattan is a challenge unto itself. Pedestrian traffic can be worse than vehicular traffic, and with no rules of the road—people rushing by in opposite directions, no lanes, cutting in and out, squeezing by and between, with little regard for each other. If people drove this way!! It was so crowded I could barely stay next to Alana and did my best to navigate and stay generally with her, Eddie, and Dale.

We got to the Garden and to our seats. Alana wanted to sit next to her cousin, so she and Dale sat in the middle with Eddie and me on both ends—proper dating etiquette but not so good for watching a hockey game with your best friend. Alana seemed very outgoing with Dale, but very shy with me. I didn't know if she didn't like me or just didn't know me? She warmed up as the evening progressed, but I don't think she really enjoyed the hockey game very much. But we were out with an enthusiastic crowd in the middle of the Big Apple on New Year's Eve, so the spirit of the evening was very positive. And to top it all off: Rangers 2, Blackhawks 1 (a good omen if ever there was one)! It's always way more fun when the home team wins. And we joined the 19,000 jubilant fans exiting "The World's Most Famous Arena." All in all, I left the Garden feeling pretty good about everything. I did hold Alana's hand walking back to the subway, and even put my arm around her on the subway back to Queens. She didn't mind at all. Things seemed to be working out!

Chapter 3

Late dinner at Jahn's, a local diner/coffee shop/ice cream parlor, was the first time I really had the chance to look directly at Alana without worrying that I might be staring. We sat across from each other in a booth, with Eddie next to me and Dale next to Alana—a perfect arrangement! It was easiest to let Eddie carry the conversation, but I was mostly looking at and listening to Alana. Eddie and Dale were a laugh-riot and the life of the party, but as the evening progressed Alana and I became more comfortable with each other and with the situation, and before midnight we were all laughing together, telling stories of our upbringing, our parents, our families, etc. Eddie had younger twin sisters who also knew Dale and Alana so there was a lot of overlap amongst our friends and families. Eddie and Dale both went to Jamaica High, a large municipal public high school with over a thousand students. Alana and I went to much smaller private schools, so we had no friends in common, but we listened and laughed in the spirit of the evening. By 11:30, we were finished eating, and ready to go back to Dale's house to watch Dick Clark and the crystal ball over Times Square count down the end of 1969.

I must have been doing something right because Alana leaned against me in the back seat, and seemed quietly contented for most of the ride. We were holding hands (without gloves by now) and even playing little games with our fingers. Eddie and Dale were laughing it up in the front seat, the radio was blaring the popular '60s music of the day, and I felt very relaxed. When we got back to Dale's house, the parents were not home yet, so we put on the TV and prepared to ring in the New Year's. Although Eddie and I were both eighteen and old enough to buy alcohol legally, for whatever reason we didn't, and didn't raid the liquor cabinet at the house either. I'd like to say we felt morally obligated to our dates and their parents, but I'm sure that wasn't the reason. I really don't know why we didn't. But the strangest thing happened, which even now I can't explain, and I can't blame alcohol. The sixties were a pretty wild ride—the Vietnam War was in full force, college campuses were up in arms and protesting, illegal drugs including hallucinogens were the designer drugs of choice, and sexual mores were pushing the envelope. But Eddie and I were conservative for teenagers of that era. Our drug experimentation barely strayed beyond marijuana (although I had tried LSD at school), we drank beer and little else, protested peacefully (mostly in order to miss class), and led lives typical of teenagers: young and foolish, not wild and crazy. But that evening something came over us. The crystal ball came down and "1970" lit up brightly on the TV. The masses in Time Square starting singing "Auld Lang Syne," streamers and confetti were released, horns were blaring, and people were singing. Eddie kissed Dale Happy New Year, and I got up the courage to kiss Alana…at first on the cheek, then closer to her lips, and then full on the lips! And she kissed me back. Then Eddie kissed Alana *on the lips* and Dale planted one right on *my* lips! Now this may seem very tame but to me it was extraordinary! I then kissed Alana again, while Eddie kissed Dale, and we switched partners again. This game of "switchies" continued for a while, and seemed really weird to me. Eddie knew Alana and I knew Dale, so it wasn't as bizarre as it could have been. But it seemed very strange, nonetheless, nothing I had ever done before or since. It didn't go any further than kissing for a while. Then Eddie and Dale decided to go upstairs for some privacy, leaving Alana and me alone downstairs. By this point we felt comfortable being together, and even being alone together. We didn't talk very much, and didn't do much more than kiss, but I still remember the magic of that night. Kissing is very underrated, and kissing on a first date can be the sexiest, most erotic experience of all, and it was that night for me. I never wanted that night to end, but by 1 a.m. the parents came home. There was some pretty fast shuffling upstairs, but we all managed to make it to the couch when the front door opened. Perhaps the parents were a little tipsy themselves because no one commented on the mussed makeup, wrinkled clothing, or early beard-burn on Alana's face. Eddie and I said hasty goodnights, and were on our way into 1970. He had a good New Year's Eve. I had a *great* New Year's Eve. The sun was setting on Eddie and Dale, but Alana and I were just beginning, and the golden dawn of New Year's Day was a bright tomorrow for me. My life was about to change—in fact it already had.

Chapter 4

The car ride back to my house was mostly quiet. It was late, we were tired, and we were both basking in the afterglow of a really fun evening together. Of course we discussed our sexual activity; mine was tame in comparison but very satisfying nonetheless. Eddie dropped me off at my house, and we planned to touch base the next day. My parents were already asleep, the house was dark and still, and I was glad to be alone to relive the evening. Every first date is so full of promise, usually unrealized, and desire, usually unfulfilled. I wondered if this would be different? I decided to call Alana the next day, and ask her out again. I went to bed, feeling excited…and maybe in love?

New Year's Day was spent traditionally at my great Aunt Charlotte's apartment in the Bronx; it had been for as long as I could remember. Charlotte was married to my mother's Uncle Irving, one of six siblings who were first-generation Americans, having immigrated to the U.S. in the early 1900s when they were barely teenagers. I was always fascinated by the story of my grandparents' generation. They were truly the "tired, poor, huddled masses, wretched refuse, homeless, tempest-tossed" welcomed to America by the Statue of Liberty. If America is an immigrant nation, she has been made great by that generation, maybe the real "Greatest Generation." My grandparents all came to the States from Eastern Europe at the turn of the century, with the hope of a better life. Anti-Semitism was rampant and their parents knew that the best chance for their children to survive and succeed was to send them to America. Personally I cannot imagine sending my children off to an unknown place with the hope of a better tomorrow. I also cannot imagine being a virtual child and leaving my home for a foreign land, unable to speak the language, without my parents or any other familial support. But somehow they did it. And their story is not unique. They sailed across the Atlantic, traveling third-class on ocean steamers, went through Ellis Island, and found a community to take them in on the Lower East Side of New York. Somehow they survived—they learned the language, amalgamated into the fabric of American life (as heterogeneous as it was), and worked their way into society. Most amazing to me was their academic success—my grandfather somehow was accepted into Columbia University, received a degree in Chemical Engineering, and became successful in the fur-dyeing business. His genius lay in concocting chemical formulae and designing techniques for dyeing inexpensive furs (rabbit, squirrel, raccoon, etc.) to look like mink and chinchilla. His "secret formulas" remain a secret to this day, unfortunately dying with him because he was afraid to write them down for fear that they would be stolen by his employees or competitors. My great Uncle Irving chose a different, equally accomplished, course. He, too, graduated from City College, and somehow was accepted into Harvard Law School, *as a Jew*, unheard of in those days. He graduated successfully, received his JD, and entered a law practice in New York. Sounds good, so far, no? But every family has a crazy old uncle, and Irving was mine. For reasons no one would disclose, great Uncle Irving stopped working in his mid-40s, and never held a job again. He simply stayed at home while Charlotte supported them, working as a medical transcriptionist. Exactly what happened to his once-promising legal career remains a mystery.

In any event, Charlotte and Irving had one of the very first color television sets, and for years (until color TV was perfected and prevalent) we never ceased to be amazed at this new technology. Truth be told, the colors were awful in those days—garish, unrealistic, blurry. The NBC peacock was the most striking icon of all. My uncle spent most of the day adjusting the control knobs to improve the picture, but with little success. Yet compared to black-and-white, it was still amazing. So we all huddled around the TV, watching the college football bowl games, and chowing down on my aunt's traditional buffet of stuffed cabbage, brisket, cold cuts, and home-made pastries and cake. She was a good cook, and it was always a treat that I relished. My father was not much of a sports fan, and would usually sit in a corner reading a book, but not in an unfriendly, unsociable way—he simply preferred philosophy to football, and we were all okay with that. The accommodation was mutual.

New Year's Day in New York was usually cold, blustery, and often snowy, and I always envied the short-sleeve crowd, the sunlight, and palm trees in Pasadena for the Rose Bowl and in Miami for the Orange Bowl. Every year I vowed that someday I would move to California or Florida. And "someday" I did, eventually splitting my professional career between San Diego and Fort Lauderdale. But that year I was more lost in thought than usual, and not because I was thousands of miles away. I was merely twelve hours away, remembering the night before and hoping to see Alana again. I didn't know what Alana's plans were for that day, but decided not to call until I returned home that evening so I'd have some privacy. Usually the day flew by and I hated to leave; but that day lasted forever, until finally it was half-time of the Orange Bowl, already pitch-black outside and time to go. The car ride back to Queens was interminable, with bumper-to-bumper traffic and small talk that made me want to scream. But I didn't. My parents asked me if anything were wrong since I was so quiet. In fact, they had to ask me three times before I snapped out of my funk and heard the question. But I made up an excuse, said I was tired from the night before, and they left me alone. It was certainly too soon to share my feelings about Alana. I didn't want to jinx anything by talking about it! I just wanted to get home, still my racing heart so as not to betray my inner feelings, and get to the phone. I hoped she would be home and interested.

Chapter 5

It was almost 10 p.m. when we finally pulled into the driveway. I fake-yawned a few times, then nonchalantly walked to the phone. "Who are you calling at this hour?" my mom asked.

"I told Eddie I'd call," I casually answered.

"It's late to be calling, don't you think?"

"No, I'm sure he's still up, watching the end of the Orange Bowl, and his parents stay up late."

"OK." Actually, I now began to worry if it was too late to call Alana? Would her parents be annoyed? Should I wait until tomorrow?

But I couldn't wait. I try to be controlled and disciplined, think things through, and make rational decisions (my dad's genetic influence, I'm sure). But often my emotions take over and I act impulsively, so I picked up the phone and dialed. We only had three telephones in the house: one in my parents' bedroom, one in the kitchen, and one in the downstairs hallway. Privacy was a rare commodity for me while on the phone, but I could pull the cord in the hall under the door to the basement steps, close the door, and *voila*...not exactly ideal but better than the kitchen! I expected Alana's mother to answer (for some reason she seemed like the person who would be first to the phone), and I wasn't disappointed.

"Hello, this is Brett Berson. We met last night at Dale's house. I hope I'm not calling too late."

There was a moment's hesitation, then, "Oh, hello, Brett. No, it's not too late. We have company over and they're preparing to leave." A moment's hesitation on my end. Would it be rude to ask to speak to Alana if they had company over? What the hell...I'm going for it.

"Would it be okay if I spoke to Alana for a minute?"

"Yes. Al? Brett's on the phone."

There was a pause, and I'm sure Gladys put her hand over the mouthpiece, as I heard some muffled conversation that I couldn't decipher. And then, "Hi, Brett."

"Hi, Alana. I hope this isn't a bad time. Are you free to talk?"

"Sure. My parents have some friends over. But I've done my time, and I'm excused, so I'm all yours."

She's all mine. I love it!!

"Just wanted to say hi, and tell you what a nice time I had last night."

"Me, too."

The conversation, a bit awkward at first, became more comfortable and natural.

"I know things were a little strange last night, especially when we first got back to Dale's house, but I had a great time with you."

"Yeah, I know it was weird. But I'm pretty sure that's not happening again."

What's not happening again? I wondered? The going out together part? The "switchies" part? The "after-switchies" part? Of course I couldn't ask.

"So what did you do today?" And the conversation progressed from there. Now it was becoming more personal—what she did today, what I did today, and gradually more and more into our personal lives. She knew something about my school situation, but now we had the time and the ease to discuss things further. We had already been somewhat intimate (sort of), and that broke the ice and opened up our ability to connect on a different level. I was surprised and delighted at how easy it was to talk to Alana. I did sense that she was a little intimidated, maybe because of the difference in our ages—that I was a college student and she still in high school—or maybe by the Yale thing—but we talked and I became more interested. I kept picturing her in my mind. For me (and likely all men), beauty transcends most barriers, and Alana was stunningly beautiful. I knew that I wanted to see her again, and hoped that she felt the same.

"So maybe we can get together this weekend, and see a movie or something," I asked.

"Sure. Call me. That would be great."

"Will do. Okay. Good night. Happy New Year's again. And I'll speak to you soon."

"Good night."

I came out from behind the basement door, and no one was there (a good thing). I hung up the receiver, and bounded up the stairs, two at a time, feeling even better. Nothing in my life had really changed—my school situation was undecided, I had no idea what I would be doing next academically or professionally, a once-certain structured and defined way of life was now chaos and ambiguity…but something had changed. Never underestimate the power of love.

Chapter 6

I saw Alana again later that week, and the next, and the next…I returned to school to tie up remaining loose ends and then moved back in with my parents. Their goal (and mine) was to give me the time I needed to regroup and refocus, but get this done and get back on track as soon as possible. With the ever-present threat of the draft, I knew that my "sabbatical" was limited, but I sought to live in the moment, taking one day at a time, not looking too far ahead into a foggy future without a clear goal or destination. Eddie's next-door neighbor owned a pen factory in Queens, and I took a manual labor job there, working for minimum wage driving products locally. The work was mindless, and I had plenty of time to consider my situation, options, and priorities. Alana quickly became the most important part of my life, and I spent more and more time courting her. Not a day went by that I didn't speak to her at least once, and we saw each other as often as possible.

Her parents were surprisingly welcoming and accommodating to a stranger spending so much time with their daughter. Alana and I couldn't have looked more different—she a beautiful, fifteen-year-old, blonde-haired, blue-eyed, sweet and innocent young thing, barely a teenager and entirely under the thumb and iron rule of her parents; me a long-haired, bearded, pot-smoking, acid-dropping, rebellious eighteen-year-old, hippie…But then again, going to Yale definitely had its perks as far as parents of young ladies are concerned. One night (January 28, 1970), shortly after I returned from college, I took Al to a peace benefit concert at Madison Square Garden in protest of the Vietnam War. It was an amazing affair, with all the great folk singers and rock bands of the day lending their support and performing. It was Jimi Hendrix's last public appearance. Unfortunately we got caught up in the moment, the concert went on for hours, and we lost track of time. By the time we got home it was nearly 4 a.m., and, needless to say, Gladys was wide-awake and waiting in the kitchen. Of course, I apologized profusely but the daggers from her eyes made it more than obvious that I would never (*could* never!) *ever* do that again if I wanted to keep seeing her daughter. The message came across loud and clear, and I made sure to be more mindful of the clock in the future. There was also the time we fell asleep while babysitting for my sister, and returned to Al's house in the wee hours (to daggers again). But overall I acted as responsibly as a teenager head-over-heels in love could act.

Milton was a very special and wonderful man whom I feel privileged to have known and whom I grew to love as the years went by. He reminded me very much of my own dad, a deeply religious, highly ethical individual whose heart was always in the right place. They both had grown up as first-generation Americans, descendants of Eastern European Jewry. They both grew up in the five boroughs of NYC, in poverty, and knew that the secret to success was hard work and honesty. They both recognized education as the key to escaping from the Jewish ghettos that imprisoned their parents, and they both succeeded. They both went to CCNY (the City College of New York, a public university) and built their futures on bedrock of the Puritan work ethic. Although they unfortunately never met at CCNY, I am convinced that, if they had, they would have become the best of friends and companions.

Milton's moral compass drove his actions, and he never doubted his faith or his priorities. Family always came first, and he made every personal sacrifice to take care of his own. A child of the Depression, he was a workaholic. Though straight-laced and serious, he also had a wry sense of humor that kept him grounded, and beneath the somewhat stern exterior was a bit of a rascal and practical joker. His career as an accountant involved hour upon hour upon hour of tabulating columns of numbers, collating accounts, reconciling books. As boring as that may seem to some, he was passionate about it, and found a certain beauty in figures and numbers and in getting it right. There may be few truths or certainties in life to which we are privy, but there is logic and sense to numbers, and there is always a right answer if one works hard enough at finding it. And Milton was rarely wrong. He was committed to his clients and served them extremely well, leaving no stone unturned to provide the service they deserved and to which we all aspire. He was a model to us all (as was my dad). But Milton was far more than a numbers guy. The image of an accountant is a nerd *par excellence*, a dumpy little guy with glasses and a pencil holder in his pocket who is the furthest thing from "cool" we can imagine. But despite his brilliance and love for accounting, Milton was anything but a nerd. He was amazingly cool in his convictions, steadfastness, focus, priorities, and breadth. For not only was he an accountant during the day; by night and on weekends he often assumed his alter egos, and donned the cape of Renaissance Man. In his youth Milton had studied the violin, and become a true virtuoso, likely proficient enough to have been a concert violinist had he chosen that path. His fiddle and music stand were ever present, and when he started to play he would close his eyes and be swept away by the music, with an expression of ecstasy and rapture on his face that so transcended the mundane realm of numbers on a ledger. In addition, Milton was a highly skilled tennis player and never lost his love for the game. When he afforded himself the rare opportunity of time away from work, he was volleying on the public courts at nearby Cunningham Park, or glued to the television watching the tennis grand slams. Pete Sampras, the huge serve-and-volley player and classic tennis master, was his favorite. Like my dad Milton was multi-faceted and a genius in his depth and breadth. The Yiddish word "mensch" is almost untranslatable in English but generally means a person of integrity and honor. Milton and my dad were the very essence of "mensch."

As time went by I saved enough money to buy my first car, a powder blue 1970 Mustang—what a sweet ride for an eighteen-year-old boy!! I picked Al up after school (to the envy of her 11th grade classmates!), and spent many an evening with her and her parents. Al had no siblings, and I became part of the family, the son her parents never had. And they became the family I never had. Eddie was back at Cornell and his household no longer available to me. As my sister continued to spin out of control, I found a haven of peace, stability, security at Al's house. Instead of being the forgotten middle-child, I became the focused-on new addition. Gladys worked for a local doctors' office as a radiology and lab technician, and made it her mission to straighten me out, show me the error of my ways, get me back to school, and on to medical school. That was a tough sell at the time, and I gave plenty of pushback. Suddenly I had the luxury of being myself, the rebellious son I never could be in my own home. I didn't have to compete with my brother's academic success or my sister's craziness and neediness. I was a welcome guest and valued member of the household, something I had never enjoyed with my own family. And I loved every minute of it. Alana and I became an item, more a couple than a couple of teenagers. We were together with her friends, with her parents' friends, with her extended family. I had found a new home and a new life at a time when I needed it most. She (and her parents) were my saviors—quite a role for a fifteen-year-old girl, but she handled it with ease, and kindness, and understanding. Al was precocious, and she too needed to be recognized as an emerging adult and woman, something her parents failed to do. But I couldn't be happier to assume that role. We both came along at the right time for each other.

As the months went by, I made progress in approaching my professional goals as well. In high school I had developed an interest in drama and theater, and as a senior had the leading role in the school play (*Our Town* by Thornton Wilder, playing a doctor of all things!). Manhattan is likely the theater capital of the world, and I started knocking on some doors, exploring the off- and off-off Broadway scene, eventually working backstage on a production at the Public Theater, and then as a designer and electrician for the mobile festival unit of the New York City Parks Department, staging street festivals throughout the five boroughs. I met lots of very interesting, creative, and artistic people, formed relationships, and developed a network of contacts that led to a subsequent job at a summer stock theater on Cape Cod. Theater met my needs for belonging to a community, for being an integral part of something bigger than me, for enjoying that special camaraderie, companionship, and inter-dependence that is part and parcel of putting on a show. I chose the theater as my future. Looking back all these years later, that time away from school, initially viewed by some (including myself) as a failure, was, in fact, the most productive, successful, and educational time of my life. I truly did "find myself", and, even more important, I liked what I found (and found Alana to boot!). I decided to return to Yale in September, change my major to Theater, and study at the Yale Drama School. My parents were not quite as enthusiastic about this turn of events as I, but Alana was supportive and her parents were accepting. That was more than enough for me.

Chapter 7

That summer on the Cape was the beginning of my next chapter. I was now focused on a career in the dramatic arts, and I was excited and enthusiastic about my choice. I would become a great leading man, and play all the iconic roles, from Hamlet to Lear, in all the great venues from Broadway to Britain. Or I would become a character actor, and create and recreate roles with my own interpretation and spin. Or perhaps become a designer and make my contribution that way. Worst case scenario, I would teach theater, become head of the drama department, direct plays at a small New England liberal arts college. Somewhere I'd find my niche, and be happy and successful. I had no doubt.

Of course Alana was never lost in my hopes and plans and dreams. I always expected to be with her. The major downside of my summer on the Cape was her absence. She spent that summer studying French at a school in Lausanne, Switzerland, an undoubtedly great experience, but I missed her terribly. I wrote every single day, and she did the same. It was a very busy summer, mounting eight productions in ten weeks, from start to finish, including casting, designing, set building, rehearsing, and performing. But I learned so much and met so many great people. And I even earned college credits that made up for those lost from my previous semester. So, all in all, it was terrific. But just the same, I couldn't wait for the summer to end to get home and see Alana again.

Finally we were both home and together once more. Our reunion was as sweet as I imagined, and life was so good. I returned to Yale several weeks later, intent on pursuing my two new loves: Alana and the theater (in that order). New Haven is only seventy miles from New York, a brief daydream away, and I knew I'd be making that drive every chance I could. Alana would be a high school senior, and looking at colleges. My dream would have been to have her at Yale, but not every dream can come true. So the next best thing would be Connecticut College in New London, an even shorter daydream away from New Haven.

In October that year Al and her parents visited and interviewed at Connecticut College. They stopped in New Haven on the way back home, and I gave them a tour of Yale, quite an impressive institution (despite the urban blight of New Haven) with beautiful Gothic architecture very much in the style of Oxford and Cambridge. I had been in a play the night before that closed after that last performance, and we had our cast party at Skull and Bones (a famous not-so-secret "secret society"). There had been lots of drinking and partying, and I wasn't at my best, but I knew which side my bread was buttered on, and convincing Milton and Gladys to trust their daughter with me was paramount, so I got it together. And the gods smiled on me...Milton and Gladys were pleased to tour the Yale campus with a native, and, a short time later, Alana was accepted to, and chose to attend, Connecticut College. It was a golden time.

The year flew by. I was busy at school, studying with a renewed interest and passion, performing in every production I could (of which Yale had many), and driving back and forth at least once during the week and every weekend to see Alana. Although I slept in my parents' house, I lived at Alana's, and nothing seemed more natural to me. My parents occasionally complained that I never spent time with them (which was true), but they were so busy and overwhelmed with my sister that they had little time to give to anything else, and were relieved that I was happy, settled, stable, and taken care of by Gladys and Milton (whom they had never met!). Alana and I spent some time at my house, but it was limited. We would babysit for my sister on occasional Saturday nights. My sister didn't act out with us the way she did with my parents, so that arrangement worked out for everybody. And as time went by we did what all young people in love eventually do...After some cajoling (more correctly, pleading and begging on my part!), Al lost her virginity to me (and, truth be told, I to her, although I never would have admitted it at the time), and things were better than ever. Of course the summer loomed ahead. I took a job with a professional summer stock company in Ivoryton,

Connecticut (not far from the Yale campus). Alana spent the summer as a CIT (counselor-in-training) at Camp Waziyatah for Girls, the exclusive camp in Maine owned and operated by her aunt and uncle. She'd been there as a camper with Dale, and would have Dale's companionship again, a blessing for both of them. It was once again a long summer, and again I wrote every night. But knowing that we'd be nearby in September, and *alone together* for the first time, gave me solace (and plenty to fantasize about in my sleeping and waking moments). Alana enjoyed camp, and was excited about starting college.

My friends accepted us as a couple, with some amazement at the longevity of our relationship. They all went through multiple relationships, some good, others not so, but normal for that age. We seemed to be steady as a rock, not fighting or conflicting except over minor matters that I can't even recall. We never had a major blow-up, or break-up. I couldn't imagine why we would, or imagine being with anybody else. Weird as it sounds in a nineteen-year-old boy, I had no desire to play the field, fool around, chase other girls, or brag about my experiences. I never thought of myself as being especially mature…I just had no reason to look for someone else. Alana was perfect, and I felt like the luckiest guy in the world. When Paul Newman was once asked if he ever cheated on his wife, he replied, "Why go out for hamburger when I have steak at home?" I felt the same way. Alana, too, seemed perfectly content. When I say how beautiful she was, that's no exaggeration or conceit. It was always a great feeling to know that I entered every room with the prettiest girl on my arm; that every guy was looking at her and wishing he were me; that, at the end of the day, I always went home with the prize. But it's true. I never questioned it, but was always grateful, and appreciated who she was. And, as corny as it sounds, her outer beauty was only exceeded by her inner beauty. And that's not just in the eyes of this beholder. Most guys never get to feel that *ever*; I had that feeling every single day.

I attended Alana's high school graduation with Milton and Gladys. It was a proud moment for all of us. Al looked so beautiful and so *adult* in her cap and gown, sitting on stage amongst her fellow graduates, recognized for her accomplishments. Graduations are a coming-of-age, not an ending but a beginning (as all graduation speakers reiterate), and I could barely contain my excitement that Connecticut College was Al's next step, and that an "adult relationship" was upon us, away from home and the ever-present parental scrutiny. We would be "on our own" to begin this next chapter of our lives together. The graduates that night sang in unison, "The Impossible Dream," a popular song of the day from *Man of La Mancha*, emphasizing the potential of the indomitable human spirit to soar to great heights and achieve great things, to transcend the weighty constraints of our daily lives in search of a higher calling. Little did I realize at the time that my most challenging "impossible dream" was yet to come; but perhaps this was a prophecy, not to be recognized or aspired to until years later. For the moment, my impossible dream had been realized. Don Quixote would have been proud.

The following year exceeded even my expectations. Al and I split our time between Yale and Connecticut College. Chuck's Steak House in New London became our favorite hangout (when we could afford it). Alana had a very irritating roommate her freshman year, while I had a single dorm room with a fireplace! So our preference as to overnight accommodations is obvious. Of course there was the time I forgot to open the flue, and turned a potentially romantic evening by the fireplace into a hasty evacuation into the wintry cold at the behest of the New Haven Fire Department. Notwithstanding the occasional minor bumps on the road, it was an ever fuller and richer golden period.

With our new-found freedom from parental supervision, we expanded our vistas and traveled to see my and her friends at other colleges. There was so much to do and so much fun to have, and we had it all. I never thought much of New Haven or New London as cities to visit or live in, but they both became far more attractive and desirable once I could enjoy them with Al. The towns themselves were pretty boring, but campus life was exciting. Neither school had any Greek life, but both (especially Yale) were non-stop entertainment with film societies, campus theatres, concerts, museums, athletic events, etc. If only we didn't have to take classes, write papers, and take exams it would have been Utopia! Al and I chose the occasional weekend to drive to Queens to see our folks (mostly hers) and those road trips too were enjoyable. Al turned eighteen that March and her mother made her a surprise birthday party at her home. It was my job to keep her out of the house until all the guests had a chance to arrive and assume their respective hiding places, so I took her to see a Broadway show (*Sticks and Bones*) starring one of my acting buddies from Yale. When we got home the surprise was perfect and suddenly we were both legal. I remember raising a glass that night to toast my Al, a beautiful girl, terrific in every way, whom I felt honored and privileged to be with and to call my person. Those feelings have never changed.

Did we ever discuss marriage? No, not that I can remember. We were both too young for that kind of talk, but I couldn't imagine life without her. There would be plenty of time when the time was right, and I took for granted that our day would come, no doubt about that.

The spring semester came to an end, and another summer was upon us. After having spent so much time together the past year, I dreaded the upcoming time apart. But I knew it would be temporary and September would bring more happiness, and who knows what new adventures in our relationship?

I was again working at the playhouse in Connecticut, and Alana returned to camp as a counselor. That year I drove her up to Maine. The counselors and staff all arrived a few days early every year to prepare for the campers. The campsite was a gorgeous piece of property, secluded in the midst of a beautiful wooded area, kept immaculately well-groomed, set beside a beautiful lake. The bunks were somewhat rural (as a camp should be), but lacking nothing that money can buy (as the wealthy parents expected). There were horses and riding/hiking trails galore, with a large barn, stables, and a gathering place that served as a theater (where we snuck away to make love in the hidden loft every night before bedtime). For me it was a magical end to a magical year, and when the campers started arriving, we kissed good-bye and I headed to Connecticut, choking back a tear as I saw Alana receding in my rear-view mirror.

Once I got on the highway I felt somewhat better. It was a beautiful day and I had several hours to daydream about my girl. I revved up my engine, rolled down all the windows, and blasted our favorite radio station. The wide-open country fields of Maine, Massachusetts, then Connecticut passed by as I started composing in my head my first letter, which I would write that evening. Some of my friends *enjoyed* a summer hiatus from their girlfriends. I never did, and never understood why I would want that. I guess I was just an old soul trapped in a young man's body. Now it's the other way around, I suppose.

Next stop, the Ivoryton Playhouse…

Chapter 8

The playhouse was much the same as I had left it after the final show the previous August. It ranked as one of the oldest summer stock theatres in the country, and the producer, Milton Stiefel, was quite famous in his own right. He had been producing plays on Broadway and at Ivoryton since 1939, and that playhouse had been the very first stage on which Katherine Hepburn performed (her family spent their summers in nearby Essex, Connecticut, a resort community frequented by the rich and soon-to-be famous). The theatre was closed and shuttered during the winter months and offered an eight-week season every July and August, with new plays every week performed by traveling companies that did the Straw Hat circuit in New England. The resident company filled in the bit parts that did not justify the expense of a traveling cast member (I played the donkey in *Man of La Mancha* two years running), and designed and built the sets and lighting, supplied the costumes and props (collected from the locals, who enjoyed feeling like they were part of a major show-biz production), and provided the manpower to run the show and the playhouse. The theater was so old that instead of having air conditioning it had an ice house with a large ventilation system. Ice was delivered before every performance, and maintained a surprisingly cool temperature, even onstage under the lights. When a storm blew in off the Long Island Sound, we would lose our power, and would run a small, gas-driven generator that provided just enough juice to light the stage and provide a modicum of cooling. Old though she be, the Ivoryton Playhouse was filled with class, and its roster of past performers read like a Who's Who of Broadway and Hollywood. There were autographed pictures ("To Milton, With Love" etc.) plastering the walls, a veritable treasure trove for memorabilia collectors, putting Sardi's to shame in comparison. Walking backstage and past the dressing rooms was like walking on hallowed ground, knowing that the greats of show biz had once trod those very same boards.

Arriving there was like coming home in a way. When I parked in the back on the now-somewhat-overgrown gravel parking lot, I almost felt like I had never left. Walking down the back steps into the underground cool of the basement, with those multiple and pungent so-familiar smells, was like taking a step back in time for me. The basement was filled with the sets from the last production of the previous summer, not having been touched in nine months. I stopped for a moment, took a look (and smell) around, and then walked up the backstairs to the stage.

Many of that year's crew had already arrived, and were milling about. I was happy to see several familiar faces who returned for another season. It felt good to be back. I greeted my old friends and we spent a few minutes chatting and catching up, waiting for Milton to arrive to welcome us back and start work on the first show. My dark mood at the prospect of leaving Alana behind was beginning to lift. Maybe the summer wouldn't be so bad after all.

Chapter 9

The organizational meeting went well. I'd been to quite a few of them and they were always similar, discussing the group, with everyone introducing themselves and their positions for the summer. The shows were already scheduled, there was a general pep talk, then we went off for dinner, to be followed by a bright and early start the next day. I ate at the same little restaurant across the street where I had eaten nearly all my meals the year before. Ivoryton is basically a summer community, and most of the shops close down for the winter, making their living during the two months the theater is open. To a large extent, they depend on the theater and the audience it attracts to provide their customers as well, so they are always very friendly and accommodating to the theater staff. Nothing about the town seemed to have changed at all, which I liked. The restaurant owners, the two waitresses (daughters of the owners), the cook (their son), and dishwasher (another son) were still there and looking unchanged. They recognized me and I them, and we had a brief handshake all around and a few words. The menu was the same, the food the same, prices the same, and I was glad to be on my way to my summer lodging about fifteen minutes away. The local community rented out rooms in their houses to the theater staff, and I arranged to stay with the Bards, in the same place as last year, with a family I knew and liked.

After arriving and saying my hellos (nothing different there either), I unpacked and settled down at the (same) desk to write to Al. I'd been thinking about the letter all day, and wanted her to know how much I enjoyed our time at camp, how much I missed her already (all true), and how the day had gone so far. I addressed and stamped the letter, and then wrote a brief thank you to her aunt and uncle for their hospitality. With that I lay down in the (same) bed, under the (same) comforter, and fell asleep, tired but looking forward to the next day.

Only sixty-six more days until I see Alana, were my last thoughts before I dozed off.

Chapter 10

The first few weeks of summer stock are nothing but hard work. There were eight productions to prepare for, from soup to nuts, as well as a theater to spruce up after ten months of quiet and hibernation. Having survived thirty-some-odd winters, the playhouse shared the character of New England: sturdy, able to withstand cold and snow and all that nor'easters could bring, resistant to the vagaries of the seasons, ready to blossom and open its doors at the first opportunity. Landscaping the grounds was the most challenging task of all, after ten months of neglect; but that's why we had apprentices!! The very idea of working with a professional theater company was so exhilarating that they would do anything asked of them to have the opportunity to be part of "the show." My job as lighting designer and electrician was less strenuous and simpler: checking the inventory of our equipment, testing the circuits and the lights themselves, reviewing the color charts and available filters, etc. As expected, everything was where I had left it at the end of the previous summer, so I could concentrate on designing the first few productions. The "advance man" for the first show (*Butterflies are Free*) showed up on Day Three, and we went through the script, set changes, character movement, moods as they applied to lighting needs, and the like. It was a fairly simple, one-set show, so I had little to do other than add the placement of the various lighting "areas" to the draft of the scene designer, place the lights themselves in position, and choose the colors (mostly "Schubert pink" for this mostly light comedy). I had plenty of time to enjoy the leisure and the picturesque community before the madding crowds of performers and audience would start to arrive two weeks later.

Whenever things were good I wished Alana could be with me to share those moments. There were only three telephones in the theater: one in the box office for ticket sales, one in the main office for business purposes, and the other a pay phone behind the shop. Back then, there were no cell phones, texting, messaging, emailing, or any other way to communicate except snail mail and the pay phone. I always enjoyed writing romantic letters and putting words on paper, and have even composed a love poem or two in my day. But the hours and days between letters was the hard part. Absence may make the heart grow fonder, but mine was already at its max, and the absence was painfully difficult.

I knew it would be a few days before Alana's first letter would arrive, so I tried to be patient (unsuccessfully!), and even helped out in the shop, building sets (not my job but something to keep me busy). I wrote to Alana every night (and even twice a day sometimes), describing what I was doing to keep her close and in my world as much as possible. I couldn't wait to hear from her.

As expected her first letter arrived shortly, and she picked up where we left off last year. She liked the other counselors, was getting to know the campers, enjoyed being back at the camp she knew so well from years of being a camper herself, and seemed well-acclimated. She missed me too and signed off with her usual, "Love always, Alana." I was always a more prolific and emotive writer than Al; but I knew that, and didn't expect her letters to be quite as sentimental or effusive as mine. But that was okay. I just enjoyed receiving whatever she sent and staying informed of her activities so I could relate to what she was doing. (And having been to the camp for the first time I could even picture her at the various venues.). Sometimes she would send a postcard or cute keepsake (which I vowed to keep forever). Though many miles apart, I felt very connected to Al, and sometimes in the evening would look up at the stars and make a wish, knowing that those very same stars were overhead in her sky too. When you're in love, everything takes on a new meaning and significance; it fills every song on the radio, every sunset and sunrise, every shooting star, every happy moment. And I was crazy in love with Alana.

The second week became a little busier as opening night approached. The traveling company arrived, the excitement rose, and, in a flash, the season was upon us. Despite a disastrous dress rehearsal, and frenzied flurry of activity when the roof began leaking and the AC system needed some long overdue repairs, opening night came and went, the audience (a full house) went home happy, and all was well with the world. We had our traditional opening night cast party, and the season was underway. *If only Al could be here to share this with me,* I thought (as usual). I mailed her a copy of the playbill that evening.

The mail from the rural post office by the camp in Maine was often unreliable. Several days would go by without a letter, then I would receive two or three at once. It was somewhat frustrating, but at the same time it was such a treat to get multiple letters that the upside neutralized the downside. I received two or three letters from Al that first week. She apologized for not writing more often but said that the beginning of camp was hectic and she had precious little time at the end of the day to sit down to write. *Par for the course,* I thought, and never gave it a second thought.

The first show finished its brief run, the company said their goodbyes and told us what a good job we had done (and we echoed the compliment to them), and the next group of players arrived. By then we had already completed construction on the next set, I had drafted out the lighting design, and we were ready to strike the first set, assemble the next, and start the process all over again. Such is summer theater, and I eased right back into the swing of things. Next show was our one musical of the summer, *Man of La Mancha,* and it was time for me to put back on the donkey costume. Needless to say I had no lines, but I did have to support the leading lady, who sat on my back as she sang a seemingly never-ending song. The Aldonza from the previous summer seemed a lot lighter than this year's version, but I survived with a few Aleve and ice packs. There's nothing easy about being a bit player! I also served as Assistant Stage Manager for this production (a separate job in and of itself with specific additional requirements). The good news for me was qualifying for membership in Actors' Equity (the Actors' Union) by participating as an actor and Stage Manager. I still hold that union membership to this day.

I maintained my nightly ritual of coming home from the theater around midnight, and sitting on the front porch with a small candle to write about my day. I thoroughly enjoyed sharing all the silly happenings, gossip, and little fun facts about the performers, the "stars," and my "show biz" experience. But Alana's letters seemed to be getting shorter and less frequent, more matter-of-fact and less personal. She was sharing less and apologizing more for her "very busy schedule," new responsibilities, and for having no time to write. I never really got that because I was pretty busy myself but always found time to write and share. In fact, that was the best part of my day, the quiet time in the evening, when the day's work was over, the crowds had gone home, and I could be alone with my thoughts and feelings, writing silly nothings to my sweetheart. I got a kick knowing that the very paper and envelope before me would soon be in Alana's hands and before her eyes. That was so much better than today's electronic, digital age!! My "Alonalessness" was always on my mind, and I hungered for my next opportunity to write, and even more to receive and read a letter from her hand that had so shortly before felt her breath and touch. I brought her letters close to my face, trying to smell her perfume and feel her essence, and usually imagined I could.

But soon I knew something was wrong. The words and basics were there, but the letters had a different tone—or was it just my imagination and my missing her so much? I reassured myself that everything was fine, and Al was just busy and enjoying herself—a good thing, right? But as the days went by and the accustomed letters failed to arrive, I began to feel a little sick inside. Why the silence? Why the coolness? Had I done something unawares? Was it this way last summer, and the one before? Was I just being paranoid, or was something really amiss?

Finally, midway through the summer, after a week without a letter (and then I knew something wasn't right), I received a long letter. I could feel how thick the letter was even before I opened the envelope, and at first my heart took flight, assuming Al had been too busy for one reason or another, and now was making up for lost time with an especially long and loving message. Usually I couldn't wait to open the letters as soon as I picked them up from the theater office, and started reading on my way out the door. But this time I chose to find a quiet place alone to read. I sensed that this was a different kind of letter, and I wanted some time and space around me to find out. I went to a favorite "hiding spot" of mine, where I went to get away if I wanted some solitude. Sometimes I wrote to Al from that secluded spot by the river. My heart was practically beating out of my chest as I sat down and gently fingered the return address with Alana's name. Then I took a deep breath and opened the envelope.

Chapter 11

"Dear Brett,

"Sorry I haven't written for so long, but camp has been busy as usual. I'm enjoying my bunk and group of campers. The schedule is full day and night to keep the girls occupied and their parents satisfied. We've been taking local day trips, to Kennebunkport, and Ogunquit, and being a counselor is more fun than being a CIT (and I get paid!). Dale sends her best, and it's great to spend time with her.

"Thanks for writing so diligently. Sounds like you're busy too and enjoying what you're doing. I'm glad.

"I wanted to discuss something with you. I wish we could talk on the phone but it's so difficult. I hope this comes out OK.

"I've been thinking about it, and I'd like us both to see other people this summer. I think it would be good for both of us and our relationship. We'll be apart anyway, and I'd like to feel I can relate to the other counselors without feeling I'm doing anything wrong. I love you very much and don't want you to think otherwise; but I'd like the freedom to be with the people who are here, and you should enjoy yourself too. This will only bring us closer when the summer ends, don't you think?

"I hope you are OK with this. Keep writing. I enjoy getting your letters and knowing what's going on with you.

"Take care.

"Love,
Alana"

Chapter 12

My heart sank as I read the letter. I hoped there was another page—saying that this was a big joke, only kidding, gotcha! My breath was taken away, and I looked across the lake, feeling numb and almost in a trance. How could this be? I didn't get it. What went wrong? I wanted to read the letter again but couldn't...I wanted to tear it up into a million pieces but couldn't...I *did* want to shoot the messenger...I stared down at the pages in disbelief, slowly folded the letter and put it back in the envelope...I couldn't move...I couldn't breathe...I couldn't get up...I couldn't think of anything...I felt frozen and numb. That feeling of impending doom deep inside my gut for the past few weeks was now here, beside me, around me, grabbing me, choking me, shaking me...My world seemed to be receding at warp speed...I was no longer in Ivoryton, Connecticut, beside a still lake on a warm summer's afternoon...I was somewhere else, lost in space, drifting. I couldn't cry, or scream, or feel, except to feel empty and hollow and crushed...I instinctively knew that Al's desire to "see other people" meant that she felt differently about me and about us than she ever had. The tacit, unspoken commitment to each other was abruptly over...Suddenly my heart, so full of love just a few short moments ago, now was nothing but a big, black, lonely hole...We had always been a unit, immune from outside insinuations and wedges, insulated from the influences and temptations that drove other couples asunder...I didn't even think about writing back, or calling, or running to the car and driving north...I felt too crushed to muster the energy to fight back right then, nor did I think that "fighting back" was even an option at that moment...My spirit, usually so passionate and full of life, was drained of everything...Alana, my Alana, no longer my Alana...I stared blankly across the water...nothing would ever be the same again...how would I survive this...how could I go on...I didn't care...maybe I would just sit there forever...suddenly time and place had no meaning…nothing meant anything…Alana…Brett…from evermore to nevermore…could there be life after Alana?...why have you forsaken me?...a lone tear fell from my cheek onto the now-hated envelope.

Chapter 13

Eventually I did get up and make my way back to the car. Somehow I drove myself back to the theater, not even knowing what I was doing. I had a job to do and a play to run, so I snapped back into "normalcy" to get through the evening. I focused on smiling, acting like the Brett everyone knew; but it was hard to smile and impossible to laugh. It's such a struggle and effort when the public face and the private face are light years apart. I thought everyone could see past my phony façade, but maybe they didn't. I needed to get through the show, then get away, not sure where. I tried not to think of Alana, but everything reminded me of her. I wanted to be somewhere else, anywhere else, and someplace where there was no Alana, never had been an Alana, and never was an Alana and Brett. I knew nothing and felt nothing. My body went through the motions, disconnected from my heart and soul. Suspended animation, lost in time and space. I felt like my consciousness was disconnected from my body, my essence was in another place, long ago and far away, like I was looking down on the world, and the Brett I saw operating the light board was someone else. Maybe this was the dissociative fugue state psychiatrists are so fond of talking about? Maybe this was what a coma felt like, an unconsciousness that saved me from facing the impossibly painful reality of what was happening? I wanted to cry but couldn't. I wanted to die, but wouldn't. I'd have to survive this and figure it out…but not tonight. Now I just needed to get to the end of the show, then get to tomorrow, and count the hours. I was in shock. Could this be just a horrible nightmare and would I wake up, and all would be as it was yesterday? Was that possible? I prayed to God—called in all my credits…hadn't I been a good son? Shouldn't that count for something? Hadn't I been a good older brother? Hadn't I been a good boyfriend? *Please help me.* I had no idea what my next move would be. I just needed to get to my next breath and wait and see. The Bard was wrong—not better to have loved and lost such a love as this.

* * *

Time is supposed to heal all wounds, and whatever doesn't kill you makes you stronger. I held on to those "truisms" while my heart was breaking and I wanted to die... I knew that Alana wasn't feeling my pain. How could she be? This was her idea. She wanted to "meet other people"! What does that mean? Of course I knew that it meant another guy, another relationship, another man to be close to and intimate with. It hurt too much to think about it, so I tried not to. I pictured her at camp with someone else. Who was it? Had I met him during the few days I was there? I wracked my brain to remember all the people I saw there but to no avail. I couldn't (or wouldn't) remember one male counselor. This was a girls' camp! Why would there be a male counselor there? The idea that she was smiling her beautiful smile at another guy, holding his hand, trying to catch his eye and draw him close to her—I couldn't stand it!! Why would she want this? Weren't we getting along great? Wasn't she happy and satisfied with me and the relationship we had? How could this be happening????!!!!

I so wanted to love her and hurt her at the same time...have her back but never take her back for hurting and rejecting me this way. The fact that I knew she was aloof and distant from these feelings of mine made the pain so much worse. I always thought she would be there for me, as I would be for her...That in times of need she would hear me, listen, sympathize, empathize, caress, and comfort...Now she was off doing her own thing, *with someone else,* and I was left to suffer alone, with nowhere to turn.

See other people? Why would I want to do that? How would that improve our relationship for either one of us? We were made for each other, supposed to be together. I had no desire to "see other people."

I guess I should have gone along, distracted myself with one of the female interns, put Alana and *us* on the back burner for the rest of the summer until I could find out how the rest of my life was going to turn out. That thought occurred to me, but I couldn't do it; I had no appetite for someone else. I couldn't put Alana out of my mind long enough to generate any interest in another girl, even for a brief summer fling. I only wanted to get through the summer and hope that September would be our time again, that this "experiment" would be behind us, and it would be Alana and Brett like before. I had to slap on a happy grin and hope no one drilled down deeper. I felt like a village idiot, smiling at everything and nothing, so no one would see the tracks of my tears. Inside I was a mess. I'd never been in love before. I'd never had my heart broken before…but I didn't feel stronger…I just felt sad…

As the days passed my mood stabilized to the point that I began to start using my head. My heart may have misled me but my head never had betrayed me. I felt that I could always figure things out if I could focus and concentrate. So I did my best to approach this problem logically. I knew there was nothing I could do to turn back the clock; things had changed for reasons I didn't understand and had no control over, but they were different nonetheless. The only real question was what to do from here? Whether I liked it or not, whether I could manage it or not, my best strategy would be to give Al the time and space she needed (and try not to torture myself by picturing her with another guy). Maybe I was too much? Too crowding…too overbearing…too smothering and suffocating. Maybe the best thing would be to stop writing, not call, respect her needs, and let her find her way, hopefully back to me. As hard as it was I chose to follow my head, not my heart, for a change. Days went by and I didn't write. Sadly, but not unexpectedly, neither did she. It was a horrible few weeks.

One day someone came to me with a message from the office: Gladys had called and wanted me to call her back. I knew that Milton and Gladys had been traveling for a few weeks in Europe. I supposed that she had come home, and wondered if she knew what was going on.

I went to the pay phone and called. Gladys answered.

"Hello."

"Hi, Gladys. It's Brett."

"Hi, honey. It's good to hear your voice."

"Yeah, yours too."

It was strange hearing Gladys' voice. It felt warm, and familiar, and comforting, reminiscent of a time that now seemed so long ago but was really so recent. For a moment I felt whole again, back in the warm embrace of my happy days, so near yet so far. "How are you doing?"

"Not too well."

"Alana isn't doing too well either."

"I don't know what happened. Everything seemed fine when we said good-bye at camp. I came to Connecticut, and everything went to hell. I don't get it." And for the first time I started to cry.

"I know, Brett. Alana told me. She's confused and hurting, too."

"So what is it, Gladys? Did she talk to you? Did I do something wrong? Why doesn't she want me anymore?" By this point I had lost it and was sobbing uncontrollably. All the hurt, all the pain, all the anger and missing and jealousy rose to the surface and I could barely speak.

"I don't know, honey. And Alana doesn't know either. She's very unhappy, and glad that camp is over soon. Milt and I will be driving up to take her home in two weeks. Try to be patient until then. Things have a way of working themselves out."

I was hoping for some answers, some light and a way out of my darkness. But it wasn't that easy.

"We have one more show after Alana gets home—Mickey Rooney in a play called *Alimony*. I know Milton loves Mickey Rooney. Do you think maybe you can drive up with Alana to see the show? It's only about eighty miles from New York." I tried not to, but I was almost pleading.

"I don't know, honey. I'd be happy to come and would love to see you. I'll ask Milt and Al, and let you know."

"Okay. Thanks for calling. It's been a really rough few weeks. I look forward to getting home, too."

"Okay. We'll talk soon. Keep your chin up. It's not the end of the world."

Somehow that wasn't comforting at all. It *was* the end of the world...the end of *my* world, at least. I couldn't imagine a life without Alana. I had never even thought of that. I had so many plans for things we'd do my senior year, the fun we'd have, and especially having her and her parents at my graduation. What a celebration!! I won't give up my dream, I decided, until I have no other choice.

I didn't want to be alone so I walked across the street to the neighborhood bar and joined my friends from the theatre, along with some of the actors in town that week. I replayed my conversation with Gladys over and over, trying to find a hidden message to help me with Alana. Gladys had always been honest with me, an ally when times were tough. *How could she help me now?* I thought. I wasn't in much of a partying mood so I left after one beer and went home to find some escape in sleep. But sleep wouldn't come to save me, and I spent another night staring at the ceiling, tossing and turning, wondering what tomorrow would bring, if anything. And wondering how I would survive this…

Chapter 14

A day went by. Then two and three, and a week and two weeks. I knew Al had come home and was hoping she would call. How could she not? What happened to all the love, and connection, and shared history? Everything meant *so much* to me…did it mean so *little* to her? Was I already in her rear-view mirror and getting smaller in the distance? Was she now on to someplace else, someone else, a future without me? Was I just a memory, someone who had once been in her life but now was no longer relevant or important? Did she not care anymore about me, about us? These questions were echoing and re-echoing in my head, day and night, as I tried to concentrate on getting my job done and pretending that everything was fine.

But it wasn't fine. Nothing was fine. I was moving off-campus for my senior year, and had hopes and visions of Alana and me being together, like real grown-ups in our own apartment. My closest friend at college, Dave Black, lived in Oklahoma, and was there for the summer. We had decided to room together, and since I was nearby New Haven, it was up to me to find us a place. On my days off from the theater (usually Tuesdays), I would drive to New Haven and check out the postings at the campus housing office, as well as the local newspapers. I found us a great place, and made my plans around having my own bedroom for Alana and me to share on weekends, and whenever else she could get away. It would be my first "love nest" and I was so excited at the prospect. Dave and I had no furniture of our own, so I planned to "borrow" some of the theater's inventory (beds, mattresses, dressers, couches, tables, lamps, rugs, etc.: things that certainly wouldn't be missed during the off-season), and arranged with one of the interns (who happened to have a pickup truck) to load the items at night and transport them to my new place some evening during the last week. It had been such an exciting and wonderful plan in prospect.

But once Alana began to withdraw, all the air slowly seeped from my balloon. What's the point? I wondered. Without Alana, I really didn't care about the apartment, the experience of living on my own, off campus. In fact I didn't care much about anything.

Finally, not having heard from Alana in weeks, I knew it was time to be proactive and make the call. I wish I could say I was cautiously optimistic, but I really wasn't. I had received no encouragement from her, no indication that she too wanted to be together, resume our love affair, go on to bigger and better things next year. Wasn't that the plan? Wasn't that our agreement and arrangement? Weren't we committed to each other and to being together? I guess not. But I knew I had to find out for sure…find out if she still loved me, cared for me, wanted *us* again. Maybe, just maybe, this would all work out for the best? But I knew it was a shot in the dark to really believe that. "See other people and our relationship will be better for it"? Who believes that? Why would that ever be true? Women who want out seek refuge in that ridiculous statement (just like "I don't want to be serious with anyone right now" really means "I don't want to be serious with you"!) Couples happily in love don't need to, don't want to, "see other people". Why would they? I know I didn't. But apparently Alana did, and there was nothing I could do about it. Except to find out for sure if I got the message right. So with a knot in my stomach, a hole in my heart, and an increasing fear of impending doom crowding my thoughts, I decided to call and find out for sure. I owed that to myself. And so I did.

"Hi, Gladys."

"Hi, Brett. How's everything?"

"I'm okay. And you?"

"I'm fine."

"I think you told me that Alana would be home from camp by now. Is she back yet?"

"Yes, she came home two days ago."

"Well, I haven't heard from her. Is she home now, and can I speak to her?"

"She's not home right now. A friend from camp came back with her, and they're out together now. I'm not sure what time they'll be back." I could sense an unaccustomed hesitation and uneasiness in Gladys' voice. There's something she wasn't telling me. I was desperate for information, hoping for the best, and knowing I wasn't prepared for the worst.

"Well, have you thought about coming to Ivoryton with Milton and Alana to see the show?"

"I don't know, Gary. Alana's friend will be here for a few more days, and I think they've got plans. And Milton is backlogged with work since we returned. I don't think we'll be able to make it." I knew that something wasn't right, but didn't feel comfortable asking Gladys right then.

"Okay. Well, it was just a thought. I'll be home Sunday evening, and I'll call Al when I get in."

"Okay, honey."

And with that thirty-second phone call, my heart sank. Why was Alana (and even Gladys) so distant? What had happened? How could she have fallen out of love so quickly, and for what reason? I refused to accept that this was the end for us. I thought our love was so strong that nothing would beat it down. "Till death do us part" was what I had in mind. But here it was: distance and emptiness and darkness where there had so recently been intimacy, fullness, completeness. Alana was in my thoughts 24/7; I wondered if she thought about me at all? Wouldn't she want to reach out, to connect, to talk and to see me after all this time? Like last year? And the year before? I just didn't get it, and it was killing me.

Now I just had to finish out the summer, get home, and find out for sure what was going on. The next few days were dark and cold, full of dread of what awaited me when the last show was over; when the sets, costumes, and lights would be stored away for the winter, and nothing but a brief stretch of highway would be between me and seeing (or not seeing?) Alana again. I tried to gird myself for the worst. But I'm too romantic for that. Alana was my girl, and I her guy, right? There must be some mistake. I had no choice but to wait until I got home to find out how the rest of my life would turn out. They were the longest few days of my life.

***

    I thought Sunday would never come, but it did. There was a closing-night cast party, as usual, then an end of season party for the Ivoryton staff. I remember how much fun it was last year, when I was so excited to come home to see Alana. Back then it seemed like the last few days dragged by, but they dragged by with excitement and eager anticipation, the polar opposite from what was going through my head and flooding my soul now. I didn't know what to expect when I got home and called Al…would she be happy to hear from me? Would this summer's "experiment" be over and with a happy ending? Would she have discovered that the "other people" she wanted to see were a disappointment, that the forbidden fruit wasn't better, that the grass wasn't greener? I tried to convince myself all this was possible. After all, hadn't she written that we would appreciate each other more after this brief separation and "freedom"? What kind of fool was I to believe such a thing? But I held on for dear life to that shred of hope that all my love, my commitment, wasn't made in vain…that it wasn't a mistake to give Alana my heart so completely, and to trust her…She, too, had given expressions of love, maybe not as over-the-top as mine, but seemingly sincere and profound nonetheless. Didn't she owe it to me to follow through on those loving feelings? As much as I knew I couldn't answer these questions for myself, and as futile as it was to replay them, I couldn't put them to rest or put Alana out of my mind. She had been so central (and essential) a part of my life for so long. At that age, two and a half years feels like a lifetime. Now I feared that lifetime was ending. The drive home was both too long and too short.

    I knew that my parents were away (as were my brother and sister), so I came home to an empty house. The "pathetic fallacy" was never more alive than when I walked through the front door—the house was deathly quiet, as was my soul…the house was empty, as was my heart…the air was heavy, as was my spirit…the house seemed forlorn and forsaken, as did I. I've never felt more lonely or alone.

    I waited a few hours, then picked up the phone to dial the number I had dialed a thousand times before. I had always felt a tickle of excitement in my belly when I called Alana; this time was so different. I had no idea what to expect. Until now all things were possible, even potentially the reunion and reconciliation I had fantasized when we said goodbye in June. Maybe I had completely misunderstood and misinterpreted everything, and had tortured myself and agonized over nothing. Wasn't that possible?

"Hi, Gladys. It's Brett."

"Hi, Brett. Are you home?"

"Yes. Is Al home? Can I speak to her?"

"Yes, she's upstairs. Hold on a second. Al (I heard Gladys calling). Brett's on the phone. Just a second. She's coming." I could hear a hand over the mouthpiece and some garbled voices. And then, "Hi, Brett. How are you?"

"Hi, Al. I'm okay. I just got home a little while ago, and couldn't wait to call. Is this a good time?"

"Well, my friend, Zoltan, is still here. He was the fencing instructor at Waziyatah this summer. He's leaving tomorrow. He goes to school at Wayne State in Detroit, so will be flying there from LaGuardia. I'll be taking him to the airport. His flight's at two."

"Okay. Can you talk for a while now, or would you rather wait till tomorrow?"

"Let's talk tomorrow. We have a lot of catching up to do. I'm helping him pack now, so we're kind of busy."

"Okay. Call tomorrow when you get back. I miss you and can't wait to see you."

"Okay. I'll call you tomorrow. Bye."

Nothing had been said, but everything had been said. Her "friend" was still there, sleeping in her house, sitting in *my chair* at the kitchen table, laughing and part of her life with Milton and Gladys. *He was living my life.* My worst fears were realized. Another day to wait. And I was all alone.

Chapter 15

I had nothing to do but wait for Al's call the next day. I tried to entertain and distract myself with TV, books, and radio, tinkering at the piano (I wasn't very good but it was something to do), and spent most of that night on the porch and in the backyard, staring up at the stars, hoping the hours would pass. Time seemed to be standing still. Finally it was daybreak, "the first day of the rest of my life," as they say. Perhaps I had reason to hope after all. Al's friend was leaving for Detroit. Maybe it was just a meaningless summer fling that would end as quickly as it had begun. Were it that, it would still hurt, but I would forgive Al in a heartbeat, no questions asked. It could only have been a few weeks long. How could that compare with the years and experiences we shared together? Certainly her feelings for me must trump those for him! Now that we were home, back in our world, things would be right again. I waited an eternity for Al to call. And around 5 p.m. the phone rang.

"Hello."

"Hi, Brett. It's me."

"Hey, Al. Did your friend get off okay?" I choked on these words but tried to sound nonchalant.

"Yes."

"So how have you been? Tell me about your summer."

"It was okay."

"What have you been doing since you got home?"

"Well, my friend from camp came home with me. I showed him around the neighborhood. Yesterday we went shopping for some furniture for my dorm room. I'm going to have a single this year so I can decorate it however I want! The salesman said we looked so much alike he thought we were brother and sister! That was funny."

I listened very hard to sense the feeling behind Alana's words. She didn't sound sad or sorry at all. In fact she sounded kind of content and happy, not at all what I was feeling. She was very matter-of-fact.

"That is funny," I answered, though I felt no humor at all. "I'd really like to see you!"

"Yes, well, it's getting late and I have a few things to do with my parents tonight." In the "old days," I would have been immediately and eagerly invited over, a welcome "guest" in her house. Whatever she had to do with her parents we would have done together, *as a family*. Why was I not welcome now? I didn't need to ask the question.

"How about tomorrow? In fact there's a double-bill at Fresh Meadows—*Lady Sings the Blues* and *Cabaret*. How about we go?"

"Okay. That sounds good. Call me in the morning."

"Okay, Al. Talk to you then."

"Bye."

"Bye."

And we hung up. I felt no warmth or passion or interest whatsoever from Alana. I was bursting inside with love and desire, and getting nothing in return. Relationships are two-way streets, and ours had always been that, until now. I was traveling at breakneck speed, but Al was strolling along, oblivious to where I was or where I was going. Clearly she wasn't on board. Despite my hopes and prayers, she was receding in the distance, fading from my future dreams. And it all happened with a whimper, not a bang…like a raging fire that was fizzling out. At one time our love was like ten candles, burning strong and bright. Now it seemed that, over the past few months, gradually each candle had burnt out until there was but one faint candle left, flickering in the wind, about to go out any second. And then there would be none—just a faint plume of smoke where once there had been fire and light, just a cold and dark wick where once there had been warmth and joy. She had lost her mojo for me, an ending I never expected.

The next day I called at around 11 a.m. Al said she wanted to go to a matinee (and gave no reason why). I was anxious just to see her, so planned to pick her up at 1. I made the same ten-minute drive I had made a thousand times before, and parked in front, just like I always did. I rang the front door bell and, after a minute, heard footsteps.

Then the door opened. Alana was as beautiful as ever, with gleaming blonde hair, even blonder with highlights from the summer sun. I didn't hesitate but stepped into the kitchen and leaned forward to kiss her. She turned her head so my kiss landed on her cheek, not her lips as I had intended. Things were definitely different.

I had rehearsed this moment for hours, not knowing how she'd act when she saw me, or how I'd react. A warm, tender hug and kiss was what I had hoped for; a cool awkward turn-away was what I got instead. I put my hands on Al's shoulders to look directly into her face, her eyes. The weeks of longing, missing, not knowing nor understanding, finally overwhelmed me. As hard as I tried I couldn't contain myself, and a tear formed and trickled down my cheek. Al looked away, wouldn't lock eyes with me, and started to step back and pull away. I wanted desperately to pull her to me, and squeeze her so hard so she couldn't get away, and maybe she would realize that mine were the arms in which she belonged. But I knew Alana well enough to know *that* strategy wouldn't work. She would never allow herself to be controlled or manipulated. She was always her own person, unyielding and impenetrable unless she opened the door. She was clearly in no mood to open the door to me that day. So I let her drift back and away, not knowing where to go from there. I told her how great she looked, how much I had missed her, and that I looked forward to being back with her again. She answered in requisite colloquialisms, putting out very little. More than hurt, I was confused. She wasn't the girl I drove away from two months ago, the girl who was my partner, my person. She was entirely different in mood and affect. She was cool, distant, and almost resentful that I was intruding. What had happened to cause this alienation? I was the same. Why wasn't she?

After a few minutes of painful and awkward small talk, we left the house and drove to the movie theater. Our conversation was punctuated with monosyllables, pauses, and silences. I searched for things to say to lighten the mood. I can't say there was tension exactly. It was more like nothing, like strangers who have little to say to one another. We had been soulmates a few short weeks before. Now we could barely look at one another.

Once inside the theater we sat down as we had done countless times before. In the darkness I repeatedly stole glances at Alana, trying to read something in her face or body language that would let me know she was still my girl. The movie started and I placed my right hand on her thigh. She was wearing shorts, and I felt her warm, smooth skin, so familiar but now so unresponsive. In the past she would always put her hand on mine, and we'd interlock fingers. Our hands would make love together in their own special way. But not today. She didn't pull away or take my hand away. She didn't do anything; there was no response whatsoever. As the movie continued I kept hoping for a signal that she was with me—a caress or, even better, leaning her head on my shoulder. But for two-plus hours there was only my hand searching for recognition and acknowledgement. None was forthcoming.

> *My Love is like to ice, and I to fire:*
> *How comes it then that this her cold so great*
> *Is not dissolved through my so hot desire,*
> *But harder grows the more I her entreat?*
> *Or how comes it that my exceeding heat*
> *Is not allayed by her heart-frozen cold,*
> *But that I burn much more in boiling sweat,*
> *And feel my flames augmented manifold?*
> *What more miraculous thing may be told,*
> *That fire, which all things melts, should harden ice,*
> *And ice, which is congeal'd with senseless cold,*
> *Should kindle fire by wonderful device?*
> *Such is the power of love in gentle mind,*
> *That it can alter all the course of kind.*
> -- Edmund Spencer

I gradually began to feel physically ill. The butterflies in my stomach multiplied and grew louder and stronger until I excused myself and vomited in the men's room. I came back to my seat. Still no response, not a look, not an "are you alright?", not a squeeze, not a sound. I tried once again to reach out to Al, to touch her, to connect with her, but my hand again met nothing but a cold, stony passivity.

I couldn't believe that the girl I loved so much had disappeared without a trace, without a reason, without an explanation. Nothing made sense, and I didn't want to believe that she had moved on. I wanted to stay, see both movies, hoping that simply being together would rekindle the old passion, even if it took some time. But the distance between us got the better of me. I felt sick to my stomach. Finally, I whispered to her that I wasn't feeling well and needed to leave. She got up and we walked outside into the bright September sunlight. We sat down on the curb outside the theater, all alone except for an occasional passerby. I wanted to tell her so much, to ask her so much, but she seemed unapproachable. I asked her what was wrong, and she didn't answer, just looked away, off into the distance, shrugged her shoulders, and said nothing. So I thought it best to go home, regroup, compose myself, and try again tomorrow. Maybe she was just having a bad day and didn't want to talk about anything. Maybe in her mind there was nothing to talk about. I just didn't know. I had waited seemingly so long for this day, and now it seemed my chance for reconciliation was slipping away. Would there be a tomorrow to talk about things and move forward together? I just didn't know.

So I took Al home. She got out of the car, didn't invite me in, turned, and walked away. I watched her disappear through the front door, without so much as a wave or a glance. I drove back to my house, still empty. I vomited again when I got home, more confused and upset than ever. I hoped that Al would call to see how I was feeling, maybe offer to come over and talk. But the phone never rang. Day turned into night turned into morning and not a word. She truly seemed not to care anymore, and I just didn't get it. In truth, to this day, I never really have.

Chapter 16

The next day I decided not to call Alana. As painful as it was, I realized she had other things (Zoltan?) on her mind, and I was a low priority, if I even was anywhere on her radar any more. Until she was ready to talk openly and honestly I was better off without her. I couldn't allow a repeat of what had happened the previous day at the movie theater. Other guys have been jilted, licked their wounds, and gone on. I had no choice but to try to picture a life without Al. That very idea would have been inconceivable two months earlier, but times change, people change, and she had changed. People who are rejected always seem to want an explanation, as though that would ease the pain. But once I understood that Alana was no longer available to me (for whatever reason), I needed to feel the pain, to try to hate her if I could, to put her out of my thoughts, though I knew she would never leave my heart or my memory banks. But I couldn't spend every waking moment obsessing about her, about what had happened, and why. I afforded myself the luxury of time to heal, knowing full well that the scars of a broken heart may never fully disappear. Years later, I would see on the highways of Southern California what became my favorite bumper sticker:

"Work like you don't need the money;
Dance like nobody's watching;
Love like you've never been hurt."

The first two I conquered, but the last was asking too much, and maybe even not desirable in the big picture. I don't think I was a better person for having loved and lost, but I was more sensitive and empathetic. I didn't become jaded or cynical, or vow that I would never fall in love again. It's been said that "without a hurt, a heart is hollow." Mine became fuller. The experience of Alana taught me how much love I was capable of, how wonderful and gratifying and magical it is to be in (requited) love. The experience of Alanalessness taught me that a broken heart may make me want to die, but won't kill me; and I'll live to fight (love) another day. Once I figured that out, I was able to get up off the floor and rejoin the living, although it would be quite some time before I rejoined the loving. I emotionally shut down, which was likely a saving defensive posture. I knew I had to take things one day at a time and build a new life without the girl of my dreams. But I had faith that things have a way of working themselves out.

    My twenty-first birthday was the following week. I hadn't spoken to Al since the day at the theater, but fantasized that she might send me a card, or even call to wish me happy birthday. Twenty-one seemed like an important age, a milestone. But nothing happened. I suppose she did me a favor by not leading me on. It was over, and there was nothing I could do about it. Her actions were brutally clear and honest. I should be grateful and thanking her for that. But gratitude and thanks were two emotions I wasn't feeling at the time. Strangely, I spent my birthday with Al's parents. They took me out to dinner, and Gladys got me a cake (and a coffeemaker for my apartment). I was never mad at them, and spending time with them was familiar, comfortable, and comforting. I sat in my same chair at the kitchen table, and in my usual spot on the couch in the red TV room. Everything seemed like before, except Al wasn't there. I never brought up Alana's name, nor did they. I supposed that Gladys would say if Al asked her about me. I admit that I always hoped she would do so. Milton and Gladys and that house in Holliswood were all I had left of the happiest, most loving years of my life, and I was reluctant to give that up. In fact, it would be quite some time before I did.

Chapter 17

My senior year at Yale was forgettable but not forgotten. The high hopes and expectations I had had were dashed, and I returned to New Haven (to my new apartment furnished with bits and pieces from all eight summer productions) to finish my credits to graduate. Having become a member of Actors' Equity by appearing in one of the plays that summer, I threw myself full-bore into the pursuit of a career in theater, onstage or backstage, and started attending every audition I could find, in New Haven, on Broadway, off Broadway, off off Broadway, and anyplace with a stage and a company. I soon began to see the same people every week at all the auditions, actors who had a dream but not a career. They were all waiting: waiting for that one big break which would bring them recognition and calls from agents, and waiting tables by day to pay the rent. Rarely did that big break come. After a while, and after not landing any roles, I came to the sad realization that most of these other aspiring actors were so much better than me, and, in fact, were so much better than I'd ever be. I had no special connections, and no desire to spend my life chasing the impossible dream while serving meals as my day job. So I gradually became less and less sanguine and enamored about my future in the theater. My second semester I took a dumbed-down version of a physics course ("Physics for Poets") which somehow met pre-med requirements (my parents and Gladys especially were happy about that!) and I began to circle around to thoughts of a career in medicine if my theatre life fizzled as it seemed to be doing. The Yale campus was full of student activities and I kept myself as busy as possible. I performed in and designed multiple college theatrical productions. I joined the staff of the *Yale Daily News*, which, obviously, came out every day (duh!), and signed up for the closing shift, from midnight until the paper was put to bed, usually around 4 a.m. When you're twenty-one you don't need much sleep; I would catch a few hours before my 8 a.m. classes, and go full-speed all day (excellent preparation for my later life as a surgical intern and resident, when I got even less sleep!).

Did this flurry of activity make me stop thinking about Alana? No, not at all, but it helped some.

My roommate Dave Black was a most intelligent and interesting guy. Dave grew up on a ranch in Oklahoma (the "Lazy B"), liked Country & Western music, and wore cowboy boots before it was cool to like country music or wear cowboy boots. He was certainly no hick or country bumpkin, and I was so grateful to have Dave's companionship. Dave knew Al from the year before, and I spent countless hours sharing my sadness and grief, even desperately (and pathetically) asking "Why?" Of course he had no answers but he heard me out, always listening patiently and sympathetically. He was a good friend.

Years later, when I first saw the movie *Forrest Gump*, I realized that Forrest's impossible love for Jennie was not unlike mine for Alana—she hurt him, rejected him, and left him time after time; but he never stopped loving her, no matter what or when. And he was always there for her, ready to take her back in a heartbeat, even knowing that she likely would break his heart again. My feelings for Al were kind of like that. Like Forrest, I was destined to love Alana come what may. Was Forrest a fool? Or a hopeful romantic? I prefer the latter.

We, as a couple, were invited to the wedding of Al's freshman-year resident advisor, Betsy, over the Thanksgiving holiday. We had become especially close to Betsy when one month Al missed her period and we were both freaking out. Betsy was the voice of calm and reason and talked us through it (just a false alarm, but very alarming to us nonetheless). I was surprised (and cautiously optimistic) when Al asked me to escort her. I wore my nicest suit, bought Al a corsage, and thought she might be softening towards me, regretting her decision and reconsidering breaking up, and even remembering the good times. I tried not to let myself get too excited. But my wounds were still fresh, and it was so easy to allow myself to slip back and believe the unbelievable. Of course when things seem too good to be true, they usually are. As one of the wedding gifts I bought what is still my favorite and most romantic piece of music, Beethoven's "Kreutzer Sonata," an amazing expression of love-making between a violin and piano. On the cover I wrote, "For your holding-hands times," a message to Betsy and her future husband, but, of course, really a subliminal message to Alana. I'm always moved by a wedding, and I hoped that Al would be, too; that our hands would touch; we would dance the night away, and fall in love all over again. Unfortunately, none of that happened. Al spent the requisite amount of time with me, but was much more interested and involved with her friends from college, especially a guy named Randy, and I watched her laughing at his jokes and smiling that beautiful smile as I was crying inside. It wasn't a good day for me.

About a month later, when I was home for Christmas break, I was at Eddie's house when Alana dropped in unexpectedly to visit Eddie's sisters (former high school classmates). When I heard Al at the front door I was surprised, scared for some reason, then decided to take the plunge and talk to her. We spoke briefly in the vestibule. I was hoping for a sign that Al was glad to see me; maybe she even came there hoping to see me? But after a brief hello, she went upstairs with the girls, and a short time later left without saying goodbye. Miraculously I wasn't as crushed by this encounter as I thought I would be. It seemed that I had faded into the background of her past, just a memory with little to no emotion attached. This was the new normal, and I had better get used to it if I wanted to move on to other healthy relationships. Easier said than done, but I realized that my feelings for Alana were never going to change, and I was lucky to have had experienced them. The opening scene of a popular movie of the day, *Carnal Knowledge*, portrays a conversation between two teenage boys at summer camp on the cusp of their sexual awakening. One asks the other, "Would you rather love or be loved?" I had seen that movie with Alana, and, at the time, I felt quite good that I had both, so never had to answer that question for myself. But later on, when I was no longer so fortunate, I came to the surprising realization that, at this point in my life, I would choose the former, to love with all my heart, as I did Alana. That feeling (active, fulfilling, enriching, explosive even) is a gift, way better than simply being on the receiving end. For me, as far as love is concerned, it's way better to give than to receive, and, amazingly, the more one gives the more one *has* to give. The feeling sustains, indeed magnifies, itself. That epiphany changed my whole way of thinking about Alana. She could withdraw her love for me, but not my love for her; though unrequited, it was still quite a feeling, and I felt fortunate to have the capacity to experience it, and fortunate to have met the Muse to bring forth those feelings in me. Maybe I was just trying to come to grips with my loss by rationalizing a silver lining? I needed to find something positive in the past few years, and not feel that I had just been chasing my tail and giving my all to a lost cause with nothing to show for it in the end but a heart in tatters. But maybe I had grown, and learned something about myself, and Alana had been instrumental in that discovery and maturing process. Somehow I could live with that.

    I returned for my last semester at Yale, finally feeling that I was healing, not yet recovered but on the road. For Spring Break Dave and I drove down to Florida to visit my cousin at Rollins College, outside Orlando. We went to New Smyrna Beach on the Atlantic coast, and I remember thinking how much better it would have been to spend that time with Al instead of Dave (no offense, Dave). I gathered a bunch of sea shells, and, on a whim, put them in a box and mailed them to Alana. I was still fishing, hoping to land the one that got away. A few days after I got back to New Haven, I got the strangest phone call and request. I suspected I would hear something from Alana after she received the shells; but I never expected what happened next. Al said that she was taking a photography class, and as a project she wanted to photograph me in the nude!! What a proposition!! Why me??!!!! I was both gratified that she wanted to use me as her model and relieved that she likely wasn't intimately involved with anyone else at the time. Again I fought the expectation that this was a new beginning for us, although it was certainly tempting to fall into that trap, given her suggestion. Of course I said yes immediately, and once again was cautiously optimistic. That weekend Al drove to New Haven, and I stripped down for her. She posed me and spent the whole afternoon taking photo after photo. I was all too happy to oblige, wondering what would happen next. When the last picture was taken, she came over and sat down next to me on the bed. I was naked, excited, and it obviously showed. I was careful not to make any advances (other than that which was beyond my voluntary control) because I didn't want to scare her off or do anything to push her away. I was so happy just to see her, and spend the day with her. In a way it was like old times, and I didn't want to do anything to ruin the moment. To my surprise Al reached over and gently pulled me towards her. We kissed, this time not on the cheek. We kissed again, and then we made love. The whole time I couldn't believe this was actually happening. I had fantasized about this so often and now to be intimate again, after so much distance and so much longing, seemed impossible. I must be dreaming. It was fantastic!! Please, God, don't let me wake up!

And then she dressed and got ready to leave, without a word about her feelings or when we'd see each other again. But by this time I had grown to the point where I felt able to tell her how I felt, how much I loved her and missed her, not to make her feel guilty, just to let her know. She smiled, gave my hand a squeeze, and was on her way. I guess it just wasn't her time. Of course it would have been over the moon had she reciprocated. But for that moment it was enough for me to express myself in a way I hadn't for so long. I never felt more alive. And I slept soundly for the first time in months.

Chapter 18

Lovemaking, human intimacy, the all-encompassing embrace of two warm intertwined bodies, the soft touch of human flesh—powerful medicine when one's heart is broken, something for which there is no substitute. And our last romantic interlude had been therapeutic in that way. I could still feel Al's skin against mine and smell her hair. Whether or not we'd have another chapter was beyond my control or knowledge. If she would agree I would certainly agree. But what more could I do? I heard once that 10 percent of life is what we do, and 90 percent is how we react to things that happen to us. And I must agree. I needed to forgive Al, to drill down deep to find it in my heart (what was left of it) to change my perception, interpretation, and appreciation of our relationship. Anger is likely the most destructive of emotions—malignant and overwhelming. I had to give that up, for my sake. Al could control her actions, but she couldn't control my reactions, and that was what I had to work on. I wish I knew how. But even recognizing that I could be in charge of myself, rather than be at the mercy of someone who I loved but was no longer there for me, was intellectually, if not emotionally, comforting. Food for thought. But I knew I couldn't hang on to a memory or a dream. I needed to live in the moment, and I certainly wasn't doing that.

I didn't hear from Alana again that semester. Graduation came and I saved a ticket for her, hoping that somehow she would want to come and be part of that celebration. Instead, my parents and sister came. Dave's family couldn't come from Oklahoma, so we all (including Dave) went to eat at Morry's (a famous Yale eatery) after the ceremony. It should have been a day to remember as nothing but goodness and happiness; but I felt a certain undeniable emptiness even as I received my degree. If only Alana were there it would have been the perfect day. But the sharp, raw pain had been replaced by then with a deep, dull ache that never seemed to go away. I had learned from Dr. Eric Segal (a classics professor at Yale who incidentally wrote the wildly popular *Love Story*) that wisdom comes through suffering (Aeschylus), and I guess I was wising up to the reality of my Alanalessness.

I returned my furniture to the playhouse, drove to Boston with Dave to drop off a few things at my brother's apartment (he had graduated from Harvard Medical School, just gotten married, and was on his honeymoon), and returned to New York. I had resigned myself by then to shift my career focus from theater to medicine. I moved back in with my parents to start the process of completing my pre-med requirements at Columbia University the following year and applying to medical school.

My first stop after unpacking was to visit Milton and Gladys. They had always been such strong supporters, from the time I first met them when I took my leave of absence from college. They never doubted that I would find my way, and I appreciated their confidence. Over time I had developed an ever-closer relationship with them, even without Alana's involvement. A part of me always hoped they would convince her that she had made a big mistake and I was the only guy for her; or at least that she would come to that realization herself, share it with them, and they would encourage me to call. None of that happened but it was enough to remain part of their family.

When I got to Palermo Street I was happy to pull up front and ring the bell. Was I surprised when Alana answered the door! I'm not sure why I was so surprised—it *was* her house, and the school year was over. I guess I had become so accustomed to visiting just Milton and Gladys that Alana being there seemed strangely out of place. The last time I had seen her was that wonderful and surprising rendezvous in New Haven with the photo shoot and all that went with (after) it. It could (should) have been very awkward, but somehow we had gotten past that. Neither one of us seemed taken aback or embarrassed. If anything, I was pleasantly surprised, and surprised at how pleasant and comfortable it felt. The anxiety of last summer was long gone. Maybe that love-making session had been more therapeutic than I knew. But somehow it was okay to see her. In fact, she even seemed pleasantly surprised herself (also a surprise for me!). Milton and Gladys were both home, and all congratulated me. Alana gave me a peck on the cheek but even that was okay. We sat down at the table, me in my accustomed seat, Al in hers, and had coffee and pie a la mode. It seemed like old times once again.

When it came time to leave, I had a moment alone with Alana (surreptitiously arranged by Gladys, I'm sure). I told Al that I missed her not being at graduation, and asked if I could take her out to celebrate, just we two. There was no rehearsal, no preparation, just a from-the-heart, sincere request. And, surprisingly once again, she said yes. A day full of surprises. So I went home feeling surprisingly (!) good, and thought of how we should celebrate. I doubted there would be love-making involved this time, but who knows? Maybe our time had come.

A week later I came to pick up Al and we went to Manhattan. I had bought tickets to see *Grease* (the original Broadway production). I made reservations for dinner afterwards. The show was great. Al was in a good mood, and we spent the whole evening talking, like good old friends. I remember sitting behind a middle-aged couple who brought their young child to the show. At intermission they asked if we would watch their daughter while they went to the restrooms. They must have seen us as a responsible young couple ourselves, and it felt so domestic and so natural for me. I was still crazy in love with Alana; there was no doubt about that. But by this time I was comfortable and secure with those feelings. I (and my feelings) had been through so much, and we both had survived. Alana, no matter what happened, could never take that away from me. Perhaps she didn't (couldn't) appreciate my true feelings, or respect them, or value them. But they were real nonetheless, and I enjoyed loving her the way I did. I had no unrealistic expectations anymore, just that same cautious optimism that had characterized my approach since last summer. Perhaps cautious optimism—rather than all-in love, passion, and commitment—was a safer way to go. Not as fun, and certainly not my first choice. But I didn't *have* a choice over that, and I knew it. So I enjoyed what I could, and tried not to agonize over what I couldn't. Another valuable lesson I learned from Al.

After the show, we went to a nearby restaurant for dinner. I still remember what I ordered (lobster thermidor). We spoke about a lot of things, but avoided the 800-pound gorilla in the room. Much as I wanted to have Alana back in my life, I could easily tell that she wasn't interested in resuming what we had before. I suppose we could have been friends, but that mature I wasn't, and I could never deal with knowing that there was a love interest in her life who wasn't me. That much I knew about myself and was sure of. Of course I was hopeful that evening, but when we said good night (one more kiss on the cheek) I knew it was really over, and time to move forward. I had graduated from college, and I needed to graduate from Alana and Brett. It had been a very long year for me. I expected to see Milton and Gladys again (which I did regularly), but not Alana (which I didn't). I knew I would always be in love with Al, but I finally had come to terms with my Alanalessness.

    As Yale and Alana retreated, my life continued. I never forgot Al (who forgets their first love?), but knew that she was lost to me. I returned to Palermo Street on a regular basis, both to see my surrogate parents and hopefully to hear about Alana. I didn't feel comfortable or appropriate fishing for information; I was always afraid that I would hear what I didn't want to hear, that she was involved with someone else and never mentioned my name. I assumed that if Alana expressed interest or asked questions about me, Gladys would speak up. But she never did.

    Long after Al and I were no longer a couple, I continued to drop by to see Gladys and keep my hopes and dreams alive. Milton would come home late from work, briefcase bulging with papers, and, despite his surprise at seeing me in my accustomed spot at the kitchen table, would welcome me like the son he never had. I'm sure he was always surprised to see me, and wondered, *What the f___? I thought this guy was long gone. Why am I still feeding him?* But he was always most gracious and courteous, and I never felt anything but welcome and included in his life and family, despite my ill-defined role. I truly loved that man. I regret that Alana and I didn't reconnect while Milton was still alive. I would have loved to re-enter his life, and let him know that all those dinners and times at his home were not for naught. He truly meant something to me, the father I never had after my dad died so young and prematurely. I have since dedicated a memorial plaque in Milton's name at the temple, and visited his grave with Gladys on numerous occasions. I will say Kaddish for Milton for the rest of my life, as I do for my own dad.

Year after year I returned to my second home, always wondering (hoping) that my first love would be there and we'd have another inning. But it never happened.

Despite our break-up and the long healing and rebuilding process, I was never able to get fully past Alana, and she remained deeply and dearly embedded in my heart and soul. For reasons not clear to me then or now, except spiritual in nature, we somehow continued to remain in each other's lives, at least tangentially and peripherally. Most lost loves are over and done with, and the individuals involved, regardless of the hurt, move on. But I never did, and Al and I were destined to remain in touch, one way or another, whether by accident or "intelligent design." When it was clear to me that theater was not an option as a career, I proceeded to pursue a future in medicine. Another big circle that was completed! Since I had majored in theater at college I had few of the pre-med requirements. So I enrolled in the General Studies Program at Columbia University (specifically designed for post-baccalaureate candidates who had completed their undergraduate degrees in other fields but who chose to pursue an alternative pathway and needed additional credits to move on to postgraduate studies). Interestingly, years later, Alana, who had majored in Psychology as an undergraduate, and subsequently received a Master's Degree from NYU in Special Education, also followed this same track, and spent two years at Columbia completing her pre-med requirements before entering medical school. Our paths never crossed at Columbia (I being several years her senior), but that would have been an interesting and fortuitous turn of events. Who knows? Perhaps our reconnection would have happened then and there, and saved us both so many lost years…but it didn't, and maybe that wasn't the right time. Man plans and God laughs…

In any event, I completed my required courses, studied for my MCATs (medical college aptitude tests) at the Stanley Kaplan educational center in Brooklyn (where Alana also studied years later…no, our paths never crossed there either), and was accepted at

FIRST LOVES ARE FOREVER

New York Medical School (where Alana also received her medical degree in years to come; sadly, our paths never crossed there either). Looking back it seems like there were so many opportunities for us to meet again, so many times in our separate and individual lives that we traveled the same highways and byways; but for some reason we just missed each other, time and again. So many close calls. But it just wasn't our time.

As the years went by, I moved from relationship to relationship, never able to fully commit myself for reasons I didn't understand. I wanted a steady, long-term involvement but couldn't seem to find the right person. Perhaps subconsciously my heart still longed for Al. In medical school I met Arlete de Moraes, an exchange student from Brazil studying at Manhattanville College. I had thought *my* upbringing, being the middle of three children, was difficult and fraught with parental insouciance. Imagine being the eleventh of twelve children, as Arlete was—the "end of the harvest," as she said ruefully. It seemed that she too was damaged goods from a difficult childhood and broken love affair, and despite the language, cultural, religious, ethnic, and all the other differences between us, we connected on a deep level and became serious about each other and our relationship. It was the first time since Alana that I fell in love again.

One New Year's Eve we were invited to a party by my childhood friend Eddie, who, interestingly enough, lived about a block and a half away from me (again!) in Manhattan. New Year's Eve was always bittersweet for me; I could never quite forget my first date with Alana, and what could have been.

In any event, Arlete and I went, and, lo and behold, the first person I saw when I walked into the apartment was Alana. She was sitting on the couch and looked up as I entered the room. I had no idea that she would be there, and, like years before, she took my breath away. She was there with a girlfriend. At first I was speechless, but then, without being too obvious, I maneuvered my way over to say hello. Al didn't seem as surprised as I, and perhaps even knew that I would be there. Arlete was by my side and Al realized I was with a date; she kept an appropriate distance, but I thought I saw something warm, inviting, and nostalgic in her eyes. Try as I might I couldn't keep my eyes off her, much to the dismay of Arlete. Of all the gin joints in all the towns in all the world...I left the party shortly after midnight, and Arlete knew my mind was far away. We walked quietly through the cold, still, winter air the few short blocks back to my apartment.

"You and she were lovers?" she finally asked, breaking the silence.

"Yes," I answered. "Once upon a time, long ago and far away."

"You're still in love with her, you know." I didn't answer. We never spoke of it again.

After medical school I spent two years as a general surgical intern/resident at New York Hospital, where, interestingly enough, our paths did cross. By that time Alana was at Columbia preparing for a future in medicine. She called and came to see me to discuss medicine and surgery. I was surprised to hear from her, but, for some reason, not all that surprised. She had remained ever-present in my life, despite our being physically apart and incommunicado. I was on-call that day to the emergency room, and I remember she brought a dozen bagels with her (strange the things we remember!). She shadowed me for several hours while I saw patients. I didn't understand why she chose that time and place to contact me; we hadn't spoken in so long, and clearly I was not on her radar romantically. Or was I? I was both curious and, once again, cautiously optimistic, but tried not to let my imagination get the better of me. I was happy to see her, glad that she was invested in, and passionate about, a career she was committed to, and it was a very pleasant afternoon. It just felt so good to be with her! I knew full well that my feelings were still very much alive, and I fought the temptation to reach out to her, discuss our past together, or maybe a present and future. She had initiated this reconnection, and it was up to her to start that conversation. I tried to convince myself that I was just an old friend, no longer a significant other, nor likely to become one. But my heart and mind were at odds, and I couldn't help but hope that our time had come. When we left the ER, and had a few minutes to ourselves, we went back to my apartment (across the street from the hospital). We sat on my couch and made small talk about the day. But my mind wasn't on the small talk or the ER. I saw only my Alana, the golden girl of my dreams, the one who got away. It was both strange, and at the same time natural and familiar, to be sitting, talking, sharing this way. At one point, as we sat next to each other, our faces inches apart, Al looked up at me and said, "Can I give you a kiss?" "Sure," I said, surprised and not knowing exactly what to expect. Our lips met, and moments later our tongues were playfully touching, caressing, exploring, connecting as they had done so long ago. As we "disengaged," I had no idea where this would lead, but I had no doubts or reservations, and pulled Al closer to me again. This time she resisted. "I'm sorry, I shouldn't have," she said. "But I still have very strong feelings for you. I've got a lot on my plate right now, Brett, and am not ready for a serious relationship. It wouldn't be fair to you to have a casual hookup. Been there, done that a few years ago, and I shouldn't have then. I know how painful it was for you and how selfish of me. Knowing you as well and as long as I do, I know you can't accept or be happy with what I'm able to give you now. I'm sorry. Please don't be angry." I looked deep into her eyes, and said nothing. "I really should go," she said, and stood up and gathered her things. We walked silently back to the subway station. Before she walked down the steps there was one more lingering embrace, like old friends who were more than old friends. And I watched her as she walked away. I just didn't get it. It seemed that we were destined to go round and round, ever reaching for the brass ring, always touching but never able to own it. I lingered outside the station, wondering if maybe she would come back up to see me, hug me, walk back with me to my apartment to continue where we left off, to right the wrong of yesteryear. But no such luck. She had disappeared into the night again, and would not be back.

    I entered my apartment, so alive minutes ago, now dark and lonely. I put the stylus on the LP, and the haunting voice and words of Ella Fitzgerald (*"Every time we say goodbye, I die a little..."*) washed over me, echoing and re-echoing across the years and memories and heartaches.

    I still wasn't over her, and wondered if I'd hear from her again. I kept my feelings in my secret place, undisturbed. I hoped that Gladys would have some information for me, but she gave me nothing and life went on.

Several months after our day together in the ER, when I least expected it, I got a phone call from Al out of the blue. She asked if I'd like to come visit at her apartment in Long Island. She had afternoons off on the days she didn't have class, and she invited me over for lunch. I was reluctant at first, with very mixed and conflicting feelings, not wanting to stir up my own passions and hopes only to be disappointed and frustrated again, but, as usual, cautiously optimistic, and hoping for the best. Why would she call and ask me over if she had no interest? She undoubtedly knew how I felt. But, as usual, my heart won out (nothing ventured, nothing gained). I tried to minimize my expectations (unsuccessfully), but couldn't pass up an opportunity to see Al, catch up, and maintain whatever connection still existed. And who knows? It seemed that somehow we couldn't live with each other, and couldn't live without each other. I no longer tried to figure it out, but just accepted it for what it was and went to see her at her then-residence in North Shore Towers. She lived in a very comfortable, one-bedroom apartment, and seemed really glad to see me. I asked how she was, and she seemed happy enough, though she didn't share any details of her personal life or volunteer any of her feelings about me (much to my disappointment). We had lunch, exchanged small talk, and I kept wondering and waiting if there would be more. But this time no kiss or hug, just two old friends with history getting together. When I left I wondered why she had called; it must be our destiny. Like a rope tied in a knot, the more we tried to pull apart, the tighter the knot became.

I recalled the words of Deepak Chopra:
"Yesterday is history;
Tomorrow is a mystery;
Today is a gift; that's why they call it the present."

I could only live in the moment, glad that Al still thought of me and reached out, and leave the future in God's hands, where it belonged. As it turned out, I wouldn't hear from Al again for the next twenty years.

After my residency, I spent several years as a research fellow in Skeletal Pathology at the Hospital for Joint Diseases in Manhattan, and our paths nearly crossed once more. During our frequent phone calls and connections, Gladys told me that Milton had been diagnosed with kidney cancer, and would likely require removal of his kidneys and lifelong dialysis, a very dismal and depressing prospect. But they were fortunate enough to be referred to a surgeon at the Cleveland Clinic who pioneered a procedure called "bench surgery" in which the kidneys were removed from the body, the tumor resected, and the kidneys re-implanted. It was landmark surgery, yet very promising, and way better than the prospect of being hooked up to a machine three times every week for the rest of his days. Gladys and Milton went to Cleveland, and I spoke with them every day from my Bone Lab at Joint Diseases. Little did I know at the time that Alana, then a medical student, went to Cleveland to be with her parents and likely was there during my frequent phone calls. Why we never connected then I'll never know; but somehow we didn't. One more missed opportunity. Fortunately Milton made a full recovery, and Al and I remained strangers during a time when we both needed each other and were open and available for a new beginning. Again it wasn't the right time.

Al completed medical school, and I my fellowship, traveling parallel paths but never intersecting. I entered my residency in orthopaedic surgery at Long Island Jewish Hospital, and Al accepted a position in General Surgery at St. Vincent's Hospital. So near, yet so far, and we each followed our own separate roads, though we could have reconnected at any time had the Fates been kinder.

One evening while at work in the Emergency Room, I received a somewhat frantic phone call from Gladys. She had fallen outside while walking Al's dog Slip, and fractured her hip. She needed care and reached out to me. Of course I advised her to be brought right to the ER and I would be waiting there for her. Gladys was admitted to the hospital, and had surgery for her fracture the next evening. Of course I followed her case very closely (although I did not participate in her surgery for obvious reasons). I came by to see her twice a day (and to poach from her breakfast and dinner trays), every morning before rounds, and in the evenings when the work day was completed. I knew that Alana was likely to show up, but for whatever reason we never were there at the same time. I was still single, she as well. It would have been so sweet and special to reconnect at that time, but such was not the case. Man plans and God laughs…Once again it just wasn't our time.

Gladys recovered, went home, and, whenever I had a free moment, I continued to come by, always to see my surrogate parents as well as to hope for some positive news about Alana. But no such good news was forthcoming. God plans, and man waits and wonders…

I eventually met someone else, and, with Alana apparently uninterested and gone from my life, I became engaged and got married. Jennifer was my wife's child from a previous marriage, an infant at the time when we were courting, and an important part of the equation for me. I had an instant family, and was optimistic and committed to making this work. I still (subconsciously) held steadfast to my dream (my, I am stubborn!!), and when I got married Milton and Gladys were there. I wanted the people most important to me at my wedding. Of course I couldn't invite Alana. But Milton and Gladys were the next best thing, and meant so much to me. They met Jennifer (toddling along at one and a half years old, and walking down the aisle with me as the flower girl). At my wedding, Eddie witnessed the signing of my Ketubah, and, after my first dance with Sharon, Gladys approached me to dance with her. It was a sweet but poignant moment. I had always pictured dancing with Gladys at my wedding, but in my dreams my bride was always Alana. Of course I was glad that Milton and Gladys were there; but there was also a profound sadness and emptiness that they weren't to be my in-laws, and this was likely the last time I would see them, given my new life and new living arrangements. Eddie and Gladys—a circle *in*complete, a life unfinished and unfulfilled. Sometimes things *don't* have a way of working themselves out. This iconic moment of my life was sadly one of those times. Alana was ever-present but never-present. I would have to build my life without her. And so I did…

Tragically, when I was a Chief Resident, my father became ill with terminal metastatic pancreatic cancer, and died shortly thereafter. I moved to California for a second fellowship and a new life far away. Although not fully aware of my motivations at the time (I had been offered other fellowships and job opportunities nearby), I needed to move away and start over, which is what I did in San Diego (as far away from New York as one can get in the continental United States). And my life and dreams with Alana were out of sight but never completely out of mind. I thought my life on the East Coast was over, and it would be a new beginning. I was looking only forward, not backward. Dwelling on the past has little to commend itself. I visited Milton and Gladys after my father's funeral and shiva to say my goodbyes, fully optimistic that my future would have a way of working itself out (as Gladys always reminded me).

Alana remained buried in my heart, further and further down memory lane.

PART III

Chapter 1

May 28 (continued)

The Roslyn-Clermont Hotel (Room 222)

 I stepped over the threshold, and felt like I was stepping through the looking glass, into a fantasy world where anything was possible. The days and weeks (nay years!) of imagination flooded my mind, heart, and body with a tingling from head to toe, a rush of excitement, anticipation, and trepidation. My life didn't exactly flash before my eyes; it was a more complete experience than that, of sight plus a well of emotion that was gushing to the surface. I had no doubt that the Alana I would meet that morning would be very much the same Alana I had known as a teenager, the very same Alana I had pictured off in the distance, over the horizon, so many times before. I knew I wouldn't be disappointed, no matter what I saw. I only hoped she would feel the same.

 I looked into the half-darkened room and finally saw her. At first glance, she seemed way more tense than I felt. We let the door close, and stood a few feet from each other, quiet, gazing, not moving, living in the moment for the first time in a long time, taking each other in. How did she look? As beautiful as I remembered, with the same shoulder-length blonde hair, sparkling blue eyes, and radiant smile. That part of me which I had left behind so long ago burst through, reborn, rejuvenated, yearning to live and love again. Our eyes were locked and we both stepped forward at the same time to seal the moment with a brief kiss (this time on the lips) and a long hug. Whether she looked the same or not, Alana *felt* the same to me, and I put one hand on her hair, the other around her waist, and we stood there, cheek to cheek. I, never at a loss for words, was speechless then. But words seemed unnecessary and superfluous. The moment transcended all that had gone before. I knew right then that finally I was at the right place at the right time with the right person, and I wanted that hug to last forever.

We gradually, reluctantly, loosened our grasp to look again into each other's eyes. Had I witnessed this scene in a movie or play I likely would have thought it unbearably corny. *If that wasn't me I'd laugh,* I thought. But instead it felt so natural, and real, and iconic. There's a reason things become clichés, likely because they're commonly experienced and true. There was *nothing* old, tired, or worn-out about that moment. It was new to me! Although fully clothed, I felt completely naked and exposed, covering and concealing nothing, wanting Al to see me and see into me. The eyes are direct outgrowths of the brain, the only externally visible part of our central nervous system, thus truly the windows of our mind. Looking into Al's windows I could still see the eighteen-year-old Alana. It was 1972 all over again, *before the fall*. It seemed that nothing existed beyond the walls of that hotel room, neither in time nor space. It truly was a dreamlike moment.

We stepped back, and took each other's hands as we continued our gaze, looking across the years to familiar and comfortable landscape. We had done so much talking during the past month that we didn't need words right then.

I suppose a real cliché would have been if we ripped each other's clothes off, fell into the bed, and ravaged each other for hours, making up for all the lost time, the disappointments we had felt in life, filling our hunger for satisfaction. But in truth we were a bit too old (not that there's anything wrong with that, and not that it didn't occur to me!). Instead we instinctively realized there was no great rush, and time was on our side. In truth I think Al was more nervous than I, very much like our first time. So we sat down next to each other on the edge of the bed instead, and held hands for a few minutes. We gradually loosened up, and started talking and laughing the same way we did on the phone. Besides our personal history, the most common ground we shared was our careers as surgeons, so we naturally talked about that.

My very first day as an intern I learned the most valuable lesson of my professional life. I approached the ward at New York Hospital to which I was assigned with false bravado (*I'm a frickin' doctor!!*) but basically scared to death. (*I'm no doctor; what am I doing here, taking care of patients???!!!!*) The first person I saw was my first-year resident Bob, who saw the terror in my eyes and empathized, remembering his first day as an intern. He came up to me and introduced himself, and he seemed like a wise old man to me: comfortable, confident, at-ease, and relaxed. In truth he had been standing in my shoes a short year ago, and was likely younger than I was! But he seemed in a different world. He put his arm over my shoulders and said, "Relax. There's nothing to be worried about. I'm here to help you, and you'll get through this, the same way I did, the same way a gazillion other interns did." Bob said the words I'll never forget: "*The most important thing is to keep a sense of humor about things. No matter how crazy things seem, stay grounded, focused, and don't lose your sense of humor. Otherwise you'll never make it!*" And with that, my perspective changed, and I never forgot that wisdom. *I had people!* and wasn't alone. Now I could be an intern.

Despite the gravity of medicine and patient care, and the decisions doctors make every day (every hour), the only way to survive and avoid burn-out is never to lose your sense of humor. Alana and I had been there, shared a common history, and were both experienced enough to appreciate that life is a tragedy played by comedians, and laughter is the best medicine for patient and practitioner alike. I guess we related the way old soldiers do, looking back on times and experiences that were terrifying once but now comical, even commonplace. I told Al about the last patient I had seen before leaving Tuesday evening, a woman with carpal tunnel syndrome for whom I had prescribed Vitamin B6. The patient followed up, saying that she felt somewhat better (I was happy), but that she couldn't find B6 in her local pharmacy; so instead she bought B12 tablets and broke them in half!! Just as good, doctor, right? It made perfect sense from a lay person's perspective, but of course it was ridiculous and absurd from a scientific perspective. I would never laugh at a patient, but inside I was screaming!! And that funny little story broke the ice, we both relaxed, and laughed, and started sharing "war stories."

Al lay back on the bed, laughing hysterically, that same laugh and beautiful smile I remembered so well from so long ago. She hadn't really changed at all…the years had been good to her, despite her life's experiences.

"You can't make this stuff up!" she said as we shared a moment reserved for old soldiers who had been in the trenches, lived to tell their tales, and laugh about them. People (patients) say the darndest things, and we both knew how to appreciate the absurdity, and laugh with, not at, those entrusted to our care. Years ago we were both rebels, searching for our path and our way to change the world. Now we were looking back on lives of service, and the positive contributions we had made. We had both come a long way. We were like two peas in a pod, connected by a bond that reached back to our adolescence, like Forrest and Jennie, and continued through our years apart, unbeknownst to us. We had followed parallel paths without even knowing it, and here we were, together at last, perhaps the way God meant it to be?

Once the mood had lightened and we were talking like old friends, I took from my pocket a little surprise I had been saving…the last letter Alana had written to me almost four decades before. It was that same three-page letter I had received that broke my heart. Why I kept it for so long I had no idea. I certainly never expected to see Alana again, and it certainly didn't bring a smile to my face to reread it. Quite the contrary! But I had kept it all these years, tucked away in a briefcase I had used at Ivoryton that summer, along with memorabilia from the theater and my theater days, such as playbills, set and lighting designs, color wheels, and the like. The letter had remained untouched for a long time and was still in pristine condition, looking very much the same as it did when I first opened it. To make the scene even more poignant, there were actual forty-year-old tear stains that smudged some of the words, a touching reminder of the power of ink on paper.

The letter had Alana's return address from camp, my address at the Ivoryton Playhouse, and Al's handwriting and signature, not very different from the way she writes today. She was very surprised when she saw the envelope, and had no idea what was inside. Her recollection of those days (so burned into my memory) was sketchy at best, more a haze than the series of sharply focused, discreet moments I had buried deep down inside until recently.

"I have something to show you," I whispered as I gave her the envelope.

She took out the letter and began to read. Not until midway through did she get the significance of that piece of paper, why it had so much meaning for me, why I had held onto it for so long, and why I had brought it with me that day. Initially I thought that I had brought it along as much as a curiosity as anything else, a relic from the past, something we would both find amusing. But reading that letter silently together as we sat next to each other closed a big circle for me, a circle that had started when I first read it alone by the lake at Ivoryton. I began to tear up all over again when I read the part about "seeing other people," how it "would be good for us and our relationship," how "we will love each other even more when we got home after the summer". Knowing now what I didn't know then was the saddest part of all for me. Back then, I still *was* hopeful, and it took a lot of grief born of denial before I faced the truth. I suppose I had kept that letter, and brought it with me to show to Alana, because I wanted her to know how much I had been hurt that summer of '72. I really didn't want to hurt her, but I wanted her to know how much she had hurt me, how deeply I had cared, that she might feel my pain, still so raw after so long. We didn't say much about the letter after we had read it. There wasn't much to say. I didn't expect or want an apology, or even that elusive explanation of "why?"

Now it *was* time to seal the deal. That letter, once an ending, was now a beginning. We lay back together on the bed, and this time kissed to start anew, and it was amazing. We spent the morning in bed, and, strangely, it didn't seem strange at all! I remembered Al as the best lover I had ever had, and my memory was spot-on. Everything was finally as it should be.

Al said that she wanted to go out for lunch. I preferred room service. I didn't want to leave that room and that bed *ever*. I was afraid getting up and going out, into the real world, would be like waking up from a dream. Once awake, it's usually impossible to return to the same spot in a dream, and that's what I feared. But Al insisted, so we got up, dressed, and went to Wild Honey, a local restaurant. We sat in the corner. I didn't want to make her feel uncomfortable but I couldn't take my eyes off her. "You're staring at me," she finally said.

"No, I'm gazing lovingly," I answered, and I'm not sure we said much else. We held hands under the table, and I squeezed hard so as not to let her get away, practically and symbolically.

"I need to use the ladies room," she said as she tried to pry her fingers from my hand. "Don't worry. I'm not going to disappear. I'll be right back." I guess my mind and heart were an open book to her, as they always were, as I always wanted them to be.

After a few nervous minutes I saw her return, and I thought that maybe this wasn't a dream after all, or maybe a dream that wouldn't end.

After lunch we went to a beautiful nearby arboretum, and walked amongst the blooming fragrant flowers. Roses (the flower of love) were plentiful. It was a marvelous afternoon.

Then we returned to the hotel and our Room 222. We picked up where we had left off a few hours earlier. It was a perfect day, perhaps the best day of my life. I was completely satisfied in every way—body, spirit, heart, and soul. I couldn't believe how great I felt. The intervening years seemed to evaporate, and we were Al and Brett once again. Being with Al in person reinforced my conviction that she was the same person I knew back then, the same girl I had fallen in love with, and was still in love with, truly the girl of my dreams and the love of my life. I wondered if I was the same guy, but dared not ask her. Not once did I think about facing reality and overcoming the considerable obstacles before us once we left that hotel room. The day was too perfect to ruin with, "Now what?" As a born idealist and romantic I had no doubt that we could work through whatever lay before us. As long as Al was on board and in love, then the other hurdles seemed trivial and solvable. We were at the fork in the road, and we had chosen our path; only one road lay ahead, only one life before us. Thoreau remarked, "If you have built your castles in the air, then that is where they belong. Now proceed to put foundations under them."

A piece of cake, I thought, as long as Al was my princess.

Chapter 2

In the late afternoon our day in the sun had to end. Reality called. We both had other lives and obligations beyond each other and Room 222. Maybe when you're teenagers in love the world ends at your embrace and there is nothing else. But when you're approaching sixty, as I was, a physician with a family, the real world can be a demanding and heartless place, not to be ignored.

So we showered together, to wash away the smell of sex and intimacy, and said our goodbyes outside. It was a bittersweet moment, with the emphasis on the *sweet*, very unlike our last goodbye. Alana owned a hot-red, sporty Jaguar, and I was renting a Ford Fiesta. She was always high-class and top of the line, and I mostly a "schlepper," getting the job done, taking care of business, more substance than style, very much like Milton in a lot of ways. With one last embrace in the parking lot, knowing now that the "teasing" of the past month had risen to a decidedly different level and that we would see each other again, we said goodbye. I was glad to be alone in the car, driving back to Manhattan to bask in the afterglow of this day in white satin, and luxuriate in new-found fantasies of tomorrow's tomorrows. I didn't even mind the traffic on the Long Island Expressway and was glad to enjoy time with my thoughts and amazing memories of an amazing day.

Everything was the same, but nothing was the same. I called Sharon to tell her I was on my way. She asked me how my day had been, and I told her that everything had worked out well (not a lie at all, just not the whole truth, I thought). Once back in Jennifer's apartment, we made plans for driving to New Jersey for the rehearsal dinner, and the rest of the weekend. I functioned on autopilot. Suddenly my "reality" was my life and plans with Alana, and everything else was almost a fugue state.

Needless to say, I couldn't stop thinking of Al, and struggled not to let my distraction and new-found excitement shine through. Al and I emailed all weekend, every chance we could ("I'm still tingling all over" was my favorite line from her!), wonderful romantic loving messages, the honeymoon of our new life together. It was too risky to call. My daughter's wedding was two months away and I couldn't (wouldn't) risk a major blow-up at home now that would ruin the wedding. She needed this wedding to be as perfect as possible, given the disaster of her prior broken engagement, and I would not deprive her of that for selfish reasons. So I was especially careful to keep things as normal and routine as possible, despite bursting within. I hoped Al would understand, and thankfully she did.

Al's life too was "the same" but not. She returned to her house, her husband, and son. They apparently knew and suspected nothing of our tryst, and she kept it that way. She had very little relationship with her husband; they spent limited time together (primarily for appearances and professional reasons), and the trust and intimacy had long ago left their marriage. Pierce was the glue that held it all together, but he was a teenager on the cusp of becoming a full-fledged man, seeking his own independence and his own life, and spending more and more time out of the house with his friends. So life at home was fairly empty for Alana. It wasn't too difficult to maintain that status quo without suspicion while having a whole separate semi-fantasy life with me. Our situations were not dissimilar. The planets were aligned and our clocks were in synch.

Chapter 3

The drive back to Florida was actually fun for me. I was feeling exhilarated, excited, and delighted at how well our assignation had unfolded, very much like I felt after our first date from a past lifetime. I was in such a good mood, reliving our day together, daydreaming about our future together. Even spending time with Sharon seemed more tolerable, knowing that my life sentence was soon to be commuted. There was some small talk, but mostly long stretches of silence with music playing, and I was in a much better mood than on the drive north. I'm not a very good liar, had never cheated on my marriage before, and worried if my ebullient spirit might betray me. But Sharon seemed oblivious and asked no probing questions. So far, so good.

I wondered how to concoct a scenario to see Al again and, hopefully, soon. My job never involved traveling, and I rarely left Florida alone. But I knew that moving forward with Alana would demand face time to confirm and solidify what we had started, and to build for the future. We had made a great beginning, but it was crucial to strike when the iron was hot and exploit the giddiness of the past month. The long drive over the endless monotonous I-95 allowed ample time to let my mind wander. I explored multiple mental scenarios that would enable brief visits to New York for "legitimate" reasons, considering the pros and cons of each. I've been blessed with a somewhat analytical mind, and easily assessed the "risk/benefit ratio" of each potential excuse to get away. The whole thing still had an air of fantasy about it, almost a mind-game, and was a delicious escape from the unsatisfying and hopeless ennui that had somehow become my life. Maybe that's why I didn't feel guilty about it. It still didn't seem really real yet. Sharon seemed normal and unaware of any new developments in my life or hers. I'm sure that had she imagined any foul play she would have thought herself clever by "casually" quizzing me with presumably innocent questions that were obviously pointed. But such was not the case. There was no fallout yet from my imagining, dreaming, or even seeing and relating intimately to Alana. The shit hadn't yet hit the fan, so to speak. And I hadn't considered the true practical implications of this dangerous game I had started playing. So I was young and foolish once again, naively enjoying my good fortune with no anticipation of the difficult and foreboding terrain that lay ahead to get from Point A to Point B. Seemingly in no time, I exited the highway into Fort Lauderdale and arrived home, physically tired to be sure, but more alive and energetic than I had been in years. As I entered the house, I remembered leaving several days earlier, closing that very door and knowing that when I returned it would be a new day and possibly a new life. I had tried to convince myself then that nothing could go wrong, but even *I* knew that was my hopeful romantic talking, and that anything and everything could go wrong. But now I was back, the weekend had passed, and I couldn't have hoped for or scripted a better outcome. Despite my bravado, false confidence, and enthusiasm borne of past failures tempered by dreams of future successes, I knew deep down that fantasies are just that and too often end up being great disappointments rather than unbridled successes. I knew that actually seeing and being with Alana would be the true test of whether all the talk of gossamer fairytales would be victimized by the ordeal of human sensibility in the arena of brute fact. But I entered the house a new man, with a newfound life and spirit that had been absent for too long to fathom. I lay down with the delightful prospect of writing to Al as soon as possible and continuing this exciting adventure. Oh, what happiness…

Chapter 4

Although it had been barely a month since Al's first email, I was already committed to moving forward with her, convinced that this newfound passion was real and alive and not just based on memories of days gone by. We emailed as often as possible. When I was on my laptop writing to Al, Sharon always thought I was catching up on work, so never interfered or suspected anything. I continued to wonder if she speculated anything amiss, but she gave no inkling that anything was wrong. Perhaps I hid my inner self better than I thought; perhaps she didn't pay very much attention to me or my moods; or perhaps she was so busy with Jennifer's upcoming nuptials that nothing else mattered. In any event I was able to speak with Al three times a day from work, and write as often as I could. She always took my calls, made time to speak freely and uninterruptedly in her office, and answered my emails. There was never a shortage of topics to discuss, and I continued to live from one phone call and one email to the next, with the afterglow of each contact lasting longer and longer, and a sense of peace and security gradually settling in and rattling through my bones. Not only was the bloom not off the rose, but it became fresher, newer, and more exciting every day. We both wondered, and talked about, whether part of the passion and hunger was the forbidden fruit aspect of our clandestine love affair? Would it still be as exhilarating when we both were free of our entanglements and together? But that was idle conjecture, and giddy chatter; we talked about it but neither of us believed it for a second. The next step, and we knew it, was planning our next rendezvous, and getting away with it.

Al told me that her son was scheduled to attend a lacrosse clinic in College Park, Maryland (on the campus of UM) at the end of June, and she could arrange to drive him to and fro, no questions asked, no eyebrows raised. It seemed like the perfect opportunity to me. So she made plans on her end, and I concocted a story on my end which seemed to make sense and I was able to sell without too much effort or interrogation. We also started thinking and making plans for our next get-together, hopefully in early July. Our mutual eagerness to start scheduling future meeting times and places was very telling, and implied an unspoken agreement and commitment to play out this hand and see where it led. It was too soon to make long-term plans but clearly we were both ripe and ready to appreciate this sudden and unexpected gift we had been afforded and to make the most of it. Al's desire to see me justified my increasing interest and devotion. I spent most of my time concentrating on ways to make this work, to give us a chance to experience the changed reality, the new life we had been shown although not yet given. I felt almost schizophrenic, leading two disparate lives, knowing that one day these two universes would inevitably collide, and the Big Bang would hopefully create a new, viable, and better universe for me. I consoled myself with the faith that it was in God's hands.

So at the end of June we met in Baltimore and stayed at the Hotel Monaco, a classy European, old-world-style hotel on the Inner Harbor, the perfect spot for a few wonderful romantic days together. When we checked in together, Al said, "It feels really weird to me checking in to a hotel room with someone other than Martin." Somehow it didn't seem weird to me at all.

The weekend was as magical as I had dared hope. We walked about the city, enjoyed unfettered time alone together without watching the clock, strolled hand in hand along the water and lingered over candle-lit dinners. We talked more and more about ourselves, our lives since 1972, our respective families, hopes and disappointments, primarily regarding our spouses. I expressed my true concern that maybe she was still committed to, even in love with, her husband Martin. She took my hand, looked me squarely in the eyes, and said with no hesitation that Martin wasn't even in my class. I liked that…

The weekend ended too quickly, Al dropped me off at the airport, and before I knew it I was back on the plane to Florida. Al had given me one of her favorite books to read, *The Art of Racing in the Rain*, a real tear-jerker about a man and his dog. I spent the last thirty minutes of the flight reading and crying, somewhat from the story but mostly because I was overwhelmed by the events of the past few months, my reawakened love for Alana, and my growing realization that lightening can strike twice in the same place, and second chances do exist.

I carefully wiped the tears from my eyes before exiting the plane to meet Sharon at the curb.

Chapter 5

My new life accelerated. I continued to gravitate towards Alana and a future with her in New York as I receded from Sharon and Florida. The wedding plans were essentially completed, and my outer life and public face continued apparently unchanged, with work filling most of my days, with increasingly frequent, ecstatic intervals of Alana. She was navigating her own journey away from Martin and towards us. Her situation was more complicated, with her son still living at home and with another year in residence before he went off to college. Pierce was clearly Alana's top priority, the apple of her eye, nearly her *raison d'être*, and she made no bones about that. She would do whatever it took to keep him whole, regardless of the personal sacrifice. Pierce was very close to his dad, and Alana agonized over the ramifications for Pierce of separation and divorce. She knew her marriage was empty for her, but the family was an anchor for Pierce. When Martin had suddenly left four years ago, without warning and no clue to Pierce that his home life was about to be dismembered and dismantled, the fallout was severe. Pierce was shaken to the core, and, as a fourteen-year-old, had no understanding how his father could move out and his parents no longer be the stable, secure, eternal unit he had always known them to be and expected them to continue being. Pierce was older now, but Alana still feared for his safety and reaction to this painful *déjà vu*.

But Martin seemed clueless. Of course Alana worried that she would be found out. Before our trip to Baltimore she had mistakenly left one of my emails on her desktop in the den, for all the world to see. When she realized her *faux pas*, she called me in a panic, convinced that Martin had seen it and the jig was up. Martin said nothing, but, since he feared and avoided confrontation at all cost, Alana was still nervous that he (and perhaps even Pierce!) had unintentionally come upon and read that email . Upon my return from

Baltimore my staff told me that a "doctor" had called the office looking for me. When he was told I wasn't available he was unusually persistent about asking where I was, and when I would be back. The staff innocently but unwittingly revealed that I had gone on vacation to Baltimore. I never found out whom that "doctor" was, but I had my suspicions. Still not a word from Martin. Al felt that the tension at home seemed to be building, but she couldn't be sure whether Martin knew anything, or if she was imagining and being unduly paranoid. As with my situation, life continued for Al on its usual course, working, caring for Pierce, socializing with friends, taking care of business. But the backstory was increasingly crowding the plot of our daily existence. Al was already convinced, even prior to our reconnection, that she and Martin would never have the marriage she wanted and hoped for. The truth is, they never had. When Alana first learned of his extramarital affair several years before, they had reconciled to a degree for the sake of Pierce, had gone to counseling, and worked on improving communication. That process was somewhat helpful. But after Martin's last bout of cheating and betrayal, maintaining the status quo was increasingly difficult. Chances are, had I not responded to her with such passion and alacrity, Al would have remained in the marriage, with she and Martin leading separate lives, there but for fortune and their son, playing out a time-worn, pointless, and hopeless existence, seeking satisfaction and gratification in work, friends, and Pierce. But unlike Martin, Alana did not sleep around, had never cheated on him, and had no intention of doing so before we reconnected. Very much like me, she had emotionally and romantically shut down, given up that part of her life, and made do with what was left...her own life of quiet desperation. "It could be worse"—the pathetic justification for a life unfinished and unfulfilled.

So Al was surprisingly ready to give Martin his walking papers, and pull the trigger. He couldn't be surprised that she was unhappy with the marriage, especially since she had confronted him about his most recent dalliance. But there's a great divide between confrontation and "Get out!" He likely would not be prepared for that. But Al was moving in that direction as she and I became closer, Martin remained his own distant, uninvolved, and cheating self, and Pierce grew older, more mature, and more independent. I could see that it was only a matter of time for her and for me.

Chapter 6

I continued to deceive Sharon about my need to travel for a "new business initiative," and Al and I planned to meet in early July. Pierce was going away with his father for a long weekend, and it was the perfect opportunity to spend a few delicious days together. This time we would take the next step, and stay at Alana's house. Other than her Labrador retriever Rex, the house would be empty. I looked forward to getting an insider's look at Al's home and life in her community. She hadn't yet shared me with any of her friends so we would keep the weekend on the down-low, which was fine with me.

I escaped from Florida without a hitch, and Al picked me up in Islip at a small, very user-friendly airport that just so happened to have direct flights to Fort Lauderdale. I hadn't been to Long Island for quite some time, and never to Alana's home town. In fact, I had been away from New York for so long (over twenty years) that it was a nostalgic return. When I initially moved to the West Coast I couldn't wait to leave, and now I couldn't wait to return. California, for all its attractions, was distant and alien to a born and bred northeasterner. Florida was even more so. I relocated to Florida not only because of the job opportunity but also because it seemed at the time to be a comfortable, friendly, "familiar," and inviting area. I'd grown up thinking that Jews retired to Florida—that's just what they did. And I expected to find a large contingent of retired Jewish people who would welcome me into their community and invite me to their Seders. But I wasn't aware of the changing times and new demographic of South Florida. The previous generation's Jewish population had largely disappeared, replaced by a new culture of Latinos--either Cuban-Americans displaced from their homeland by Castro's revolution, or Central and South Americans seeking a better and more prosperous future on the golden shores of the U.S. I was accustomed to some Hispanics from the Mexican and Chicano population in San Diego, but

South Florida was a quantum leap from there, with the majority Latin, mostly first-generation, still speaking primarily their native Spanish. It was not the easy adjustment I expected when I moved back East.

Al's home town, on the other hand, was pure Americana, pre-revolutionary, with colonial homes, national historic landmarks, cemeteries with ancient tombstones marking graves of early colonists, a memorial to Nathan Hale, and a largely non-Hispanic, Caucasian population whose families dated back generations. While I knew few native San Diegans and Floridians, most Long Islanders had deep family roots, and generations to come likely would settle near the family homestead. It was a refreshing change, one that I hadn't anticipated but sorely needed.

Returning to Alana was such a thrill. I barely could sleep the night before, nor contain my excitement. The moment I got to the Fort Lauderdale airport I switched into a new mode of existence, and the weight lifted from my shoulders as I entered that sweet mood of delicious anticipation.

We drove from the south shore to the north shore of Long Island on a glorious sunny summery day, the kind of day I remembered from New York and San Diego (Florida had its own brand of summer: hot, humid, sweltering, oppressive, insect-laden, not the best time of the year). We put the top down, and felt the rush of the air going by, compounding the inner rush of our newfound love and passion. The drive was no more than thirty minutes, just long enough to chat, feel comfortable, and bask in the pre-glow of what would be a weekend to remember. We drove down Main Street through the center of town, a cute and quaint area with small shops, abundant restaurants of all varieties, flowers, and American flags bedecking every street lamp. I felt very much at home.

Al's house was on a corner lot of a quiet cul-de-sac. Unlike Florida, there were no large cookie-cutter developments or gated communities. The homes were older, traditional, settled in, and lived in. Each house was different from the one next door in size, design, and style, so unlike Florida. This was the architecture and type of neighborhood I grew up in. Although I had never been there before, I felt like I had. We drove down a wide street with large old maples and elms adorning both sides. Al made a left turn into the driveway and suddenly we were "home." Al clearly was very proud of her house and couldn't wait for me to see it. She had bought it twenty years earlier, and had essentially rebuilt most of it, including major extensions and additions, all of which she had played an integral part in designing, and oversaw each step of the construction. Martin was largely an absent husband and parent, always seeming to be out of the house working. He had constructed for himself the image of being the fine, upstanding, hardworking physician totally devoted to his patients, sacrificing his home and family life because he had no choice given his profession. He had hidden behind that mask their whole marriage. Unfortunately, as they say, there's a level below the level you know. In actual fact, his extramarital activities were ignoble and selfish, as Al found out to her great surprise and disappointment. In any event, Al was clearly the rainmaker, homemaker, and home director, in charge of all the domestic issues and chores while, at the same time, a full-time, busy general surgeon in her own right. How she managed to juggle all these roles was amazing to me, and a testament to her extraordinary talent and drive. She had seen what a happy and successful marriage looked like from her parents growing up, and she had learned her lessons well. Martin and Pierce were two very lucky guys to have Al holding things together and making it all work out. She was a doer, with a strong sense of responsibility and dedication to her family, and a Puritan work ethic borne of nature and nurture, one that would have made her dad proud.

    The house itself was lovely, a ranch built like a French country cottage, with old world charm, elegance, and taste. As Al took me from room to room I noted certain pieces of furniture and decorations that seemed oddly recognizable—a large armoire off the kitchen, an occasional painting or two on the walls, a grand piano in the living room. They seemed familiar because they *were* familiar, pieces recovered and restored from her childhood house that I knew so well—essentially my own childhood house—that she had transplanted here. I truly was home again.

Chapter 7

The weekend was amazing!! All that I could have hoped for and more. The bliss of our last togetherness in Baltimore carried over, and we enjoyed each other from beginning to end. I was still in the shadows, so we were careful not to let the neighbors see some strange guy on the property while Martin and Pierce were away. It was just the two of us, which was fine with me. Al spent considerable time cooking a special meal for us, an incredible rack of lamb with all the trimmings, and I learned for the first time that she was a gourmet chef to go along with all her other qualities and talents. My admiration for her grew by leaps and bounds. I had never known the domestic side of Alana before; it was most agreeable, and made me love her even more (if that were possible).

We spent Friday evening at home, settling into the TV room to watch a light romantic comedy (*Chocolat*), the perfect fun and mindless entertainment as we sat cuddling on the couch, sipping red wine, the iconic domestic scene. The house was very livable and inviting, small enough to be warm and cozy, large enough to accommodate a family, user-friendly enough (one story, large rooms, comfortable furniture, well-designed flow and ease of passage from one living area to the next) to be a place to grow old together. I could picture myself living there with Al for the indefinite future, making a life there on that quiet piece of Heaven, God's little acre, so to speak. Perhaps it was too early to think that way. But I had no doubts that we would weather the upcoming storm, surmount the considerable obstacles (although admittedly I was too naïve and in love to even speculate what they would be), and build a life together, possibly there, possibly elsewhere; it didn't matter to me as long as Al were by my side. And once again, it was *déjà vu* as I remembered how I felt in New Haven when I moved into my single dorm room Al's freshman year at college, or the sense of hope, optimism, and inner warmth when I moved into my off-campus apartment that would be our love nest (so I thought at the time). But despite the disappointments of the past, I recalled none of those; they were yesterday's news, and bygones. This, here and now, was my life going forward, and I deeply inhaled the delicious aroma of this prospect, and had no questions or fears.

Our only companion for the weekend was Rex. As previously noted, he was a wonderful, huge, love-muffin, nothing but goodness. When I looked into his eyes I saw sweetness, kindness, and gentleness that belied his 120-pound frame and huge head. Sadly Rex had been the victim of bad joints (common in Labrador retrievers) and had undergone multiple surgeries, including hip replacements for severe arthritis. A complication from his last surgery had left his left hind leg lame and useless. He had no control over that extremity, it was more of a liability than a help, and interfered with his ability to use his other three legs. Dogs can do quite well with three legs, and amputation of the defective limb, as extreme and horrible as it sounds, would have been in his best interest. But he was too old to undergo another major surgery, so he was destined to schlep that useless leg along, like an albatross he had no use for but couldn't get rid of. It was so pathetic watching this big, beautiful animal so crippled and barely able to walk. Yet he clearly loved Alana, no doubt about that, and would drag himself to her wherever she happened to be in the house. He never could have navigated stairs, so it was a blessing for him that the house was a ranch-style. Going outside to do his business was a major chore in itself, and Alana had configured a sling and harness system to lift him up to assist him out of the house. It's no easy feat carrying a 120-pound, helpless dog, but Alana did it three times a day, such was her love and devotion to her best friend. As usual, Martin did nothing and left the burden for Alana…I was learning more and more about this cruel, selfish, heartless, and aloof man…I guess times change and people change. Perhaps he was more of a mensch in the early days of their relationship but he withdrew and became a virtual stranger and non-entity in his own house and home. It seemed that the entire burden of keeping things going fell on Alana's shoulders as Martin played the role of selfless physician, privileged to contribute nothing to his own family because of his presumed admirable self-sacrifice for his God-given role as doctor. But, in actual fact, he was a very self-centered and deceitful scumbag (pardon my French). The weekend was eye-opening for a lot of reasons.

Regarding Rex, since I was an orthopaedist I had a good understanding of the musculoskeletal and locomotor system in people, and dogs are not all that different. The principles are the same, and I specialized in hip replacements, so Rex's problem is one I had seen before (in humans) and I wanted to help if I could. When I was in Florida Al had advised me of Rex's condition and sent X-rays, so I knew what we were dealing with. Since surgery was not an option, I thought that an elaborate brace might stabilize his bad (dislocated) hip and improve his quality of life somewhat. So that was my initiative and project. After an extensive online search and research, I contacted a veterinary prosthetist in Canada to discuss Rex's issues and find a solution of some sort. After several back and forth emails we came upon a design for a brace that might work. To fabricate a custom-molded brace required a body mold of poor Rex, so Alana procured fiberglass casting materials from the hospital and we set about the challenging task of casting this gentle giant. Being the good soul that he was, Rex was amazingly patient and cooperative during the casting process, which involved wrapping him in wet, pliable fiberglass from head to toe (tail), including his hind legs, and keeping him still while the material hardened. I've never had a human patient that was as understanding and compliant as Rex. Despite the discomfort, he was a good soldier and let Al do whatever she had to, while he stood stock-still, seemingly understanding that his owner (his best friend) was only looking out for his best interests. The relationship between dogs and people is very special. I've always felt that children are highly over-rated and dogs highly under-rated in terms of their undeniable family connections and indisputable commitments and loyalties.

Once the cast was on and hardened, we had the daunting task of removing it to send it to Canada for the brace to be fabricated. Al had also borrowed a cast-cutter from the hospital, so we gradually and strategically cut through the cast to remove it intact. Sounds easy, but in reality not at all. The cast needed to be tight and form-fitting so the brace would fit, and removing it involved cutting with a sharp blade directly over Rex's fur. He was a trouper, and never flinched, even though we cut his skin several times, causing some superficial bleeding. Finally it was off. What made the situation even tenser was that we had tickets to see a concert that night—Crosby, Stills, and Nash, a group popular from our earliest days, whom we had seen in concert before in our prior lifetime together. Connecting the past to the present was a delightful exercise that brought us back to our youth and reinforced the memories and long-standing connection between us. And I really liked that!

Fortunately we got to the concert on time. It was held at the outdoor amphitheater at Jones Beach, another of our frequent haunts from days gone by. The whole evening was magical, full of nostalgia for the past as we heard the old favorites, and we continued to have an appreciation for our new beginning. The weather was balmy, clear, not too hot or humid, with a beautiful full moon gracing the concert stage. Everything old was new again.

On the drive back home, with the top down, I relived the old days in this very same locale, and marveled at the amazing turn of events that brought me back to this time and place with this girl. I've always been a somewhat spiritual person, firmly believing in a higher Being looking down benevolently on us and somewhat controlling our destiny (although I also believed in free will). I have never been more religious or more of a believer than I was then. This completely unexpected turn of events elevated me from the depths of a lost life gone badly, to the heights of a present and future brimming with promise. Who but a benevolent God could have choreographed this romantic *pas de deux*? It's God's will, I thought, as we headed toward home.

Chapter 8

The rest of the weekend was a dream come true. We were two young lovers again, isolated and insulated from the slings and arrows of outrageous fortune, with seemingly no responsibilities beyond the property line. Family, friends, patients were nowhere to be found, and we could bask in our togetherness. The young prince was back with his princess, and the ravages of time, experience, disappointment, and heartache were long ago and far away. We made love when it felt right; we cuddled and connected from beginning to end. I knew the weekend would end, and reality would rear its ugly head, but I was able to compartmentalize and avoid thinking about it. Sharon called several times, and I spoke calmly, evenly, and (hopefully) nonchalantly, maintaining the illusion of being on a business trip, while inwardly resenting her intruding into my new world. I carefully perpetuated the ruse, hopefully without raising any suspicion.

I knew that the Big Bang would come, and I would have to face the music. Alana told me over and over that "coming clean" would not afford the cleansing and forgiving confrontation I hoped for. "Honesty is the best policy" is *not* the best policy here, she said. From a woman's perspective, she knew that a husband coming clean about cheating is the unpardonable sin, and nothing good could come of that approach. I was so happy for myself that I innocently expected everyone else to share my exuberance. Of course Al was right and I would need a different explanation.

But that would not be today or tomorrow. I knew that I would do nothing to rock the boat until after the wedding (in three weeks), and then would deal with it. I would not allow the sweet nectar of the weekend to be soured by the certainly difficult times ahead. There would be time enough for that.

Sunday afternoon Al drove me to the airport. Packing and leaving was so painful and difficult, knowing that Armageddon was not far away. Although my entire stay was no more than forty-eight hours, it seemed like a whole new life, and was one more step on the road to rebuilding and salvaging a life gone wrong. Jennifer was flying from New York to Florida also, to spend the next few weeks preparing for the wedding, and we had arranged in advance to fly together. Al dropped me off ten minutes before my scheduled meeting with Jenn, and was careful to leave me at a separate terminal to avoid any chance of an unexpected and inexplicable encounter. Here and now was certainly not the time to bring Jennifer and Alana together. I looked intently at Al, squeezed her hand, gave her a quick kiss, took my suitcase from the back seat, and watched as she drove away. I missed her already!! And I sent a brief text to that effect. She responded with an "xoxo," and that would have to do until next time, whenever that would be. I met Jenn as planned, with no apparent mistrust, and we proceeded through security and to the gate. I knew that I had to keep up the charade for three more weeks, until the wedding. Then Jenn would be settled in her new nuclear family, and I would feel freer to start my own process of extrication/emancipation (from Sharon, from Florida, from my work) and subsequent rebuilding and reinventing. Despite the uncertainty and angst, I also felt exhilarated and empowered, a strange confluence of life at the crossroads.

Chapter 9

We returned to Florida, and Sharon seemed to be none the wiser. The wedding was so all-encompassing that there was little time to explore or question my recent mood and behavior. I lived two lives: one that was picking up speed, and one sputtering to a stop. I threw myself all in to the innumerable last-minute wedding preparations. I was happy to have the distraction, to take the focus off me and to keep Sharon and Jenn occupied. I continued working, speaking to Al from work whenever I could, and sneaking in an extra phone call or two when I could escape alone with Shanee for a late-night walk. Sundays were by far the worst days of the week because I was at home all day and unable to get my Alana "fixes." Whereas I had previously lived for Sundays and dreaded starting the week again, now it was quite the opposite, and I couldn't wait to leave the house early Monday morning and call Alana as soon as she got to her office, usually around 9 a.m.

But this Monday my cell phone rang shortly after I left my house at 6 a.m. *Must be the answering service*, I thought. But I was somewhat taken aback to see Al's name on the caller ID.

"Hi, Al. What a nice surprise to hear from you so early! How's everything?"

"Not so good. Not good at all!"

"Why? What's the matter? What happened?"

"Martin found out about your being here this weekend. He saw some of your shavings in the sink, and stains on the sheets. I didn't deny it, but it was awful last night. We slept in the bed as far from each other as possible. I was almost falling off the edge."

"Gee, I'm so sorry. But I'm not sorry. This is exactly what he deserves. You think it's any better because he takes his cheating out of the house? Does that give him an excuse and a free pass? What did you do that he hasn't done, multiple times?"

"But it's here, in his bed, in his face."

"So? Y'know what that says? *Fuck off*, mister! You're a prick, and a cheater, and two can play that game! That's the message he should have gotten. And I hope he eats his heart out! I'm not sorry."

"Yeah, but you weren't here. It was really unpleasant."

"He's a jerk, and an asshole, and he has no right to be offended, not after what he's done to you and your marriage, time after time after time."

"Yeah, I get it. But it was still horrible."

"I know, and I'm sorry you had to go through that, and I'm sorry I didn't clean up better after myself. But this is the truth, and this is reality. It's going to come out sooner or later, so maybe sooner is better. What are we waiting for? Are you going to forgive him, and reconcile with him?"

"No, I'm not. I was just hoping to do it on my terms, not this way."

"Okay. I'm sorry, not for him but for you. But maybe it's not so bad that it's out in the open. He has a competitor for your love and affection and attention. What's good for the goose is good for the gander. He's in no position to make you feel bad or guilty. In fact, not to be mean or cruel, but you should rub this in his face at every opportunity. Look at what you, and Pierce, have gone through, and had to put up with! He's a loser, and a loser for you. For selfish reasons I hope he's overwhelmed, and moves himself out. That would make it so much better for you. Fuck him. That's all I can say."

"Yeah, I get it. But it's very stressful being here and dealing with this now. I'm not sure what will happen when he gets home tonight. I don't want Pierce to suffer. I think I'll tell Martin to move into the guest bedroom. I can't have another night like last night."

"Yeah, maybe that's the best idea. I'm sorry that you're so upset. Try to get a grip, realize that it's not the end of the world, and it's inevitable. Whatever drives it, he needs to get out of your bed, and out of your life. He's done you wrong repeatedly, and this is not your fault."

"I know, but it's Pierce I'm worried about."

"Alright, I'm at the office. Let's talk later."

"Okay." And so we hung up.

Wow, this is an interesting new development, I thought. *What a slap in the face, to know your wife slept with someone else in your marital bed! I hope it kills him, just as he hurt Al. The plot thickens, and the process may be heating up. I can't say I'm unhappy about this new turn of events. I hope Al is okay.*

Chapter 10

Being the non-confrontational, self-loathing, cheating bastard that he is, Martin got past his "discovery" and they amazingly didn't speak of it again. Were it me, that would have been the only thing I could think about and speak about; but that's just me. I also wouldn't have cheated on Al and acted as though I was the victim not the perp.

In any event, the next night Al asked Martin to move out of the master bedroom and into the guest bedroom next door. The tension was rising, and they could no longer share the same bed. Martin still left most of his clothes in the master, and came into the bedroom to use the shower in the morning. But at least Al had the room mostly to herself, had privacy at night (all the better for us to talk and text!), and the separation process had begun. Of course Pierce was aware of these new living arrangements, and Alana had an open, frank discussion with him. She didn't want to indict his father and cause Pierce more pain and confusion than he'd already undergone. But Al believed in being open, candid, and honest, including with her son. Nothing good comes of lies and deceit, she felt, and Pierce was old enough to face the facts. He'd already been through this several years earlier; now he was older, more mature, hopefully better able to cope with the truth, the fact that most marriages end in divorce, and with the changing reality of his own nuclear family. Nobody said it would be easy for any of the involved parties, and Al knew that. But she also knew she wasn't going to share her life with a serial womanizer, even if pretending that all was normal would have been easier for Pierce. Martin had crossed the line over and over, and there's a price to pay. Their marriage had reached the tipping point. Al was done.

So there was a new normal in Alana's household, at least temporarily. Looking ahead Al tried to consider when to have "the talk" with Martin (and with Pierce), and what to do next. All the while she was working full-time, in fact overtime, as a busy surgeon, trying to take care of her patients and her practice, manage her home life, and put on a happy public face despite the turmoil boiling over within. Quite a challenge! The situation was too hot to handle, and the volatility approached the breaking point more than once. Something had to be done, and soon. I wished I could help her, but from a distance all I could do was listen and be supportive. I knew that my own home life was not much better, but everything was on the back burner until after the wedding. Then things would start to pop.

Chapter 11

Because of all the frenzied, eleventh-hour wedding preparations, time went by quickly for me. One of my happiest moments was going with Jenn to pick up her wedding dress. It was actually the very same dress we had bought for her earlier (canceled) wedding, kept in storage all this time…perhaps not the best karma, but having already spent $15,000 on this one-time-use only item, I was willing to "take a chance." Jenn wanted me to go with her for her final fitting, and to learn the proper technique to bustle the dress after the ceremony. Her closest friend, Ana, whom she had known since summer camp years ago and who was her maid of honor to be, had come to Florida early and was staying with us to share in the pre-wedding joy and excitement, and help out as needed. Over the years I had gotten to know Ana well, and she was a terrific girl, a great friend to Jenn, and generally all-around a first-class person. Ana came with us to pick up the dress. When Jenn stepped out from the dressing room in that beautiful gown, I choked up and let it go. So much had happened since I last saw that dress, some very bad, and some amazingly good. Now seeing it on her, with the wedding a week away, and her as happy as could be, another big circle closed, the past was behind us, and we were both ready to start fresh with new lives full of hope and promise. Of course she didn't know that my tears of happiness were not only for her.

The wedding weekend couldn't come soon enough for me. I was deathly afraid that somehow I would be outed despite my increasingly neurotic precautions. But Alana remained my little (*big*) secret, and before long I was packing the car to drive to the venue, a nearby hotel on the beach, where we would be staying for the weekend. Steve would be bunking with me (for propriety) and Jenn and Sharon would be in the bridal suite until the wedding night. Shanee came too (how could she not?), and stayed in the hotel, making a brief appearance at the rehearsal dinner and the reception (as well as providing a convenient excuse for me to get away "to walk her" and speak with Al).

I called Al one last time before I got dressed to go down for the wedding pictures, with the ceremony to follow. It was a beautiful (*hot*) day in Florida, and equally beautiful (but considerably less hot) in New York. Al was sitting in her backyard by the pool, Pierce was off with his friends, Martin was "working" as usual, and Gladys had come by to visit.

Al was very aware of my concerns that the wedding go smoothly for Jennifer, and I kept her abreast of each and every step of the way. "So it looks like you made it," she said, with an obvious impish grin on her face that I could "see" over the phone.

"Yes, so it seems. Thank God. I've been counting the days, and think I'm home free."

"I know how worried you've been, and I'm glad you can put that behind you. Now I want you to have a wonderful time at your daughter's wedding. This is her moment, but yours too. Don't think about me, don't think about us. Just enjoy every minute. I'll be thinking about you."

"Well, y'know, I'm always thinking about you, and will tonight as well. But I think it should be great! Jenn looks beautiful and happy, and I couldn't be happier, for a lot of reasons. The reception should be over late, maybe after 1. Can I call you then?"

"Sure. I'll wait for your call. No rush. Just relax and have a good time."

"Okay, my love. Maybe there will still be one more wedding in my life? We'll talk about that another day."

I walked Shanee back to the room, put on my tuxedo, and headed to the ballroom. Another step on the journey, a big one for Jenn, and for me.

Chapter 12

The wedding went by in a flash. Standing under the chuppah, during the ceremony, Sharon became faint, nearly passed out, and had to sit down. She was fine, just overwhelmed by the moment, and recovered quickly. She returned to the bema in time for the breaking of the glass and the exit music. It was just a minor distraction and nothing more. I so feared for the integrity and sanctity of this wedding and wanted nothing to ruin it.

The band played until nearly 1:30 a.m., and Jenn and Steve danced every dance. I felt more relaxed than I had in a long time. This evening had been lurking in the back of my mind for the past three months, and finally it was here and gone, and I couldn't be more relieved. Now Jenn and Steve would be on their own and I could plan my own future. I felt that I had given Jenn all I could and all I had, even waiting for her to be married before leaving my own lifelong unhappy marriage. She really had no right to hold it against me, I thought, and I wasn't just kidding myself but truly believed that. I wasn't sure exactly what my next step would be, or how I'd take it, but the time was upon me, and I felt both excitement and trepidation. In my heart of hearts I had faith that it would all work out for the best, and I just had to keep my eye on the prize (Alana). As I remember, Gladys had once told me long ago, "Things have a way of working themselves out."

With Shanee as my companion, I called Al around 2 a.m., and she was awake to answer. I gave her all the details, and she listened attentively (or maybe dozed off, I couldn't tell for sure). In any event, she seemed relieved for me; we would talk again Monday and make plans for me to come visit.

Sunday was a morning-after breakfast for the out-of-town guests, then home to resume our lives, although mine was really just beginning. Al and I had never specifically talked about it, but we both knew that we were on the cusp of ending our marriages and figuring out how to make a life together. I started inventing different mental scenarios to tell Sharon I wanted out, and rehearsed them in my mind over and over. Despite my fears up to now that Sharon knew something was going on, I became convinced after the wedding that my paranoia had gotten the better of me, and she was totally in the dark. She knew that I wasn't happy, but I seriously doubted that she suspected me of having an affair, and had absolutely no idea that I would leave her. How should I say it? What reason should I give? When should this come down? I obsessed over these questions for days until I realized that it really didn't matter. No matter what I said she would be shocked, angry, vengeful, etc. ("Hell hath no fury like a woman scorned" echoed and re-echoed in my head.) But I knew I had to act, and soon, if I wanted to keep building my future with Alana. At some point these brief, unaccompanied trips of mine would raise suspicions, and I felt it better if I were proactive, choosing the time, place, circumstances, words, etc., rather than being confronted and attacked unawares, trying to explain something for which there is no satisfying or adequate explanation.

I returned to work Monday morning looking forward to speaking with Al. It felt like a new phase of our relationship, and the time to help each other navigate the undoubtedly choppy waters ahead. (That was quite an understatement, but this was all unchartered territory for me, so what did I know?)

Chapter 13

I hadn't seen Al in three weeks, and felt that we needed some face time, especially now. So we agreed that Al would take off the following Monday and I would come to Long Island for the day. That was a lot of travel for one day but that was fine with me. I would take an early flight, sleep on the plane, and return on the last flight back. My home life remained unchanged, and Sharon even took me to the airport and would pick me up when I returned. I felt a little guilty that she was essentially complicit in my traveling to meet my lover. I offered to drive myself but she insisted, and rather than raise any suspicions I simply went along with her offer. I knew that the end was coming soon, and this likely would never happen again.

So I flew to meet Al. She picked me up in Islip, and had planned a day for us visiting the wineries on the North Fork of Long Island. Al was much more of a wine connoisseur than I (in fact, I pretty much drink Scotch exclusively, and can't tell a fine French vintage from Manischewitz), but I was happy to do pretty much anything, as long as it was with her. The weather was beautiful and we spent the day sampling multiple wines from the local vineyards. For me it was just another day in paradise. But I (and Al) knew that the storm clouds were rapidly gathering on the horizon, and there was no denying that. It wasn't a simple, carefree fling anymore. We had reached the point of no return by choice, and for us there was no going back. The future was indistinct, but way better than the past we were so happy and eager to get away from.

As the sun was setting Al dropped me off at the airport. I knew (as did she) that maintaining the status quo was not sustainable, and things would have to change in the very near future. We chose not to spend the day dissecting and analyzing our situation; instead we spent a day in the sun, holding hands, walking through the vineyards, tasting the nectar of the vine, and laughing—exactly the kind of day we needed.

There would be time enough to face the music; this one lovely day was for lovers to enjoy. And we did.

Chapter 14

The flight back to Florida was less happy and enjoyable for me. I knew that I needed to act, and soon. Because of severe thunderstorms, my flight was diverted to Tampa, and then sat on the tarmac for two hours until the storm had cleared. Another example of the Pathetic Fallacy. Finally we were cleared for takeoff and shortly thereafter landed in Fort Lauderdale.

Sharon was waiting for me, and the drive home was normal on the surface, despite the angst I felt within. I wondered how Sharon could be so unaware of my thoughts and feelings. Was I such a good actor? Or was she so removed and insensitive to my behavior? Regardless, I wanted to see Alana again and soon, and this ongoing charade was impossible to continue.

Al, too, wanted a resolution to her abysmal situation. Twisting in the wind without traction or control is horrible, and not for her. The tension at home was suffocating. They were now sleeping in separate bedrooms, and Martin made no effort to reconcile or improve things. Perhaps Al was hoping he would, and she remarked to me several times that despite everything, he made no attempt to "woo" her, buy her flowers, take time off from work to show any interest or affection. He was the same old Martin, going about his business, and maintaining his peripheral role in the life supposed to be for better or for worse, till death do us part. His idea of romance was lost on Alana, if he had any inclinations in that direction. Nothing was getting better; Al and I were talking, sharing, and getting closer, and she and Martin were traveling on parallel, if not divergent, paths.

So she planned an evening out with Martin for dinner, a dinner date if you will, to talk things over. She felt that the temperature at home was too hot to have a clear, calm discussion, and Martin could (would) never commit to a time they could talk without interruption (always using his all-important work as an excuse, since, needless to say, he was the busiest and most important man in town, without question!). So they "made an appointment" and dinner reservations. Al thought things through thoroughly before their meeting.

And she decided it was time, and they were through. They sat at a familiar restaurant where they had dined many times before, and to the casual observer they probably looked like any other couple, out together to enjoy a quiet meal together. But this was no typical dinner out. Personally I can't imagine having this discussion "in public" and managing to swallow and hold down a meal. I would rather be alone, say what had to be said, and have the option of picking up and leaving if the conversation got out of hand. But that was just me, and my relationship with Sharon. Al was a different person in a different relationship. I suppose that over time she and Martin had grown so far apart that their lives were entirely matter-of-fact, with little emotional involvement. Confronting the failure of their marriage was like talking about the weather, with their feelings so encased in years of frustration and disappointment that the here-and-now was insulated from the what-could-have-been. I so wished I could have been a fly on the wall to witness how this scene played out. Al later replayed the conversation for me; she told Martin that their marriage was over as far as she was concerned, and there would be no third chances and turning a blind eye to his unforgivable indiscretions. She had had it, and wanted out, and wanted to move on with her life without him. His behavior was no longer acceptable or tolerable in any way, and he had placed her in an untenable position as a wife and partner. This partnership needed to be dissolved.

Despite all that had gone on, Martin was shocked. In an uncanny way, he saw *himself* as the victim, and, as had happened years before, he didn't understand why he was considered at fault for their failed marriage. All was permissible for him, to his way of thinking, and he was being treated very unfairly. But, unlike their previous near implosion, this time was the real deal, the unpardonable sin. Al had already moved on, and Martin knew it. Despite his despicable behavior he would not go down without a fight, not that he was fighting for Alana (he had given no indication of that), but he was fighting to preserve his own skewed vision of what was permissible *for him!*!! No one in their right mind would consider his actions acceptable and tolerable in a marriage, but he was not in a right mind. He afforded himself a special set of rules that entitled him to a wife and son devoted and committed to him while he could seek personal satisfactions and pleasures outside his marriage and home life. This psychopathology baffles me to this day. I wonder what type of marriage his parents had, or his siblings? Regardless, it was beyond the pale, and Al had been tormented beyond measure. Martin didn't deny his affair, nor did he seek reconciliation with the promise of changing his behavior. He just didn't get it. And Al (and I) didn't get how he "didn't get it." His attitude was inconceivable and incorrigible. Their last candle had burned out.

It wasn't an easy dinner for Al, not that she wished to reconcile, but she regretted so many lost years and dashed hopes, so enormous an investment with so little in return, so many years of disappointments and now so many regrets. Martin's behavior—cold, passive, distant, and removed—recalled so many years of anger and pain. Change is hard, but this change was inevitable, and it was time. Al felt at peace with her decision.

The following morning (a Sunday) I found an excuse to leave the house, and parked my car in a nearby secluded spot so we could talk. We spent two hours on the phone, and Al recounted the entire conversation. She had finally "pulled the trigger" and seemed settled with her decision. Martin would continue living at home for the rest of the summer, until Pierce's college applications and school visits were completed, and then move out. It's hard, even inappropriate, to celebrate a long-but-failed marriage, so our conversation was somber and reserved. The solution to Al's predicament was in progress, and I knew I needed to act as well. My life at home was becoming increasingly intolerable: living a lie every day and pretending that all was well. I just couldn't stand it anymore. There was no great urgency for me to act, but there was also no reason for me not to act and take my next step. And I wanted to show Al that I was committed to her, to our relationship, to moving forward as a couple to a destiny written when we were teenagers. She had done her part and showed her commitment. Now it was up to me. I would not disappoint her, and I decided that very day to begin my own process.

So when I got home, I sat down with Sharon. There was no "appointment," no formal "we have to talk." Instead, I simply told her that I was not happy with our marriage and hadn't been for as long as I could remember. Jennifer was now married, and building her own life distinct from us. I wanted us to separate. It was long overdue.

Sharon listened and heard me. To this very day I don't know if she was shocked or even surprised. Tears came into her eyes, and she said, "Now you won't be there to help me raise Jennifer's children." She didn't ask any questions, nor did she get angry. *Perhaps she doesn't believe me?* I wondered. *Or thinks I'm going through a phase, a mid-life crisis?* In any event she said we should go out for lunch, which seemed like a crazy idea to me after what I had just said. But she asked, so I agreed. Certainly it was the least I could do. I just felt relieved inside that I had started (and hopefully ended) the conversation. I had no appetite for lunch, and certainly no appetite for further discussion, explanation, coming clean, or attempting reconciliation through counseling. But I owed Sharon a lunch.

So we went to The Cheesecake Factory, a favorite of hers, and sat silently together at a table. It was hard to look at her and make small talk, so we said nothing. Our last candle had gone out long ago, and now it was more a matter of adapting to the changed reality rather than rekindling a fire that was cold and ashen from years of neglect. Of course I was sad at the realization that the end was finally here. Despite my love for Alana and excitement at what lay ahead for us, I still had a long history with Sharon. I had spent so much time focusing on the failures and disappointments; but for some reason, over that quiet and still lunch, I recalled the hope we had at the beginning, the joy of raising Jennifer, the happy times, though they were few and far between. The cup was way more than half empty; the few drops at the bottom were bittersweet, and it was the sweetness I was now recalling and missing. If only things could have been different...but I knew they never would be.

Hope springs eternal in the human breast;
Man never is, but always to be blessed:
The soul, uneasy and confined from home,
Rests and expatiates in a life to come.

– Alexander Pope, *An Essay on Man*

My hope had been depleted long ago. What is love if not hope, and faith, and optimism? My marriage had been running on fumes for the longest time, and it was past time to lay it to rest. I couldn't wait to get home, take Shanee for a walk, and speak to Al.

Chapter 15

"Hi, my love."

"Hi, Brett. So how's your day going?"

"It's done."

"What's done?"

"I pulled my own trigger today, and told Sharon it's over, and I want out."

"Really? What made you decide to do that?"

"Well, you did it last night, and I want you to know that we're in this together. I wanted to step up to the plate and be a man. I wanted to show you that I'm totally committed, and now we're both in a position to change our lives for the better, and work together to make our dream come true."

"Wow, I'm just surprised. I didn't expect this today."

"Are you not happy?"

"No, of course I'm happy. I'm just surprised. I appreciate your wanting to follow my lead. I just didn't think you'd act so quickly. How did it go and how are you feeling?"

"Okay. It was an unpleasant conversation, as you can imagine. Sharon didn't see this coming, I'm pretty sure. But at the same time she didn't act totally surprised. I can't believe that it was shocking to her, not after the way things have been going the past few months."

"Well, things are going to be different for both of us at home now. At least you won't have to hide what you're doing and make up excuses all the time."

"Yes, that will be better. It was very stressful being so secretive. But I still haven't told Sharon about you, and don't know if I should."

"No, I definitely don't see anything good coming of that. She doesn't need to know about us. That could only make things worse for you."

"Yeah, you're right. On the one hand I'd like to share my happiness about you with everyone. But probably not a good idea right now."

"Agreed. Martin obviously knows about you. I don't want Pierce to find out. I'm sure Martin won't tell him."

"Yeah, Jennifer too. They'll find out when the time is right, hopefully once they've gotten used to the idea that their parents are no longer together. I don't want Jenn to blame you, or Pierce to hate me."

"Right. What are you going to do about your living situation? Are you staying in the house?"

"I don't know yet. We haven't really said anything to each other. I'm sure we'll discuss it before bedtime. I can't imagine sleeping in the same bed as Sharon anymore. I'll never get any sleep that way!"

"Well, you'll probably have more to talk about when you go back home. Text me later and fill me in."

"Okay, will do. Talk to you later."

Chapter 16

When I came back to the house I was anxious as to how Sharon would act. There was no Jennifer present to mitigate the mood (as Pierce was for Alana), so anything was possible, from silence to a free-for-all. So I walked back in to face the music. *Que sera, sera.*

Sharon was sitting at the kitchen table. The TV was off, and the house quiet. The silence was deafening, the tension crushing. I sat down at the table, and neither one of us spoke for several minutes. Then I decided to start things off.

"I know how sudden this must seem to you; but you must admit that things have not been very good between us for a long time. You said yourself a few weeks ago that after the wedding, we'd stay together but you'd do your thing and I'd do mine. Now that's no way to have a marriage."

No answer.

"Being physically apart will be much better than being together but really not together. We've drifted so far apart over the years that we're barely a couple anymore. Our paths cross but our minds and hearts really don't. We're too young to accept this as the way it's going to be for the rest of our lives. I'm sorry but I want something more. Jennifer's married, starting her own life. We need to restart our lives. I didn't mean to hurt you or shock you earlier, but I see no other way."

No answer.

"Would you like me to move out?"

Until now Sharon had been looking down at her hands in her lap. At this point she looked up at me. She had clearly been crying. I tried to read her eyes—was she angry? Full of hate for me? Hurt and sad? Confused? All of the above? I couldn't tell.

"No," she finally said. "You can stay here. Why don't you sleep in Jennifer's room?"

"Okay," I answered.

I was hoping for more of a reaction, a sense of what she was thinking. But it was enough for now. At least it was a start. Without another word I collected a few clothes from my closet to wear in the morning, and closed Jennifer's bedroom door behind me. I was exhausted. I texted Al, and she answered right away, seemingly very concerned about how I was feeling. I guessed it was a shock to her, too, what I had done that day. But not to me. I had *not* acted impulsively. I did what I had to. I didn't know that that day would be perhaps the most important "first day of the rest of my life", but I was glad the deed was done. It was inevitable that this happen and now I didn't have to agonize and obsess over how and when. That was behind me. Al seemed a lot closer now. We both still had a lot of work to do.

I slept poorly, but got out of bed in the morning with surprising vigor and energy. The door to the master bedroom was closed and I left without seeing Sharon. The drive to work was more peaceful than I remembered. I didn't even think twice about running away as I drove past the I-75 exit to Key West (a daily daydream pre-Alana). Work would be the same as always, but now I had a new initiative. Exactly how to get to Point B was unclear, but I was clearly on my way.

I spoke to Al before I started seeing patients. She was glad to hear from me, fully understanding how unpleasant things were and very supportive. Al's life remained virtually the same on the surface: same house, Martin still in the guest bedroom, Pierce going about his business, friends, neighbors, and community unaware and unchanged. My life not so. Sharon and I had few friends and no extended family to speak of. Jennifer wasn't around so it was just the two of us, and whatever stability we had together was now gone. My work situation was the same, but my partners were all busy with their own practices, and we rarely socialized or shared our personal lives. On the one hand, that would make it a lot easier to build a new life without Sharon; on the other hand, there was no bedrock to plant my feet on and weather the storm. I felt adrift without traction…except for Alana. My actions were predicated on our building a future together, and I felt strong and confident that we would be successful. But it was hard being 1500 miles apart and limited to a few phone calls and texts. I knew it wouldn't be easy. I even knew that it wouldn't be perfect. The only thing I was afraid of was that it wouldn't be. But I held on tight to my blind faith, and if we wanted it enough we would make it happen. It was up to us.

At the end of the day, coming home from work, I again had no idea what would await. Sharon had had time to digest the events of the day before. Who knew what kind of a mood she'd be in? I even wondered if she'd be violent, waiting with a loaded gun, or something crazy like that. It wouldn't be the first time a spurned spouse decided to get even. But instead, when I walked into the house, I found Jennifer there. Apparently Sharon had called her the night before, and Jenn took the first flight in the morning to support her mom and find out for herself what was going on. At first I was taken aback, not knowing why Jenn was there. I gave her a hug and kiss, and asked her why she had come so suddenly.

"I told Jennifer everything," Sharon blurted out.

I had no idea what "everything" meant, and I was upset that Jenn had been brought into the middle of this mess now, just two weeks after her wedding, when she should be on Cloud Nine loving life. How wrong to burst her bubble and burden her with this, even before anything definite had been decided (as far as Sharon knew). Fortunately Alana remained unknown to Sharon so at least she wouldn't be accused or blamed. But still…what the fuck? I knew that more important than anything was handling Jenn properly now. She and I had had a beautiful, loving relationship from the beginning. She was my only child; I loved and cared for and about her dearly, and desperately wanted to protect her from the pain and fallout that a parental divorce undoubtedly entails. But what did she know?

I knew that I'd never be able to have a heart-to-heart with Jenn if Sharon were present. Maybe at some point we could all discuss this together, objectively and rationally, but not yet. Everything was too raw and too fresh. So Jenn and I took Shanee for a walk, and we talked. I'm usually not naïve about life but I admit to being naïve about the profound impact divorce has on the children, who are the true unsung victims. Jenn was an adult and married. She had many friends whose parents had divorced. Steve himself was the product of divorce, and had managed to maintain close, meaningful relationships with both his parents even as they refused to speak on the phone or even acknowledge each other for twenty-five years. I figured Jenn would do the same, not hurl blame or point the accusing finger, but accept our failed marriage and be there for both of us. Jenn must have sensed over the years that her parents were unhappy, that the marriage was not working. Of course she'd understand and not take sides... Boy was I wrong! Jenn had already been poisoned by Sharon's bile, and told me how upset she was! *What was going on?* she wanted to know. She said that she had sensed things were different and something was wrong these past few weeks, but thought she was imagining things with all the hoopla of the wedding. I didn't know what to say or how much to tell her. I thought there would be time for that later. But here it was, in my face, demanding answers...So I told her the truth, up to a point. I explained that my marriage had become increasingly dysfunctional to the point that I needed some air. No child wants to hear the gory details of their parents' intimate lives and unhappiness, and I spared Jenn that. I wouldn't talk badly about her mom *no matter what*. I owed that to both of them. But I stood my ground and explained that I deserved some happiness, and wasn't likely ever to find it with Sharon. Jenn didn't disagree, or curse me out. She knew how difficult her mother was, and that I had borne the brunt of her nastiness, nutsiness, and *issues* over and over, year after year. Jenn grabbed her first opportunity to leave town and get away; now it was my turn. Of course she was visibly shaken and upset by the news and this unexpected turn of events, and said she hoped we would try to work things out. Not knowing what else to say, I told her we would do our best, knowing all along that such was not in the cards. We got back home and Jenn slept with Sharon and I in my new digs. It was very weird, punctuating the new normal. But I knew Jenn had to see it as it was, and face it in no uncertain terms. Things were, and likely always would be, different for all of us. I felt terrible about hurting Jenn. Married couples who insist that their kids would rather see them separate and happy with other partners than unhappy together under the same roof are deluded and clueless. No kid wants that. Jenn (and

Pierce) certainly didn't. I knew Sharon was hurting and desperate, but I've always resented her bringing Jenn in so early, counting on Jenn to take care of her when the roles should have been reversed. Jenn herself needed all the support she could get. I hoped Steve could be her rock, and, given his own experience, teach her how to facilitate close relationships with both parents, such that they could still be Dad and Mom even when they were no longer husband and wife.

Jenn returned to New York, and Sharon and I began the painful process of deconstructing a twenty-five-year life together. In my ongoing naiveté I thought that we would come to a meeting of the minds, and learn to tolerate, if not embrace, the new circumstances, gradually accepting the impending divorce, and try to survive, if not unscathed, at least as intact as possible. Throughout our marriage, for whatever reason that I could never understand, Sharon had always said that she "would never take anything from me" in the event things didn't work out. I never questioned her about that because there was no need. Even when we separated twenty years before, the "D" word remained taboo and unspoken, so her taking things from me was a moot point. Sharon liked to play the self-sacrificing martyr, and I assumed this was just another Sharonism, Sharon just being Sharon. But now here we were, and I knew enough to realize that divorce is all about the taking, and never taking enough. Would her years of vowing never to take anything from me hold true now? I doubted it; but if we could remain civil, and remember that we had spent twenty-five years together, had raised a child and made a life, perhaps that would temper the fury and ease the transition.

But we never had the chance to even try to develop a new relationship: no longer spouses, but exes and still Jennifer's parents. Reconciliation was never a consideration for me. There had been too much pain and disappointment over the years. In truth I had left the marriage emotionally and spiritually long ago. But I had always done my best to maintain an air of civility and consideration. Sharon not so. She immediately and completely withdrew from me and from her life, a sudden and total crash and burn. She stopped working at her part-time job (surely a mistake at a time when she most needed human contact and relationships, a support system and network, even if just casual workplace acquaintances). She spent every moment that I was home locked in the bedroom. She would never come out, or answer when I knocked on the door. On the rare occasion I was allowed in to fetch something I needed, the blinds were drawn, no lights were on, just a series of candles. Incense was always burning, old mindless situation comedies (usually *The Nanny* and *The Golden Girls*) played endlessly on the TV, and she became addicted to word puzzles. She spent every waking moment in this surreal state. The TV was on at all hours, and I'm not sure she ever ate or slept. She started seeing a psychiatrist, who prescribed various medications. She seemed to be on a downward spiral, and I felt very responsible and guilty. I never meant to hurt her, just to get away from her. But her decline was unmistakable, though I hoped not irreversible.

I was very concerned she would overdose, but there was little I could do to stop or help her. I fully expected to come home to an ambulance and police car, and see her wheeled out on a stretcher. No matter how badly she had treated me, that I didn't want. I knew that she spoke with Jennifer, and I spoke to Jenn as well. But Jenn would never mention anything about Sharon—I supposed they had a pact of silence and confidentiality where I was concerned. Whenever I voiced my concerns, Jenn would shut me down.

It's very hard to live in a house with someone who hates you, won't talk to you, and may be dangerous to herself or to you. It's alarming and disarming! I locked my bedroom door at night, but rarely heard a peep except the never ending bray of Fran Drescher's nasal and whiny voice (torture enough!). I felt responsible, and almost welcomed the craziness. It put a stamp on the failed marriage that would surely make it easier to put in my past.

Chapter 17

I felt that I really needed to be with Alana, but it was never as simple as taking a few days off and hopping on a plane. I had patients and surgeries, as did Al. She also had Pierce, and a community (professional and personal) that still included Martin. So we planned a mini-vacation for later in August, when we would spend a few days together at a bed-and-breakfast in the Hamptons. I didn't need to account to Sharon for my whereabouts any longer, so I was eager to go. I could easily rearrange my office schedule with a few weeks to plan. Al would make a suitable excuse to Martin and Pierce.

And so we spent a few glorious days together, for the first time free of spousal obligations, ready to truly be together without guilt or distraction. It just so happened that my 25th wedding anniversary fell during the middle of that getaway. Jennifer knew I would be "away on business," and asked me to spend it at home with Sharon instead. "It would mean a lot to Mom," she said. But I had no intention of sacrificing time with Alana, especially not now—and to what end? There would be no reconciliation. That wasn't even a remote possibility for me. We had passed the point of no return, and there was no turning back. *This should have happened years ago,* I thought. But I never would have left with Jennifer still at home, or even still single. That had been my pledge, come hell or high water, and I wouldn't break it. So I had stayed as long as I needed to, and wouldn't beat myself up, either, for not leaving sooner or for leaving when I did.

Returning to that cold, seemingly empty house (even in the 95 degree heat of summer in South Florida) became increasingly stressful. Would there still be a house to return to? Would one of those candles or the burning incense start a fire, accidentally or on purpose? Would I receive a phone call from the police, the hospital, a neighbor, or, worse, from Jennifer, with the news that Sharon had died in a blaze? Didn't the crazed wife in *Jane Eyre* set the house on fire?

The joy of my few days away with Alana evaporated on my plane flight back to Fort Lauderdale. As hard as I tried, I couldn't keep the afterglow alive as I contemplated what awaited me. I knew then and there that I would have to make some major changes as soon as possible. Moving out was the obvious and most pressing, and I would address that upon my return.

Fortunately the house was still intact, and Sharon again barricaded behind closed and locked doors. I knew that she would hear the front door open and Shanee barking, but I afforded her the courtesy of knocking on her bedroom door to let her know I was back. No answer. I knocked again, slightly harder. The TV was blaring and still no answer. I wondered if I should be more forceful. Suppose she were ill or worse? But I instead listened closely (in fact, put a stethoscope to the door) and heard some stirring so I decided to leave well enough alone. I went to my room and unpacked. The status quo remained for the next few days.

The more often I saw Alana the more I wanted to see her. Enough was never enough, and my hunger and appetite seemed to grow exponentially the more I was fed by her presence. I couldn't get enough of her! I couldn't wait from one phone call to the next, and hated to hang up. But life had to go on, and the process had to be played out to its (il)logical conclusion.

Because my home environment was so taxing, I spent precious little time in the house. I took Shanee for long walks and long talks. Crazy as it sounds, she seemed to understand me, and her attention and affection were my only comfort at hand during these difficult times. When I sat down next to her and looked deep into her eyes, I swear I could see my father in there! For real!! Jews don't believe in reincarnation (until the Messiah comes), but Shanee was the sweetest dog imaginable and I'm convinced that my father's life force and spirit were reborn in her.

In the house I reached out to Alana as often as I could, with every means available. There were long stretches when she was tied up with her work and/or her family, and I amused and occupied myself by devising strategies to express my love over a distance. One evening I doodled hearts with our initials, and texted photos of these to Al. I listed "My Favorite Things That Begin With The Letter 'A'" (of course Alana topped the list, followed by Andy Pettitte, Art Garfunkel, Atticus Finch, Al Bundy, Al Pacino, *a* cappella, and All Things Bacon). I compiled "My Favorite Things To Look At" (with Al #1, followed by the Grand Canyon, Mona Lisa, and sunset over the Manhattan skyline). Of course it was all a fun and meaningless distraction, but in truth it wasn't so meaningless, and a nice diversion for passing the time as I sat alone in my daughter's bedroom with the door locked, and my mind thirty-eight years and 1500 miles away. In many ways it was fun being a teenager again!

    The following weekend was Labor Day, and I dreaded the thought of three days at home with Sharon. I so wanted to see Alana, and fortunately Pierce was going away with Martin to visit and tour some college campuses. The stars were aligned for a long weekend together, which we both sorely needed. We made plans to go to Lake Placid in upstate New York. Al's lease on the Jaguar was expiring, and, reluctantly and regretfully, she traded in the car for a white Audi sports convertible, a really nice set of wheels but nothing compared to the pizzazz of the Jag! The drive up to Lake Placid, in beautiful weather with the top down, was exhilarating and emancipating. We were away together, just the two of us, and we left all our worries and cares behind. I'd had a strange personal history with Lake Placid many years earlier. Although I had never actually been there before, I was supposed to go for the 1980 Winter Olympics. I was a surgical intern at the time, and the previous year had done research with a sports medicine guru at the Hospital for Special Surgery. He served as the medical doctor for the US Olympic ski team, and invited me to join them for the competition in Lake Placid. Of course I was thrilled at the prospect, not only of being at the Olympics, but of being part of the medical team attending to the athletes. I couldn't imagine a more fun and exciting adventure! Of course as an intern my life and time weren't my own, and when I asked my chief resident for a few days off, he almost laughed in my face and turned me down cold. "You're on-call every other night, and no one is available to cover your schedule," he snarled. Apparently granting such a request was unheard of; he seemed offended that I even asked! How rude, I thought; but it was beyond my control. So Dr. Marshall and the other team physicians flew to Lake Placid without me in a small private plane. The plane encountered severe storm conditions en route, and crashed into the side of the mountain. There was one empty seat on the plane with my name on it. There were no survivors. I guess it wasn't my time. God had other plans for me, and her name was Alana. Lake Placid had ever since carried a certain bizarre mystique for me. Thank God for my call schedule—it had saved my life. Maybe Gladys was right—things do have a funny way of working themselves out.

Now here I was, on a beautiful late summer day, driving to Lake Placid with Alana. Had things been slightly different I would have died on the slopes in that wreckage. Instead I was with the girl of my dreams, planning a romantic getaway, and a future that had been hijacked by life (and could have been hijacked instead by death). God works his magic in mysterious ways. The weekend in Lake Placid was like a dream: walking around the lake on beautiful hiking trails, seeing and smelling the first sense of autumn and resonating with the natural transition that was now part of our lives, enjoying our holding-hands times, and finding peace, quiet, and contentment far from the madness that characterized our lives at home. From near death thirty years ago to near paradise today—another big circle had been completed in a magical way.

I returned to New York feeling refreshed, re-energized, and more hopeful than ever. I knew that it was time for legal advice to extricate myself from this worsening untenable situation. I didn't know any divorce attorneys personally or professionally, so I called one of the med-legal attorneys I had worked with. Her office was in my building, one floor below mine, and I had taken care of her family members so we had more than just a professional relationship. I briefly explained my situation, she expressed her condolences, and referred me to the divorce lawyer she had used many years before, whom she recommended without reservation.

I called Sandy Stein that very day. I needed to do something, needed legal representation, and advice. Her staff put the call through, she said she was very interested in my case, and would see me that afternoon. My office schedule was full, but now everything took a backseat to resolving my marital situation and moving forward with Alana. So I moved patients to the rest of the week, closed my hours early, and arrived for my 3:15 p.m. appointment. Sandy was a late-middle-aged woman, a named partner of the firm, who saw me immediately (after the requisite paperwork). Her office was cluttered with charts, files, and generalized disarray (sometimes a good sign for a busy lawyer who appears disheveled but is actually disarming and clever as a fox). She briefly reviewed my intake form, and then cut right to the chase.

"So who is she?" she asked.

"Who is who?" I asked innocently.

"The girl. Who is she?"

I was a little surprised and unnerved by her question. Was it so obvious that there was a new "she" involved? Apparently so.

"Well, she's my high school sweetheart. We reconnected online and have been connecting ever since."

"Tell me about her."

So I proceeded to describe Alana, who she is now, who she was then, and where we were going. I hoped that my enthusiasm would be contagious. But it wasn't.

"Why do you think she's 'the one'? What do you really know about her now, and what she's been through since high school? Y'know, most of the time, these flings never work out."

I resented her tone, and use of the word "fling." What I had with Alana wasn't a "fling." Far from it. We had a real relationship, a history. We were committed.

"Well, I'm more of an optimist and romantic than you. I realize that you've probably seen it all by now, hundreds, if not thousands, of divorces, marriages "made in heaven" gone awry. But I respectfully disagree that my relationship with Alana is like all those others. I believe this is going to work out, long-term, and I'm committed to that."

"Okay. I've heard that before. I looked your wife up on Facebook. Is this her?" And she showed me a Facebook wall with Sharon's picture.

"Yup, that's her."

"Well, I can't tell you what to do, just give you advice. I actually haven't handled a divorce case for several years. I've been doing primarily administrative work for the firm. My staff was very surprised when I said I'd see you. They asked me 'why now?' And I don't know but I decided to represent you if you want me to. Am I the first lawyer you're consulting?"

"Yes. I was referred to you by someone I know and respect, and consider highly reliable herself."

"Yes, well, let me tell you something. I have lots of friends who come to me and say that their husband did this, their husband did that, and they want out of their marriages. And I listen to them, and then tell them to go back to their husbands and make up. Divorce is more horrible than you can believe. It's not a battle, it's a war, and by and large just ain't worth it. Let me ask you something: How would you feel if your wife met someone and became involved with him?"

I took no time to answer. "I'd be delighted."

"Well, if that's how you feel, then you're ready for divorce. But I suggest you think about it. If you feel strongly, then you can retain me and give me a check today for $5,000 to start the ball rolling. Or you can just pay $500 for today's consultation, and we'll talk again in a few days, after you've had the chance to think it over. It's up to you."

"Well, it can't hurt to think for a few days. I'll pay you for today's consultation, and we'll take it from there."

"Fine. Let's do it that way. I'll do some research on your situation, your assets, income, lifestyle, etc., and give you a call."

So I wrote out a check for $500. I had hoped to find some answers that day, and a savior, or at least a shark, who would carry my colors, encourage me that everything would be okay, fight to the death, and lead me to the Promised Land. But what I was hearing was far from that.

It was nearly 5 p.m. when I left, and Sandy was ready to leave also, so we took the elevator down together.

"What I can advise you now is not to leave any paper trail. Don't buy Alana any expensive gifts, don't use your credit card, spend nothing but cash—for plane tickets, hotel rooms, dinners, jewelry, etc. Nothing that can be traced and come back to bite you later on."

"OK," I said. That was the one good bit of advice I had heard all day. I wasn't sure it was worth $500, but I could call on Sandy if need be. Now I was more confused than ever.

Chapter 18

I left the offices of Stein & Stein feeling very disheartened and uneasy. This was far from the discussion I had anticipated. I thought I'd be on my way, with a champion to carry the ball for me. Instead, I was practically told to give up the game and forfeit the fight.

"No way," I thought. "I can't believe things are as black as that. Now I get why she doesn't handle cases anymore. She doesn't believe in divorce. It's that simple. And she advises all her would-be clients to forget the whole thing. How can you run a business that way and expect to turn a profit?"

We met on a Tuesday, and I planned to spend the following weekend on Long Island. Were it not for Al, I don't know how I would have survived the next few days. We spoke multiple times during the day, emailed, texted, IM'ed, etc. Late at night I would call, after another day had passed, and we both were alone in our respective bedrooms, while our respective spouses lay alone in the rooms next door. "What's wrong with this picture?" I asked myself as four lonely people contemplated their pasts and wondered about their futures. One night, while I was talking to Al, Sharon started pounding on my locked door. I hung up the phone and opened the door, wondering what was so urgent. Had she actually started a fire? In that case I doubted she would have tried to save me. When I opened the door she looked disheveled, half-asleep, likely drugged, and asked me who I was talking to. I told her a friend, and left it at that. She turned around and walked back to her room, locking the door behind her. Very bizarre, and it was getting to me. I couldn't wait for the weekend.

Friday afternoon I drove to Fort Lauderdale airport, ticket in hand, so looking forward to my weekend away. My time with Al was my salvation, a shelter from the storm of what my everyday life had become. While waiting in the terminal by the gate, my phone rang, and, to my surprise and somewhat dismay, it was Sandy Stein. *Why is she calling me now?* I wondered. Thinking it might be important, and hoping for some badly needed good news on the legal front, I answered.

"Hello, Brett. It's Sandy Stein."

"Hi, Sandy. I'm at the airport on my way to Long Island. It's a little noisy here. Is there anything urgent, or can this wait until I return on Monday?"

"Nothing urgent, but I did some research on your case and wanted to share my findings with you."

It seemed odd that Friday afternoon would be her time for sharing. I was in such a good mood, on my way to spend the weekend with Alana, and so didn't want anything to bring me down. But my scheduled take-off wasn't for another hour so I decided to hear her out.

"Okay. What's up?" I asked.

"I checked into your Manhattan apartment, the one you bought for Jennifer to occupy while she's in school. The bottom line is that Sharon can claim that you and she planned to keep that apartment after Jennifer graduates, and move in there together, or at least snowbird there six months and in Florida six months."

"But that was never our plan, and we never lived there together. We bought it expressly for Jennifer to stay in while attending Pratt, rather than renting a place with that enormous expense and having nothing to show for it when she finished. The plan was never to keep it afterwards."

"Well, so you say, but Sharon can argue otherwise. And she'd have a good case. You might be on the hook for purchasing that place to give to her, or at least give her the funds to purchase another comparable place, to maintain the lifestyle that she would say you and she were planning for retirement. In the eyes of the court, just because you want out of the marriage doesn't mean that she should suffer. Honestly, Brett, if you're telling me that your plan is to leave Sharon, retire, and be financially solvent enough to move to New York to be with Alana, I can't tell you that you're being realistic, nor that I can represent you with those expectations. I don't see how it can be done."

I couldn't believe what I was hearing, and felt myself getting hotter and a little dizzy. That apartment cost nearly two million dollars. I expected that with the ever-rising value of Manhattan real estate it would be a great investment, and I could recoup all the costs of housing Jenn when I sold it at the end. Now I was learning that it might cost me an additional two million dollars!! How could that be?

"Okay. Well, I can't really talk now. I'll think about it and we'll talk next week."

Well, that wasn't a game-changer for me, but it certainly was a mood-buster. I had enough on my mind already without this additional piece of bad news. What to do…what to do…

Needless to say I spent the next four hours in a panic. How could I work this out? The idea of giving everything up and crawling back to Sharon *because I couldn't afford to get divorced* seemed even crazier than the divorce laws. So this is what it would come to? Marriage is a better choice than poverty or bankruptcy, and people stay together, despite their irreconcilable differences, for that reason? Could that possibly be true?? One more example of my naiveté.

But no. I wouldn't give up Alana and I wouldn't give in to the absurdity of the law. If it were just a matter of working harder and longer to earn more money, that I could live with. But to be with Al I had to leave my (lucrative) practice in Florida and move to New York. Otherwise, realistically speaking, how could we grow and build our relationship? Relocating to be near Al had to be my top priority. But could my marital/legal obligations actually crush my dream? I suppose so. It was a real Catch-22. To be with Al I needed to get divorced and move to New York. To get divorced I needed to make more money. But to make more money I needed to stay in Florida!! A mad triangle with no escape! I was beginning to understand the homicidal rage that drove *The War of the Roses*, and likely many other solved or unsolved murders. But since the spouse is always the first suspect, and a spouse going through a divorce is probably the only person of interest, I probably wouldn't get away with it. Life with Sharon vs. life in the pen: a tough call.

My mind was racing during the entire flight. Usually I'm a great sleeper on airplanes, and nod off even before we finish boarding. But not this time. I'm usually pretty good at figuring things out, creating, comparing, and assessing the pros and cons of various scenarios, and making an educated decision. After all that's what surgery is—diagnosing a problem, considering the various solutions, assigning a risk/benefit ratio to each choice, and deciding which one is least risky and most likely to achieve the desired result. So if I could do that every day, multiple times every day for my patients, shouldn't I be able to figure it out for myself?

I deduced that I had three steps to take in order to end up with Alana in New York: retirement, divorce, and relocation. Now in what order should I proceed? If I got divorced first, and ended up with an expectedly huge financial burden (as Sandy had insisted would happen), I couldn't retire, and therefore couldn't relocate. That sequence is a non-starter. But suppose I retired first, thus eliminating my income as an issue? Then I could either relocate to New York with Sharon and get divorced after some time, removing my financial obligation as the "moneyed spouse," or perhaps I could get divorced in Florida eventually, also without an income to drive me to support Sharon in a style I could no longer afford, and then relocate to New York myself? How would that work? In my frenzied state of mind it seemed like it could work. Of course it couldn't, but the more I thought about it, the more I began to convince myself that this was a way out. What did Sandy know? (She'd only been practicing matrimonial law for thirty years!) By the time we touched down in Islip I had formulated a plan of action. Al was waiting for me in the terminal, and I must have looked wild-eyed and crazed from the insane ruminating of the past four hours.

I couldn't wait to tell her my plan! I had figured it out, I thought. So, speaking at a pace reserved for manic-depressives and meth addicts, I laid out my strategy and the reasoning behind it (I was so hyped up I could barely take a breath). Al listened patiently then said we needed to go somewhere for a drink (or two, or three). She could see my panic-driven state, and calmly, with some much-needed alcohol on board, she pointed out the flaws in my logic. I understood that my plan wasn't perfect—so there would be a new plan I thought! But Al held and squeezed my hand and that was all the plan I needed. I would rethink it on Monday, and I lay back to behold my Al once again by my side. Nothing else mattered but her and me, and this moment in time.

Chapter 19

My trip back to Florida was more sane and reasoned than my outbound flight. Al had persuasively convinced me that I did need another plan. I didn't know exactly where to turn, but I certainly wasn't hitching my wagon to Sandy. I needed a second legal opinion, and my sister, a senior partner in a major New York law firm, made some inquiries and gave me the name of Edna Osserman, a matrimonial attorney in Miami, who was the former president of the Florida Bar Association, a real superstar, and reportedly tops in her field. I was happy to speak to anyone but Sandy, so I called Edna on Tuesday. She was expecting my call, and we made an appointment for that evening. I was in surgery all day, and couldn't get to her office before 7, but she was fine with that and we agreed to meet at 7:30. She was a partner in a large and reputable law firm that occupied two floors of an iconic skyscraper in Miami. I was exhausted by the end of my workday (six surgeries) but had no doubts about keeping that appointment. Maybe Sandy was wrong…maybe there was another way…maybe her bias against divorce colored her very discouraging and pessimistic counsel. I had nothing to lose.

By the time I arrived, most of the offices were empty, and the cleaning crew had arrived. Edna instructed me which elevator to take (to the 42nd floor) and the password to her suite of offices. We were the only ones there, and I was glad for the peace and quiet of an office building after hours. I came directly from the operating room, still wearing my scrubs. She came directly from her health club, still wearing her workout clothes. It was a match made in heaven!

I can't say enough about Edna. She saved me and changed my life. Had she also hung black crepe about my situation I may very well have leapt from that 42nd floor, a fate seemingly preferable to my other options. We sat down in her rather cluttered office. Multiple plaques adorned the walls, from president of the bar to distinguished leader of

B'nai B'rith. She was low-key, and easy to talk to, unlike the pomp and circumstance one expects from a powerful barrister. She immediately reminded me of the actress Christine Baranski, who played a similar type of attorney on *The Good Wife*. Edna asked me some of the same questions that Sandy had asked ("Who is she?", "Are you convinced you want a divorce?", "How would you feel if your wife met someone else?" etc), and reached the same conclusion—that I was ready for divorce and reconciliation was not likely an option. But Edna had an entirely different approach. After I had told my story, she said that there *is* life after divorce, no matter how daunting the task or unfavorable the circumstances. We would get this done, one way or another, and I would follow my heart to Alana if that's where it led me. She was reassuring, confident, and supportive. Undoubtedly matrimonial attorneys must be part-therapist, and she handled my concerns with aplomb. When she asked me if I would like to proceed, I knew that she was a godsend, and I gave her a $10,000 retainer to be my person. She didn't say it would be easy, but that it was doable, and she would give me the best representation possible. I believed her, and, equally important, I believed in her.

I spoke to Al on the drive back home. I could feel that I was a different person; hopeful once again, more optimistic than cautious, confident that the dream was not only still alive, but coming true. It was a very good day.

Until I arrived home. Sharon was not only awake but out of her room, and ready to pounce when I walked through the door. She was energized, almost frenetic, pacing and infuriated. The moment I got home she pointed to her laptop on the kitchen table, open to Alana's professional website, "Breast Surgeons of Long Island." There she was, picture, bio, et al. I was too surprised to respond.

"So who is she?" It seemed everyone was asking me this question.

"Alana is an old friend of mine," I said as innocently as I could, not knowing what Sharon knew, or how.

"An old friend, huh? Well, I happen to know that you've been seeing her when you've been in New York, and writing to her, and cheating on me." Her voice was rising in volume and pitch as she spoke.

"I don't know what you're talking about," I said calmly, still not sure how much Sharon knew, and whether there was any point in denying the truth.

"Don't stand there and lie to me. I know all about it. You're a lying cheat. I hate you and hope you die!"

And with that she stormed back into her room, slammed the door, and locked it. The high of a few minutes ago crashed to a new low, and I stood in the kitchen with that same look on my face with which Bogie describes waiting for Ingrid Bergman on the train station, as though somebody had just punched him in the stomach. Now what? I considered knocking on Sharon's door, trying to talk to her, get some more information. But her anger and rage were so visceral and gut-wrenching I couldn't chance causing a further explosion. So I went for a walk with my best friend, and called my other best friend. The Florida night was still, hot, humid, and buggy, with a full moon that in other times might have been romantic and full of love. But not tonight.

"Hi, beautiful."

"Hi, Brett. How are you? How did your meeting with the attorney go?"

"Well, I'm fine. I really liked the new attorney. She was way more sympathetic, empathetic, and optimistic than Sandy, and I feel much more confident that she's the right person to handle my case, so I gave her a retainer and will be calling her again tomorrow to discuss more specifics and what she needs from me regarding the financials."

"Oh, I'm so glad. That other attorney sounds like a real bitch. She should go back to administration and stay away from clients!"

"Yes, I agree. She nearly drove me mad, as you saw when I landed Friday."

"Yes, that was not a pretty sight. You sound much calmer and more confident again. You scared me!"

"Nothing to be scared about. I do have some news. I'm not sure how it happened, but Sharon found out about us, and confronted me with accusation upon accusation when I got home tonight."

"What? How did she find out?"

"I really don't know. She didn't give me any specifics or proof, but she knows who you are, and looked you up on the web. So however it happened, the cat's out of the bag now, for both of us. I tried so hard to be careful. But it's hard to keep this kind of thing a secret for too long. I'm sure she was suspicious that I was suddenly taking all these trips out of town. That's not like me—I never traveled like this before. So now she knows, and she's even more nuts than before."

"Oh, well, it was bound to come out at some time. Might as well be now. Martin knows about us, but Pierce doesn't. Do you think she told Jennifer?"

"Hard to say. I wouldn't be surprised. It's very wrong, but she vents to Jennifer all the time, and has no problem talking shit about me to her. I haven't heard from Jenn but will call her tomorrow to check in and check the temperature, so to speak. I'm sure if she knows something she'll tell me. She's not shy about that. And if our last conversation was any barometer, she'll be pretty angry at me. I'm not looking forward to that."

"Well, at least you found a new attorney. That should make you feel better."

"Yes, it does. I've got to get out of the house, now more than ever. I'm going to start looking for a place tomorrow, at least something temporary, even a hotel if necessary. Living under the same roof as Sharon has become unbearable. I hate to go home now."

"If you think it's dangerous, don't go home. Leave tonight."

"I'll see. Maybe Sharon will be locked away and I can make it for one more night. I'll call once I'm home and let you know what's going on."

"Okay. Be careful."

"I will."

All was dark and quiet when I opened the door. The calm before the storm? I wondered. I went right to my room, closed and locked the door, and waited quietly for a few minutes, listening for any sounds of tell-tale danger. But nothing. Rather than disturb the silence I texted Al that I was okay, and we'd talk in the morning. I spent most of the night in bed with Shanee, unable to sleep, wondering what was brewing in the master bedroom. Sharon was certainly a loose cannon, and nothing would surprise me. The night seemed interminable. Finally, around 4 a.m., I got up, showered, dressed, and left. Every day seemed like a new set of hurdles and obstacles. *I'm way too old for this,* I thought.

Chapter 20

I called Al around 7 a.m.. She was up, and anxious to hear from me. No one knew better than she the out-of-control rage a betrayed spouse feels, and she truly feared for my safety. "Please get out of there," she pleaded. And I knew she was right. In between seeing patients and all the requisite drudgery inherent in a modern medical practice, I was able to find a hotel near the office and made reservations. I didn't know how long I'd be there but figured a week should be enough to come up with a plan. I could always extend the stay as needed.

I spoke to Edna, told her what happened, and she echoed Alana's concerns and advice. There are potential ramifications if you leave the marital residence prematurely (claims of abandonment), but safety first, and we'd deal with the fallout later. Edna was very sensible.

So that night when I got home I took a large suitcase from the garage and packed whatever was at hand. I took only the bare necessities. I was hoping to leave Sharon a note, and get out before she was aware I was going. But no such luck. I had left the bedroom door open, and, as I was packing, Sharon suddenly appeared in the doorway.

"Going someplace?" she asked, in a sarcastic voice with a sneer of contempt on her face.

"Yes. I have to move out. My staying here under the circumstances is bad for both of us. I'm sure you agree. It's not right for you to have to live locked in your room. I don't think you'll feel that way when I'm not here."

Sharon didn't answer, didn't try to convince me to stay, and didn't throw a tantrum. She made one request—that I take a different suitcase, since the one I had hastily grabbed was part of a set. So I accommodated her immediately, not wanting to rock the boat and hoping to make my exit before she lost control. She seemed unusually subdued. Likely the meds, I surmised. I quickly changed suitcases, gave Shanee one last hug with a squeeze (*Who knows when I'll see her again?* That thought made me very sad), and left. I backed out of the driveway and drove out of the development like a madman, half expecting to see Sharon's headlights in my rearview mirror. But no, it was a clean getaway, and I finally relaxed once on the highway. One more step closer to Al, I thought. I called her from the car. Though thousands of miles away she was right there with me as though she were sitting in the passenger seat. The *sturm und drang* of the past few weeks was taking its toll, but for the time being I was okay.

"I haven't slept, either, worrying about you. I feel much better knowing that you're safe. Now we can really celebrate your birthday! You've been through hell. We have a lot to celebrate!!"

My birthday was the next week! I had been so distracted that I forgot all about it!! Now there really was something to celebrate: not just a year older but a year better. I felt reborn in a way, that I was starting a new life. It would be a night to remember, but this time in a good way.

I checked into the hotel, lay down on the bed, and fell asleep still in my clothes. I was drained and exhausted. I saw no need to see Sharon again. It would now be Edna's battle, and, at the end of the day, I'd write a check and be done with it. Of course I still had a lot of work to do, but I imagined it would be busy work more than anything. The real cost was emotional, not financial. Those past few months had been war and peace. The worst part of the fighting was behind me. Now the work would be reconstruction. I was good at that.

Chapter 21

Life changed immediately once I left the house. Instead of angst and fear dominating my thoughts, I was now able to concentrate again on the reason behind all this drama—my rediscovered and renewed love for Alana, and the amazing future that awaited us. I had no doubts about her, and Al told me that she was "2000 percent sure" that she wanted to marry me. That was very reassuring.

We celebrated my birthday with a romantic dinner and overnight stay at Oheka Castle on Long Island. It couldn't have been more special: from the roses, champagne and chocolate-covered strawberries that greeted us in the room, through dinner, a hand-holding walk in the moonlight, wishing on a shooting star, and a blissful night and morning together. My last birthday with Al had been thirty-nine years before. I knew that I would never spend another without her.

Except for our time together, Al's "external" life remained very much the same as it had always been. She and Martin were virtually strangers, but that had been their *modus operandi* for years. There was no overt hostility, nor could there be. They passed each other (silently and impassively) regularly in the hallways of their house, their office building, the hospital, and the operating rooms. Al sporadically boiled over and keyed Martin's car in the parking lot when the spirit moved her (amazing how cathartic that can be!); but otherwise there was no contact or public feuding before their friends or medical community. Pierce was aware of the new living situation but did his best to take it in stride. When Al and Martin sat down with Pierce to discuss things openly, Pierce made it very clear that as far as he was concerned he just wanted his parents to both be living under the same roof as him. When they discussed the possibility of divorce he faced it like a man, and said that regardless of what they did, he was determined to be happy and successful, and would be. I had never met Pierce yet, but the more I learned about him the more I respected and admired him.

He seemed to be a very special kid, with a sensitivity and insight that belied his years and his tough macho image. It seemed to me that his allegiance was clearly and undeniably with Alana. But he didn't want to reject his dad, or lose him from his life. As absent a father as Martin was, and despite the pain and confusion wrought upon Pierce when Martin suddenly picked up and moved out years earlier, Pierce and Martin still connected, and Pierce was loathe to give that up. I knew that was appropriate and healthy for Pierce, and wished that Jennifer were more like him. In fact, Jennifer was much more difficult as far as I was concerned. After I moved out, Sharon got to her and once again painted me in the most vile light possible, disclosing what she had learned about me and Alana, and pushing Jenn to take sides, a terrible, selfish, self-serving tactic and so destructive to a child of divorce. When I first moved out and called Jennifer, she wouldn't take my phone calls. I called over and over, nearly in a frenzy, but she wouldn't answer the phone, or return my calls, texts, or emails. This drove me mad until one day I had an epiphany, surely a message from God Himself! People sometimes become estranged from their children, and they survive; I would survive Jennifer's rejection for as long as it lasted. I couldn't control her behavior, only my own. Maybe this was her process, what she needed, to accept and get past the shock and sadness of her parents' divorce. Maybe she couldn't deal with it. Maybe she was spending all her energy supporting and helping Sharon, and needed to share her mother's anger towards me for her to come to terms with it. And it was my job, as it always had been, to help her, protect her, give her what she needed regardless of the personal sacrifice—that's what parents do! And somehow I came to terms with Jenn's rejection and distance that way, deciding to give her the time and space she needed to deal with this on her own terms. I didn't show anger towards her, or guilt her into giving me equal time and consideration, although I certainly felt I deserved it. I would let her know I was there for her, loved her, was sorry for hurting her, and would always be available and welcoming whenever she was ready to reconcile. I stopped frantically calling, texting, etc. I withdrew in order not to be a burden, as I'm sure Sharon was. When Jenn was ready, I would be too. And that was that.

Despite the newly discovered peace and tranquility of my hotel room (and I certainly don't want to minimize those blessings!), I needed to find a more permanent solution for my remaining time in south Florida. Shula's Hotel (my temporary lodgings) was convenient and comfortable enough, with all the usual amenities, literally down the block from my office—I could've walked to work. And I could live freely, talk to Al when I wanted, without worrying that I was being overheard, away from the venom that had been spewing from Sharon for the past month. Finally I could truly come and go as I pleased without looking over my shoulder and trying to watch my own back all the time. Al and I would watch TV programs "together," and even the baseball playoffs (both of us were longtime Yankees fans, as was Pierce). I began to feel like a human being again. After some easier-than-expected online searching I found "Executive Apartments" nearby, that offered short-term leases of furnished apartments, exactly what I needed. So I signed a lease for the only available vacancy—a studio apartment tucked away in the back, overlooking a small canal. At first I thought it would be too small, but in actual fact the coziness turned out to be a blessing in disguise. After all, how much room did I really need? There was a small eat-in kitchen, a large bedroom/living room, and a bathroom with two large closets. The furniture was less than luxurious, but functional and comfortable, enough to satisfy my creature comfort requirements, at least for the short-term. Because of its location in the complex, it was quiet and peaceful. From the living room couch, in front of the TV, I could literally see the entire apartment, and this vantage was more comforting and valuable than I first appreciated. The door had a double-lock, and I felt very safe and secure inside. The apartment was very bright, even with the curtains drawn, because of the small size, the yellow walls, and the multiple ceiling fixtures, floor, and table lamps. And, of course, being in south Florida was as warm as I chose it to be. So I moved into a place that was small, warm, bright, safe, quiet, and peaceful, a place where I could rest, relax, heal, mature, and prepare for my next life, where the outside world was entirely shut out and I had my own space and tranquility. I affectionately nicknamed it "the womb." My stay there, and my gradual progressive transition from yesteryear to tomorrow, was a sentinel time in my life, and the ideal environment in which to recover, heal, and move forward, protected from the thorns of a hostile environment outside, embraced by my own inner fantasies of love and warmth inside. I had found a home.

My mood lifted immediately upon moving into the womb. I felt safe, relaxed, and comfortable. I've never placed a premium on creature comforts, so the small size and institutional furnishings weren't a problem. The bed was comfortable, the TV adequate, and the closets enough to hold my minimalist wardrobe. My rabbi once sermonized about the benefits of "traveling light" through life—physically and emotionally, with as little excess baggage as possible. And my life was the epitome of traveling light, at least as far as physical possessions were concerned. Of course I was somewhat lonely, and really missed Shanee. I specifically looked for apartments that allowed pets, and thought I might keep Shanee with me on weekends if Sharon were agreeable. I would enjoy the companionship when I couldn't travel to see Alana. So I hesitatingly broached the topic with Sharon and shockingly she was amenable. *Maybe she feels sorry for me?* I thought. In any event one Friday evening I drove to the house to bring Shanee back to the womb. Sharon was her usual cool and nasty self, and I suspected that she might change her mind at the last minute just to piss me off. But surprisingly she had Shanee ready and waiting, leash and collar on. She also insisted that I take a full bag of dog food, the food and water bowls, and Shanee's toys and bed with me, which seemed strange since she would only be with me for the weekend. But, anxious to get out of there as quickly as possible, I put Shanee in the front seat, all the appurtenances in the trunk, and drove away, never giving it a second thought. Little did I know that Sharon was playing me, but I was just happy to have my best friend with me again.

The womb was small but large enough for the two of us. I took Shanee for walks on the golf course that adjoined the apartment complex. She slept on my bed, and lay next to me on the couch as we ate and watched football together. As companions go, she was the best, and I felt more and more peaceful and comforted. She wasn't Al, but of all other living creatures to be with, she was my next choice.

Sunday evening I called Sharon to arrange to return Shanee, but oddly there was no answer. I left a voicemail, expecting to hear from her before too late. No call-back. I called again before bedtime, again no answer, again a voicemail, again no call back. I thought nothing of it, thought maybe she didn't hear the phone, or was otherwise engaged, and I would keep Shanee in the apartment when I went to work in the morning, returning at lunch to walk her, and then try to reach Sharon during the day. Shanee was very adaptable, and settled in nicely, so I had no doubt she would be okay while I was at work. I called Sharon again in the morning, no answer. And again, no answer. And so it went all day long, my calling, getting the answering machine, leaving messages, her not calling back. Things seemed very peculiar.

Finally Monday night Sharon did answer. I asked her why she hadn't called back, that I thought our agreement was that I keep Shanee for the weekend then return her Sunday night. I didn't understand. But Sharon immediately took the offensive. That wasn't her understanding at all, she said. Shanee was with me, and would stay with me. I explained to Sharon that I worked all day, from early to late, and that it would be very difficult for me to get home to let Shanee out, and unfair to Shanee as well, being locked in a small apartment all day alone. But Sharon had other plans. She didn't care if it would be difficult for me. She didn't care if it would be difficult for Shanee. It had always been difficult for her to come home at lunch to let Shanee out (even though she never worked more than two days per week, and at the Cleveland Clinic which was less than five minutes from our house), and now I would know how she felt and would have to deal with it. The issue of Shanee's comfort, safety, and well-being never entered her mind. She was using Shanee as a pawn to get back at me, and this poor, sweet, loving, kind soul would have to suffer for it.

So, if this is what it was, I would deal with it, and in a positive constructive way. I accustomed myself to having Shanee as my new roommate, and adjusted my schedule accordingly. Ordinarily I didn't take a lunch break (except to speak to Al), and changed my schedule so that I would have an hour for lunch, enough time to rush home to my apartment, connect with Shanee, take her out for a walk and to do her business, and settle her back in the womb before I went back to work. It was a bit of a hassle, no doubt, and there were occasions when I sent Jorge to my apartment to walk Shanee (which he was happy and most agreeable to contribute). But I resigned myself to this new, somewhat more harried, schedule. Shanee was now mine, and I committed myself to taking care of her. This now was my new normal, and I wasn't unhappy about it. She was my best friend, and such a good companion, I was happy to have her with me in my everyday life.

So Shanee and I spent early mornings, midday (when I could get out of the office), and evenings/nighttime together. Her very presence lit up the apartment. Knowing I would come home not to an empty space but to one with my best friend waiting for me was a blessing. When she heard the key in the door, she came waiting for me, tail wagging, tongue ready to lick and welcome me, always seemingly happy to see me. And we became reunited. My entire consciousness changed—I was no longer alone, even in my small otherwise unfamiliar apartment in Miami. The womb now had two inhabitants it was nurturing.

Of course I needed to make plans for Shanee when I left town to visit Alana. So I contacted all the kennels in the area, checked out their credentials, and selected one next door to Shanee's vet which offered "boutique services," including large individual "suites" for each dog, including a sitting room and bedroom, large comfortable beds with plush mattresses, three walks per day plus three sessions of twenty-minute individual play time, and supposedly all-natural, specially prepared meals and organic diets for each animal, unique to their breed and disposition. I wouldn't mind staying there myself! Seemed perfect. Every dog needed to be checked by their vet before their stay to verify there was no kennel cough or any other communicable diseases. I liked that too.

So I made a reservation at the "dog 5-star hotel" and an appointment with Dr. Balasky to give Shanee the once-over and verify her health status. I felt a little uncomfortable leaving her in a kennel after all these years, but I couldn't bring her with me on the plane, didn't have enough time off to drive from Florida to New York, and felt that three days would be long enough to see if the kennel worked for her but not so long as to place her in any jeopardy. Perhaps this was rationalization to a large extent because I so wanted to see Alana. Perhaps Sharon's real motivation in dumping Shanee on me was to keep me from traveling to New York? Hard to say—I wouldn't put anything past Sharon, even using Shanee to her advantage, with no regard for Shanee's well-being. In any event, I felt it was worth a try, and certainly picked the best possible lodgings for the weekend for my furry friend.

I planned to leave for New York on Friday afternoon on my usual 5 p.m. flight, and I went to Dr. Balasky's office with Shanee on Wednesday for her pre-kennel check-up. I had called Balasky's office to make the appointment. They still had my old phone number, so they called the house to confirm, and, of course, Sharon got the message. When I pulled into the parking lot, I was surprised to see Sharon standing there waiting for me. I couldn't imagine why she was there, but that was merely my own naiveté. I should have anticipated some pushback and nefarious plot brewing, and the moment I exited my car with Shanee in tow, Sharon approached me and grabbed the leash. Before I had a chance to speak, she began ranting about how awful a person I was to leave Shanee in a kennel, that she wouldn't stand for it, and I should leave immediately. I was stunned, and had no response. I was totally unprepared for this.

"She's my dog now," I answered abruptly. "Let go of the leash and let us pass."

Sharon had no intention of making this easy for me, and Shanee was just collateral damage (how evil is that??!!). In any event, there was a momentary tug-of-war as we each pulled on Shanee's leash. Then I realized how crazy this was, and how unfair to our poor, confused, suffering dog. She just wanted to be loved and taken care of, and here we were, her two caregivers, the leaders of her pack, pulling her in opposite directions as we fought our own battle. How sad, and unforgiveable…

I immediately released the leash, and let Sharon pull Shanee away. The confrontation was escalating, volatile, and potentially dangerous, and I could sense Sharon's fury being out of control. I immediately stepped back, turned away, walked to my car and drove off, leaving Sharon in the parking lot with Shanee. I'm sure she felt this was a real victory, that she had really shown me who was boss and she wouldn't let me get away with anything. Poor Shanee, through no fault of her own, was the helpless pawn in this crazy struggle. I drove back to my apartment in Miami Lakes, shocked and saddened by this very unexpected turn of events, and feeling so sorry for Shanee, and for Sharon too, driven by uncontrollable rage to this bizarre, thoughtless, inconsiderate behavior. When I returned to the womb and saw Shanee's empty bed, food and water bowls, and toys, I felt very sad and lonely. I didn't know it then but that was the last time I would see my best friend. She, who had been nothing but a loving and trusting soul, was another unsung victim of this divorce. That was a very bad day for me.

(A postscript on this awful incident: Eight months later, Sharon flew to New York to see Jennifer. I later learned that Shanee had been ill, with an open wound and an infection, and was on antibiotics and wound care, and in pain. Sharon could have asked me to care for Shanee while she was away. But she never called, and instead she herself chose to kennel Shanee, in her time of need, despite her illness and need for tender loving care. Sharon returned to Florida after a long weekend, and I got a frantic call from Jennifer a few days later that Shanee had died. I was beside myself with grief. When I learned the details of her last days I pictured her alone, ill, in pain, caged in a strange place without her loved ones around her. That vision has haunted me to this day. If I hold anything against Sharon it is that she abandoned Shanee when she needed her most, and chose her own need for anger over Shanee's need for love and affection. I still haven't gotten past that.)

I rarely spoke to Jenn for the next few months. Perhaps the most painful day of all was Thanksgiving, usually my favorite holiday, especially poignant that year. Alana always prepared Thanksgiving for the family, Martin was still in the house, and of course Pierce was home. Al's mom and relatives were the usual guests. I was alone in "the womb," comfy and cozy, but extremely lonely on this day of thanks to be celebrated with friends and family. I decided not to give in totally to my situation but would cook my own turkey (not hard even for someone as inept as I in the kitchen!) So I bought a turkey, did the basics, and put it in the oven. In the morning Al sent me a video of herself with a loving message saying that she knew how hard it must be for me, she wished we could spend the day together, that next year we most certainly would celebrate as a family, and she'd call me later. That video made my whole day (and to this day it's still saved on my phone and in the "cloud"). I knew Jennifer was visiting Florida, and having Thanksgiving with Sharon. I hoped she would call me, reach out, perhaps drive down to see me, and show some understanding, empathy, even forgiveness. I waited at home all day, but never heard from her. She had both my cell phone and land line numbers but never used them. Her absence and seeming lack of caring was the cruelest blow of all. Of course I gave thanks for the blessings I had, including my health, Jennifer's health, and Alana. But it was a very long day for me, one of the worst.

I survived that Thanksgiving, despite the loneliness and sadness, despite devouring the turkey I cooked (along with "Bruce's Yams" straight from a can off the supermarket shelf). I heard nothing from Jennifer that day or the next. Saturday morning I had an appointment with a therapist I had started seeing to help me deal with the myriad of negative thoughts and feelings that characterize divorce. Libby was young, Jennifer's age, which is exactly why I chose her from my health insurance plan. I wanted someone who reminded me of Jennifer, someone upon whom I could transfer my feelings and who might react with the mindset of a millennial. Libby did her job admirably, and helped me appreciate Jennifer's perspective and needs. That day was especially difficult for me insomuch as it was Jennifer's birthday. I had tried to call her, but she didn't answer her cell phone. I considered calling Sharon's landline but decided against it. I figured it would be another tough day to get through, par for the course at this point, and hopefully one and done. I started off the session explaining to Libby the emptiness I felt at Jennifer's absence and distance. Shortly thereafter there was a quiet knock on the door. Libby opened it, and there was Jennifer. I was very surprised to see her. I had told her when and where my session was in case she wanted to be part of it, and share her feelings with me in a therapeutic environment and appropriate venue, but she had given me no encouragement or indication that she would show up. I felt very happy to see her. Libby handled the situation beautifully, and I couldn't have scripted a better scenario. Jenn and Libby hit it off immediately, and spoke openly and unreservedly. Jenn explained how hurt and disappointed in me she was, how she never expected that I would cheat on her mom, and didn't know who I was or how to react or relate to me anymore. She had been read the riot act by Sharon, and had little to no interest in hearing my side of the story, just wanting to vent and explain her withdrawal. I tried to explain myself, and even talk a little about Alana, but Jenn would hear none of it. I could hear Sharon's displaced venom and anger in Jennifer's words. Jenn said she didn't care who Alana was, nor did she care to know my feelings about her. She vowed never to meet Alana or let Al into her life. She said she loved me, but didn't know if, how, or when she would ever feel comfortable and close to me again. I tried to answer her bitter disappointment and assault with acceptance, acknowledgement, and kindness, recalling the life we had spent together from the time she was an infant. I asked her straight up how I could rehabilitate my image in her eyes? But she turned a deaf ear to me, and let me have it again, and again, and again. And I took it all, feeling that she needed to express and release her anger before there would be any hope of reconciliation between us. She did most of the talking, a little crying, and I could clearly see and hear the pain she was enduring. I felt just awful.

At the end of the session we left together. Libby and she hugged, Libby smiled at her and wished her a very happy golden birthday (the day was November 27 and Jenn was 27 years old). Jenn thanked her, and I drove her to Starbucks to sit and talk for awhile, one on one, face to face. Jenn seemed calmer and we kept the conversation light. When I dropped her off, we hugged and she said she loved me. I said I'd call soon, and she smiled and waved goodbye. I understood that reconstituting this relationship would be a long process. But at least we made a start. Hard work never scared me, and I was beginning to realize that redeeming myself in Jenn's eyes would be a challenge I hadn't expected. But slow and steady wins the race, and time was on my side. Winning over Jenn and Pierce was the key to my future with

Alana, and I would do whatever it took to make that happen. Step 1—give them both time and space to adjust to the new reality, place their needs first, and be a plus not a minus in their lives. Hopefully with time they'd get it and gradually relinquish their anger, feeling that the upsides of having me in their lives outweighed the downsides of rejecting me. That was my hope, anyway. Time would tell.

Chapter 22

Al and I continued to speak as often as possible, both at work and at home. We wrote emails, texts, and even the occasional love poem:

A Love Poem for My Girl

A memory of love from long ago
Brought to life and allowed to grow.

Covert messages and texts galore
Allowed the nascent feelings to soar.

The Roslyn Clermont, Room 222
Convinced us both our love was true.

The Hotel Monaco outside DC
Gave us the chance to breathe and be free.

Early summer on Blue Sky Court
Showed us the life we both have sought.

Wine country and Hamptons in August 2010
Reinforced the love that might have been

And lo and behold! The coming of fall
Has brought to us the most fulfilling love of all.

The worst is over and the future awaits
With hope and passion for true soulmates.

I came to New York every few weeks for long weekends. Sometimes Al could stay with me, others not. But it was a new reality for us now. We were engaged to be engaged, once the dust had settled and the divorces accomplished. I continued working with Edna and enduring the trauma that divorce inflicts. Knowing that Al would be waiting at the end of this long, dark tunnel was my salvation and got me through. Al, too, started the divorce process. She had spoken to a matrimonial attorney years earlier, after Martin's first-known betrayal, but hadn't gone further when they decided to stay together. She returned to the same lawyer, and this time filed papers. Martin retaliated and engaged a real snake in the grass to represent him. The term "amicable divorce" is an oxymoron, and there was nothing amicable here. Florida has different divorce laws from New York, and my case, though it seemed interminable, actually proceeded much more quickly than Al's. Of course it was stressful, anxiety-producing, and infuriating. I received a Demand for Production from Sharon's attorney which was insane, a boilerplate requirement that I produce every possible check, receipt, email, memorandum, insurance policy, financial document, bank statement, credit card bill, etc, etc, etc for the previous five years. The subpoena was so far-reaching and encompassing that it reminded me of a comedy bit by Robert Klein years ago, where he satirized record company ads offering "Every record ever recorded! Yes, folks, you heard me right. For a modest charge we will send you *every record ever recorded!*" Of course the point of the sketch was to be funny in its absurdity. But there was nothing funny to me about the demands to produce *everything ever*! A brief meeting with Edna and Phil (the accountant) whittled this impossible demand down to merely a Herculean labor. But I was up to the task, and for the next few weeks I devoted all my free time to amassing, compiling, collating, and analyzing all my financials for the previous few years. At least it was a project that consumed me, and kept me from thinking about all the other impossible demands Sharon was making. There may have been a silver lining after all!

And when I wasn't adequately distracted by this task, I chose a series of other initiatives to engage in. I survived the time away from Alana, alone in the womb, by designing projects to occupy my time: I caught up on reading, including everything written by F. Scott Fitzgerald, my favorite author; Hemingway; Steinbeck; all the fiction and non-fiction Pulitzer Prize winners, etc. I enrolled in a Florence Melton Jewish Studies program at a nearby temple, and made a new circle of friends. When I became especially tense and anxious, I would default to a strategy that always worked for me: I would clean with a vengeance!! Somehow cleaning was very cathartic for me, and a way to burn off nervous energy. I started exercising, began a running program, applied for the NYC marathon, everything I could think of to (productively) control the angst that is part and parcel of the legal divorce process. And it worked...a lot better than drugs or alcohol...

Divorce is a slippery slope and challenging path to navigate, to say the least. It drives otherwise sane people to insane, crazy behavior, otherwise calm and reasonable people to frenetic, irrational acts. I hoped initially that I could allow Edna, Phil, and Melissa (Phil's assistant and a whiz at crunching numbers), to handle the details and I would remain insulated on the sidelines until the end, when the deal was completed, my best possible settlement agreed upon, and nothing to do but sign the papers and ride off into the sunrise to begin my new life. More evidence of my naiveté! Of course it never works like that, of course I had to be involved every step of the way (regardless of how anxiety-producing and unpleasant immersion in this process needed to be), and there was no escape or avoidance of this unpleasantness. I did my best to accommodate Sharon's needs and requests (within reason and according to Edna's guidance). Sharon wanted me out of the house (although I had every legal right to stay there), and I was happy and relieved to accommodate her. Sharon wanted my personal possessions (clothing, books, files, etc.) out as well, so I tried to accommodate that too. I rented a storage space in Miami Lakes not far from the womb, and made several trips in my car to move out whatever I could. But apparently that wasn't good enough. Sharon demanded that I remove everything (that reminded her of me), and wouldn't take no for an answer, despite her having no legal grounds for such a stand. I told her I was in no position at that time to remove all my stuff, had a very small apartment, limited storage space, and no resources to make such a move. In addition, Edna advised me against it, and I was entitled to leave my things in my house (which I co-owned and continued to cover all the maintenance expenses of). But Sharon thought she was clever and decided to have her own way, come what may. So she packed up all my things into boxes (against her attorney's advice), and inveigled Jenn and Steve to be co-conspirators in her transparent plan to declare my guilt and her righteous indignation. She wanted to experience that iconic act of publicly throwing her cheating husband's possessions out the window onto the front lawn, for all the world to see and empathize with her plight at the hands of a detestable scoundrel. But since I no longer lived there, she modified this scenario by having Jenn and Steve carry these boxes of my things to the post office to mail to me, a symbol of her act of freedom and declaration that I no longer lived or belonged there, nor had any rights or involvement in her life anymore. Recruiting Jenn and Steve to be her allies in this endeavor implied their support as well. If such purging helped her I didn't mind. But what I did mind was a courier unexpectedly showing up at the womb with a series of large boxes which I had no room for. The following day the same courier appeared at my office, and paraded through my waiting room full of patients with more boxes, which I piled up wherever there was a vacant spot. Needless to say, this was quite a disruption for the patients and staff, and led to all sorts of rumors and gossip, since until then my personal life had always remained personal. Of course everybody got it. Thankfully, my staff was empathetic and loyal, and did their best to support me, sympathize, and help out. Of course this behavior on Sharon's part, meant purely to make life difficult and embarrassing for me, was unacceptable. Edna spoke to Sharon's attorney and that never happened again. That evening Jorge helped me move everything to the storage unit, and things returned to the normal baseline state of divorce insanity. The crazier and nastier Sharon acted, the more justified and settled I felt with my decision to leave her and move on. I took every punch, maintained my calm and equanimity as much as possible, and kept my eye on the prize. Nothing could bring me down on the road to Alana.

Once all the financial data had been accumulated (which I did mostly on my own to assure accuracy, hasten the process, and limit my accounting fees), the proceedings had a life of their own. The financials were straightforward and transparent, and there were no custody or child-support issues. Why such an uncomplicated divorce should take so long and cost so much was a mystery to me. Edna said there was a method to this madness, and, from a purely practical standpoint, the drawn-out and torturous process served to alienate the parties involved to such an extent that they inevitably came to peace with their decision, focused on getting it over and done with, and never looked back or second-guessed. Maybe she was right. Maybe she was trying to justify the enormous legal bills. In any event, I couldn't wait for it to be over. After nine months of motion after motion, and production of infinite paperwork (time-consuming as well as anxiety-provoking), we scheduled depositions, to be followed by mediation (a requirement under Florida law). The mediator (whose name, coincidentally, was Alana, which I interpreted as a very good sign!) was an amazing woman, a lawyer in her own right, experienced, sensible, and committed to facilitating the process, putting an end to the suffering, and making the system work. It was a crazy day, with me, Edna, Phil, and Melissa sitting in one room; Sharon, her attorney and accountant sitting in a room across the hall, and the mediator going back and forth, with one proposal after another, compromising on the contested issues, and searching for a mutually agreeable middle ground. As this circus was occurring, Edna was writing the Binding Mediation Agreement, incorporating each issue as it was decided upon. Lunch was brought in, then dinner, and we sat and sat and sat and sat (Prudence redux?) for eleven hours until finally there was nothing left to discuss. The assets, income, and lifestyle issues (the three-legged milkmaid's stool upon which every divorce rests) had been addressed, and the sun was setting, both over Miami and over my marriage. Dusk is a very peaceful time, that gentle transition between day and night. As we initialed the final agreement I felt truly at peace. And ultimately Edna was right—had there ever been any regrets, the process had put them to rest. I was at peace with my decision to end my marriage, with no second thoughts. It was done.

With the agreement finally signed by all, I wrote my last check for $35,000.00 to the parties involved (I'm still not clear why I was responsible for everybody's fees, including Sharon's attorney and accountants, but I was past questioning the process…To what end?). I was too tired and numb by that time to care about anything but ending this long ordeal, regardless of the cost. Finally, Edna and I took the elevator down together, and walked to our cars. I was reminded of that elevator ride I had taken a year earlier with Sandy. What a wild and crazy rollercoaster it had been since then! I stood by her car, helped her load the mountain of files she had brought with her, and we hugged.

"Congratulations," she said. "You made it."

"I know. Just as you told me I would. And you were my salvation. I can't thank you enough."

"You didn't do such a bad job yourself, kiddo" she smiled. "I'll send you the Final Agreement, and we'll have to go before the Judge to sign it. I'll apply for a date on the docket as soon as possible."

Edna got in her car and drove away with a wink and a wave. She had been one of the few points of light for me over the previous year. I would remember her often, and always warmly and fondly.

On October 6, 2011, I met Edna at the Broward County Courthouse to complete the process. All the specifics had been worked out during the mediation, and formalized with the Binding Mediation Agreement signed by me, Sharon, and both attorneys. Now we just needed the Court's final stamp and seal to conclude and end this phase of my life. "Let no man tear asunder" thankfully is superseded by the Court system. Sharon was there, too, and approached me with her final barbs. First she said, in her uniquely sarcastic and baiting fashion, "I'm so sorry to hear that you have cancer." *Cancer!! The C-word!!* Who uses *that* as an insult and weapon? I couldn't imagine where she got that idea. I had never felt healthier in my life! But it was just Sharon being Sharon, desperately searching for the most hurtful thing she could say. I got it, and simply replied that I didn't have cancer (much to her disappointment and dismay). She then threatened not to sign the papers unless I made certain additional concessions. Both attorneys would have none of that, and stopped Sharon's rant immediately. There would be no more threats, and insults, and bargaining. The Binding Mediation Agreement was binding, and Sharon had no further leverage. Her anger and fire were quickly extinguished by her attorney, who advised her that the deed was done, and not signing the agreement would only delay her receiving the settlement and funds already agreed to, and that she needed to survive. My support obligations had already ended, and there would be no more monthly checks or credit card payments coming from me. We agreed that I would have one more opportunity to come to the house and collect my remaining possessions, and then we would be free of each other with no further obligations, legal or otherwise. Sharon signed the papers as instructed, as did I, and Edna and I appeared before the judge as a formality to officially record the final divorce decree. As I prepared for "my day in court" I wondered if, when push came to shove and I sat down before the Judge, there would be any second thoughts, regrets, nostalgia, and sentiment at this absolute and final judgment, the end of a twenty-five-year commitment and a huge chapter in my life. But thanks to Sharon's earlier behavior, I was quickly reminded why it had come to this, and I left the courthouse feeling relieved, redeemed, and released.

As Edna and I walked from the Judge's chambers down the corridor we were directly behind Sharon and her attorney. I heard her talking, obviously loud enough for me to hear and for my benefit, that she was dating a doctor, an orthopaedist no less, and was very happy with her new friend. This was likely untrue, just Sharon still being Sharon, trying one last time to get under my skin. But it didn't work; she no longer had any power or influence over me. Strangely, and reassuringly, I had no ill will or bad feelings, and, though I questioned the truth of her staged remarks, I was glad (and hopeful) that she was moving on. Sandy and Edna had both been right: when you no longer care if your spouse is involved with someone else, you're ready to move on. And I was ready, willing, and able. I drove directly from the courthouse to the airport, to raise a glass with Alana and toast this momentous occasion.

The following day was Erev Yom Kippur, and I attended synagogue services with Al and Gladys. When my dad died I inherited his tallis, the same tallis he wore when I was a child and he and I went to temple together. I remember sitting by his side, not understanding a word of the service or the meaning behind it. But I sat next to my dad, who followed the service, spoke the Hebrew, and prayed along with the other congregants. I would finger the cloth and strings of his tallis, wondering what all this meant, but knowing that if my dad believed, it must be important. And so, as I grew up, I carried my dad's Judaism and faith and belief within me. Once he died I wore his tallis to temple, every High Holy Day, and when I wrapped it around my shoulders I felt embraced and encircled by his warm and loving hands and essence, and never felt closer to him and his spirit than I did then. His tallis bag still had his name printed on the inside, by his hand, and I often ran my fingers over his writing, and, in the Jewish tradition of "le dor va dor," felt the connection from one generation to the next. I knew that one day I would drape my dad's and Milton's tallit over the canopy Alana and I would stand under at our wedding, to bear witness before God and man of our vows to cleave to each other, as the Bible said.

    I remembered a year before, alone in the house with Shanee with the alarm bell ringing, my neighbors "tsk-tsk-ing," and feeling so alone in temple. Again I looked back over the previous year, analyzing my behavior, whom I had wronged and how to ask for forgiveness. The previous year, when I met with the rabbi to discuss granting Sharon a "Get" (a Jewish divorce), I had asked him for advice. How does one repent and be absolved for behavior such as mine? I never blamed Sharon for being the bitch that she was. She had issues and inadequacies that were beyond her control and that she would have to live with and sort out. That would no longer be my problem. But I did blame myself. I had agreed to marry her voluntarily; no one had put a gun to my head. I had taken marriage vows and had intended to keep them. Although I recognized the error of my ways very early on, still I had made a commitment, and, despite my unhappiness and discontentment, I felt obligated to be a man of my word. Isn't that what God intends us to be? Men of our word? How could I ask God for forgiveness, let alone Sharon and Jennifer, whom I had hurt badly as well? The rabbi counseled me in the teachings of the Torah, 5000+ years of ethical guidelines that had kept the Jewish faith alive and ticking despite all adversities, from without and within. God would forgive me if I recognized my wrongdoing, prayed for repentance, and performed good deeds and acts of charity. As far as Sharon and Jennifer were concerned, I had no control or clear path to securing their forgiveness. As with most ethical dilemmas, the rabbis over the generations have considered this problem and come to a practical solution. Ask the wronged party for forgiveness…once…twice…thrice. If there is still no acceptance of a sincere apology after three tries, then one is absolved of any further debt or obligation in this regard. Three attempts is enough, and worthy of being forgiven. My obligation would end there. One more thing, he told me, hand on my shoulder as I left his study: "The most important thing is to get to the point where you can forgive yourself. That is when you will be at peace." The rabbi was a very wise man.

Yom Kippur that year was a far more satisfying Holy Day. I looked back over the past year, and felt reassured that I had done my very best to treat Sharon fairly, and Jennifer lovingly and patiently. Despite the craziness of divorce, I had tried to take the high road, give Sharon every possible consideration, avoid unnecessary confrontation and further pain, and offer a legitimate and generous settlement. And through this process I had forgiven myself, and could move forward, hoping for a better year ahead, God willing. Maybe that's why I had an easy fast that year.

And the best was yet to come! In anticipation of my Emancipation Proclamation, Al and I had planned a celebratory trip to the most romantic place we could think of—ten glorious days in Paris. And the trip did not disappoint. It was our first real vacation together, and it felt very much like a honeymoon, a real new beginning, and a harbinger of wonderful things to come. Our first day we spent walking through the city of light and love, hand in hand, carefree for the first time in a very long time. We smelled the flowers, had *café au lait* at an outdoor café, and walked around the Arc de Triomphe, where a smiling young Parisian girl stopped us because she saw a wedding ring on the ground and thought it might be ours. It was likely a con (as she expected to be reimbursed for her "discovery"), but the moment and setting were so lovely and exhilarating that I didn't mind at all. Upon my return to New York I put that keepsake in my special place for memories, and still have it to this day, a wonderful memento of a glorious day overflowing with warmth, love, and fulfillment—at last.

Chapter 23

    Alana's process was far more tedious and lengthy than mine. Although the plan initially was for Martin to leave the house at the end of the previous summer, his attorney advised him to stay, "to protect (his) rights," whatever that meant. Despite the obvious tension, Martin seemed oblivious and immune, and actually resentful that Alana wanted out of the marriage and him out of the house. He had somehow convinced himself that he was the victim, rather than the perp, the driving force behind and the cause of this failed marriage. He postponed his exit until Christmas, then until Easter, then until Pierce completed his senior year, then until Pierce went off to college, and finally insisted on staying until the divorce was final. His attorney was clearly an obstructionist, employing every delaying tactic imaginable, likely to increase his billable hours. Martin never questioned anything, and, on the rare occasions Alana implored him to get it done already and stop wasting time, he blamed his attorney and insisted he had no responsibility in the matter (typical Martin). Alana and Martin together took Pierce to Indiana University for orientation and to help him get settled. Things were awkward, but Al was already so accustomed to ignoring Martin and treating him as a nonentity that she endured the trip fairly well.

    With Pierce now out of the house, there was no ostensible reason for Martin to remain. But every time Alana suggested he leave, he dug his heels in even deeper, became more belligerent, and insisted he was entitled to stay. So things remained the same. Al and I continued to rendezvous at local hotels, where I stayed when I came to visit, which was now nearly every weekend.

    Al was as frustrated as I was. My divorce was long over, and she couldn't even find peace and quiet in her own home. Divorce is painful enough, but to continue to have your soon-to-be ex-spouse in your face all the time magnifies the situation 1000-fold. In addition, she couldn't bring me in to her life and community. Her friends all knew what was happening, but it was difficult to build new relationships when Martin remained ever-present and a constant thorn in her side. They managed to avoid each other at home as much as possible, but in the evening they often ended up in the TV room, sitting silently at opposite ends of the couch, but together nonetheless.

One Saturday night when I was on-call for my practice and unable to visit for the weekend, Al and Martin were both at home. Al tried once again to convince Martin that he had nothing to lose by moving out: she wouldn't hold it against him or use it to her legal advantage in any way. Their remaining in such close quarters was torture and unfair to her, she said, and potentially a very volatile situation. She was clearly at the end of her rope and her frustration was reaching a breaking point. Martin, in his own infuriating way, remained unperturbed and unmoved.

In the midst of one more such painful, seemingly endless and futile conversation (more monologue than dialogue), suddenly, seemingly out of nowhere, Martin struck out with his arm and hit Al directly on her forehead. She recoiled and nearly fell backward onto the glass coffee table, but caught herself just in time. Martin resumed his passive pose, as though nothing had happened. Still reeling and feeling nauseated and dizzy, Al went to her room and locked the door. Now she was a little afraid. Suppose he came to strike her again? This was out of character for Martin, but maybe beneath that shell of apathy he too was feeling the strain. How could he not?

Al called; I was shocked, and worried. I told her to leave the house, stay across the street with her mom, or with a friend. She should call the police, file a domestic violence charge against Martin, and force him out of the house since he wouldn't go willingly. She could no longer stay there!

But Al is strong and tough. She said she'd be okay and just wanted to lie down and go to sleep. That was even more worrisome to me! But she insisted she'd be fine, and would deal with it in the morning. Martin must have realized that he had crossed the line this time—he left the house and didn't return all night, not a call, text, or email, with nary a care or concern (except apparently for himself; how typical!).

We spoke again in the early a.m. This time Al sounded even worse, a little confused and disoriented, and she had vomited—all signs of a concussion. Her friend Judy took her to the hospital, where she was seen in the Emergency Room. A CT scan of her head was performed which showed swelling and edema, a clear indication of a concussion, *and incidentally a four centimeter tumor*. A neurologist and neurosurgeon were called in for consultation, and Al was considered stable enough to be discharged home with instructions to rest and follow-up with a specialist.

Of course the *incidental* finding of a brain tumor was far more alarming than the concussion. Al called me immediately and I arranged to fly to New York. Whatever it was we would take care of it and get through it together. Now the divorce and all its messiness seemed inconsequential. We had a real emergency on our hands.

When I got to New York, I rented a car and called Al from the airport. She said that after the events of the previous evening, Martin had spoken with his attorney and moved out that morning. They were concerned Al would press charges and Martin would be arrested and lose his medical license. Exactly what he deserved, that piece of crap! All I knew was that Al needed help, and I was on my way. I drove to her house, and there was not a sign of Martin. I dreaded to see what she would look like—would she be black and blue? Would her eyes be bloodshot and swollen? Would she be coherent? A concussion and a brain tumor—my God!

Judy let me into the house. The fire in her eyes mirrored my own. How could anyone do this to our dearest friend? We instinctively knew what each other was thinking, and words weren't necessary.

"How's Al?" I asked.

"She's in bed resting. She might be asleep."

I went to the bedroom and carefully opened the door so as not to wake her. She had an icepack on her forehead and eyes. She seemed to be asleep, but then lifted off the ice and saw me. She looked tired, her eyes were puffy, black and blue, her nose was stuffed, but otherwise she was okay.

"Hi, Brett," she said. "I must look a sight."

"You look as beautiful as ever."

"Oh, sure. But thanks for saying that."

"You know you always look beautiful to me. How are you feeling?"

"Okay. A little tired and congested, and I have a headache."

"Do you feel like talking? If not, I can just sit here while you try to get some sleep."

"No, that's okay. I can talk."

"Do you remember what happened last night?" (retrograde amnesia is a cardinal sign of concussion.)

"Vaguely."

"Do you want to talk about it?"

"No, not really."

I sat quietly, not knowing what to say, hating that Al was in pain, and homicidal that someone had done this to her. Of course the brain tumor was the real worry. Just when the drama and insanity of the past few years seemed to be over, a new and much bigger problem had reared its ugly head. Illness always seems to put things in perspective very quickly; I used to tell my patients who were moaning and bitching and complaining about one seemingly trivial thing after another that at least neither they nor their loved ones had a terminal illness. A short walk through a children's cancer ward is a gut check we all could use sometimes when we lose sight of what's important. Maybe this is God's way of reminding us that we're all a heartbeat away from myocardial infarction; a single random cell mutation away from lung cancer, breast cancer, or some other horrible disease; a single on-call assignment away from a seat on an airplane plummeting to the ground in a snowstorm; a moment away from an out-of-control car being struck by an oil tanker killing everyone involved. Life hangs by a thread, and the arrogance of hubris and self-satisfaction evaporates in a flash with a single slap from God. Man plans and God laughs. How true. My "big picture" and game plan included a lot of things, but not this. Now all the energy I devoted to reinventing myself, my life, my present and future with Al, needed to be recalled, re-energized, and rechanneled into a new initiative—saving Alana's life. With God's help I'd be up to the task.

Al drifted off to sleep…and I prayed.

Chapter 24

Judy was the first of Alana's friends whom I had met, and who welcomed me into her world. Alana had many colleagues and acquaintances, knew virtually everyone in the medical community, and, with a twenty-year history of patient care, she knew and was known by hundreds if not thousands of townsfolk. Each patient had a nuclear family, and an extended family, and they all got to know Al during their time of crisis. Not a day went by when she wasn't stopped on the street, or approached in a restaurant, by an old patient who owed her life to Al. Unlike many physicians, and most surgeons, Al emanated a warmth and compassion that served her patients well. I daresay they loved her, not just for saving their lives, but for truly caring and giving, beyond the call of duty, going the extra mile. That's the difference between a doctor and a true healer. Al's circle of intimates was small, no more than a dozen people, all of whom felt honored and privileged and proud to call her friend. She knew that to have a good friend you need to *be* a good friend, and she extended herself without hesitation or limitation to every one of them. Al's friends of course knew Martin, and accepted him, though to a person never understood that coupling. Martin seemed to be a good solid citizen (little did they know!), but he seemed out-of-touch with Al, Pierce, and her friends. Clearly their hearts and allegiances rested with Al, and when they learned of Martin's infidelity and Alana's betrayal and suffering, most sided with their best friend. As Al's ally and person, I was naturally accepted, indeed embraced, in their circle. I had been so grateful to find everyone so welcoming. I knew it wasn't because of me, but rather because of Al and their desire to be there for her in her time of need and to support her, as they knew she would support them were the roles reversed.

In a small community word travels fast, and by the end of the day it seemed like everyone knew the events of the night before. Al was a well-known figure at the hospital and in the emergency room. Despite the increasing emphasis on patient privacy, confidentiality, and HIPAA regulations, everyone seemed to know everything. One person shares a "secret" with a confidant, who then shares it with another, and before long it's not a secret anymore. The idea of a beloved friend and coworker being beaten to the point of concussion resonated with Al's network, and they all wanted to help. The support Al was receiving from her people was amazing and totally deserved. Judy did a good job of buffering us from the well-meaning nearly non-stop calls of everyone who considered Al her best friend, and that was a big club of people. Al drifted in and out of sleep as her community rallied round her.

That Sunday was one of the longest days of my life. I stayed in the bedroom, watching Al for any signs of neurologic deterioration that could indicate a brain hemorrhage and require emergency surgery. I woke her every hour to assess her mental status: Was she oriented? Did she know where she was, what day it was, who I was, who she was? How was her memory? How bad was her headache? Was she feeling worse or better? After a while she became annoyed at these constant awakenings, a good sign because she knew what was happening, and knew enough to understand why I was doing what I was doing. But it would be quite some time before we were out of the woods.

Al had no appetite and all she wanted to do was sleep. The madness of the night before, the physical trauma, and likely the psychological trauma all contributed to her desire to escape through sleep. Each time I woke her she was startled, suddenly stiffened as though in a spasm, seemed momentarily terrified until she got her bearings; she had crazy dreams of being lost in an entirely unfamiliar place, running from something she knew not what and to something she couldn't visualize, being chased with no end in sight—a metaphor of her world the past few years. She had no appetite but I convinced her to eat something, and Judy made some soup, which Al reluctantly ate between bouts of fitful sleep. Finally, as evening approached she seemed to be settling down; her sleep was more restful, her breathing less labored, she seemed to have found some inner peace (at least that was my interpretation). Judy offered to stay, but there was no need for that. She ran the Women's Center at the hospital (where Alana's breast cancer patients were diagnosed), and had a full schedule the next day. Her patients needed her more than Al and I did at that point, so she gently kissed my sleeping beauty on the cheek without waking her, and left.

"Call me if there are any changes overnight, and first thing in the morning, no matter what!" were her parting words. And I knew she meant them. Like Al, Judy is a take-charge person, sometimes a little aggressive and abrasive on the surface, but with a heart of gold. We were lucky to have her on our team, along with a host of other supporters and friends. To allow Al some peace and quiet, I turned the phone ringer off, and figured I would return messages the next day. I appreciated the concern but needed to focus on what to do next. I lay awake next to Al all night in the semi-darkened bedroom, watching her, looking for any signs of distress. Fortunately there were none. Despite my best efforts to stay up, I drifted off a few times until the sun rose and it was a new day. The first twenty-four hours after a concussion are always the most critical, and Al had passed that milestone. Hopefully there would be no new surprises.

Needless to say, Al didn't go to work in the morning. She knew a neurosurgeon nearby, and we made an emergency appointment to see him, to assess her post-concussion syndrome as well as to review the CT scan and discuss the worrisome lemon-sized mass that didn't belong. Al was by no means herself, but better than the day before, and we met Dr. Insalata in the late morning. He performed a brief directed neurological exam, short but thorough enough to dismiss an acute emergency from the head trauma.

"The fog will take a few days to lift," he assured us. "The headaches may last longer but should eventually resolve. I expect a complete recovery." At least one bullet dodged, I thought.

"Of course now we come to the trickier part," he continued, as I knew he would. "The good news is that the tumor is almost certainly benign, a meningioma, which is not necessarily common, but not rare either. It's not malignant, it's not going to metastasize, nor will it grow and expand rapidly. It's undoubtedly been there for quite some time.

Have you had any symptoms, prior to the concussion? Any mental or physical changes you can think of?" he inquired intently.

"None that I know of," Al answered. "I have noticed some word-finding problems these past few months, but thought they were part of the normal aging process."

"Any changes in vision, or sense of smell?"

"No, not that I'm aware of."

"The tumor is in a typical location, in the midline near the front of the brain where the higher cortical powers reside, as well as the olfactory center. Sometimes patients with a mass in this location report either a loss of smell, or even bizarre smells unrelated to anything in the environment. Have anything like that?"

"No, not really."

"In any event, a mass of this size needs to be removed. Otherwise, even though it's slow-growing, eventually it will crowd the vital structures in the area and cause neurological damage. It's great that you haven't noticed any changes, and I find no localizing signs on your examination. But it still needs to come out before any irreversible damage occurs."

"Okay. So how is that done? Through the nose or by craniotomy?"

"We can't really get to it via a nasal route, so craniotomy is the only option. We'll make an incision behind your hairline over the top like this," he said, as he indicated with his index finger a line stretching nearly from ear to ear. I was beginning to feel a little sick at the thought, but needed to be strong, matter-of-fact, and completely optimistic and positive for Al.

"Will you have to shave my head?" Al asked. Al had always had a gorgeous, full head of thick, naturally blond hair, and, though not vain, she prided herself on her appearance and good looks. She was by no means shallow, but she always enjoyed being beautiful, though she would never admit it. Her patients undergoing chemotherapy all lost their hair, so she was no stranger to a bald female scalp. It's no shame to be bald, but it's no great honor either!

"No, not your whole head. Just a thin line where we make the incision. Once it heals it will be barely noticeable."

This was somewhat reassuring, but the entire encounter seemed surreal at best, nightmarish at worst.

"You'll stay in the Neuro ICU for a few days after surgery and should be going home in less than a week. I know this is a lot to take in, but I'm confident things will work out fine."

Dr. Insalata was reassuring but the whole thing was scary, even to two surgeons who had spent their entire careers cutting people open, looking around, inserting and removing things. I liked Dr. Insalata and his positive outlook. I always approached my patients the same way, accentuating the positive, without ignoring the fact that bad things can happen whenever anyone approaches you with a sharp object in their hand. In orthopedics we cite the "rule of thirds": for elective surgery, generally speaking, a third of the patients get better, a third stay the same, and a third get worse. For this reason I was very conservative about my surgical indications, and advised my patients to act accordingly. But this wasn't orthopedics or elective surgery. As with Alana's breast cancer patients, this operation had to get done, despite the risks. With Al's meningioma, it seemed that the benefits of timely removal outweighed the risks of waiting. This was not a diagnostic dilemma, nor a treatment dilemma. Though it was hard to get our arms around the thought of cutting open the skull and removing part of the brain, still it seemed to be the only choice, and we'd have to deal with it, as scary and distasteful as it was.

"This is a lot to absorb, and I'd like to think about it for a day or two before scheduling the surgery, if that's alright," Al said.

"Of course. No problem. There's no great rush. But I wouldn't wait too long. Let me know when you've made a decision."

"Thanks so much for seeing me on such short notice. I'll be in touch."

We left the office walking through a waiting room of patients with God-knows-what horrific problems. Now we had a decision to make.

Chapter 25

There was very little conversation as we walked to the car. We were both overwhelmed. We knew we had no real choice, but weren't prepared to say, "Let's go." Dr. Insalata enjoyed an excellent reputation and we had no reason to doubt his clinical acumen or surgical skills. But a craniotomy!! Wow…

"I like and trust Sal, but think we should get a second opinion," Al said as we drove home.

"I couldn't agree more. Time is on our side to a certain extent. But we need to get moving on this."

"Yes, I know." At that moment, miraculously, of necessity, we made the phase shift from scared, helpless, victimized patients to take-charge, get 'er done, self-advocates. We had spent our lives giving medical advice to those in need. Now *we* were in need and we needed that same skill set to help ourselves. Al called her medical partner's sister, who held a high executive position in a local healthcare system. If anyone knew the best doctors in New York it would be her. She referred Al to a neurosurgeon at Columbia-Presbyterian, and got us an appointment for the next day. That evening was quiet and somber. Friends called and wanted to come over to help, but it wasn't the right time. Al needed rest, and we both needed time to just be alone together and come to terms with this bizarre and shocking turn of events. Our immediate focus was to decide upon a course of action. Everything else would have to wait, for now.

The following day we drove into Manhattan to Columbia-Presbyterian Hospital to see Dr. Matthew Trippi. Most of my patients Googled me before their appointments to check my credentials. We felt no need to vet Dr. Trippi. We trusted our referral source, and the institution. He wouldn't be doing what he was doing, where he was doing it, if he weren't at the top of his field. We were really only seeing him as a matter of course, for a second opinion to confirm Dr.

Insalata's diagnosis, prognosis, and treatment plan before scheduling surgery. Our appointment was in the early afternoon, and the waiting room was nearly empty.

After completing and handing in the standard forms and paperwork, we sat and waited. We were quite early and were prepared for a long wait, as per usual in most doctors' offices. What a surprise when a smiling middle-aged man in a long white coat entered, approached Alana, came over to introduce himself and shake our hands, and personally ushered us into his study! It was tastefully appointed, with a large desk and two comfortable chairs. After discussing her medical history, and answering a few questions, Al gave Dr. Trippi the CT scan and we waited for his opinion. We didn't want to influence his assessment so didn't mention right away that we had seen Dr. Insalata and share his thoughts. Dr. Trippi reviewed the scan on his desktop computer, and I scrutinized his every move and expression to try to read his mind. Was he surprised in any way? Dismayed? Had he seen this a thousand times before and this was another routine case with an expected excellent outcome, as Dr. Insalata had said? Or was there something unforeseen here, perhaps that Dr. Insalata had missed? Would he be as optimistic and confident that all would be well? We didn't have long to wait. It only took a few minutes, Dr. Trippi looked up at Al, and we heard the words we were hoping to hear.

"You have a benign brain tumor called a meningioma that grows from the membrane that surrounds the brain. It's not uncommon, and you should make a complete recovery. I have treated several thousand of these in my practice. We have a protocol here at Presbyterian, including a gamma knife program that I run. But your tumor is too big for gamma knife treatment at this stage. Let me emphasize that it's a benign tumor with near uniformly good surgical outcomes, but it has to be removed."

He waited a few seconds for this to sink in, then, anticipating our questions (which he'd undoubtedly heard a few thousand times before), he continued.

"The only way to approach and fully and safely resect the tumor is through a craniotomy. The tumor is midline but appears slightly bigger on the right, so we'll probably do most of the work from that side and visualize the other side to remove what's there as well. The olfactory nerve is the structure most at risk, and you may lose your sense of smell for some time; but that should eventually return, hopefully within a year. It is unlikely the tumor will recur, but if it does, with adequate follow-up, primarily MRI scans, we can deal with small recurrences at an early stage with gamma knife radiation, and further open surgery won't ever be needed again."

Dr. Trippi's manner, compassion, and clear confidence borne of experience bolstered by likely excellent results were quite something. I liked Dr. Insalata but Dr. Trippi seemed to be a cut above. His matter-of-fact explanation and reassurance washed away any doubts, not only about what should be done but who should be doing it.

"Do you have any questions or other concerns?"

"No, Dr. Trippi. I think I understand. Just to be perfectly honest I did see Dr. Insalata at University Hospital yesterday, and am here for a second opinion. His recommendations were very similar to yours. I do have one question, even if it sounds stupid."

"There are no such things as stupid questions from patients, only stupid answers from doctors. Shoot."

"Well, I know this is silly, but would you have to shave my hair?"

"Actually, no. I part your hair directly over the incision, and tape it down to isolate it from the field. There would be no shaving necessary. I would use a small metal plate to fix the osteotomy. I find it aids in the healing and post-op pain. The plate never has to be removed, is made of titanium, and won't set off any metal detectors. I also place a great premium on the post-op dressing. I stay with you in the OR after the actual surgery is done and apply the head dressing myself. It's quite snug and molded over the incision, scalp, and forehead for compression and to minimize swelling. Some patients find it uncomfortable but I've found it makes a big difference in minimizing the scar. The dressing stays on for three days, then I remove it, and no further dressing is needed. You can shower at that time, but we advise not to scrub or wash your hair for a few more days after that. We keep our patients in the ICU for twenty-four hours, where they can be monitored by the nurses, who are really expert and excellent. We have an MRI scanner right in the ICU so if for any reason we need to do a post-op scan you don't have to be transported to Radiology but can have it done right there.

"When you leave the ICU you'll go to the Neuro floor. We have a special private ward which is really gorgeous, all private rooms, overlooking the Hudson River and George Washington Bridge. When I had surgery that's where I stayed, and it's amazing. Even the food is good, although you likely won't have much of an appetite during your hospital stay. Any other questions?"

Al and I looked at each other. Words again were unnecessary. Dr. Trippi was the man for the job.

"No, thank you. You've been very thorough. What's the next step?"

"Speak to Patricia at the desk. She'll give you all your instructions. There's no great rush but I'm going out of town for the Christmas break so either before or after then."

"Thank you so much, Dr. Trippi. We'll be in touch."

So there it was. Now the path was clear. We left the office feeling way better than before. We even spoke jokingly and played music on the long ride home stuck in NYC rush-hour traffic.

"Okay, then. Check your schedule and let's pick a date."

"Yes. I'm pretty busy until Christmas. I also have to tell Pierce, and think he'll want to be here for the surgery. Maybe the first week in January, before he goes back to school."

"Sounds good to me." It was somewhat comforting and settling to have a definite plan. Al was okay for the time being, and, hopefully, would be fine afterwards. But, wow, brain surgery!!

"At least they don't have to shave my head," she said, smiling for the first time in days.

Vanity, thy name is woman, I thought, although I would never have said it out loud. I would figure something out with my partners to take several weeks off from work after the New Year to be at the hospital and at Al's house to help her recover. "We'll get through this and it will be fine," I repeated over and over in my mind, a recapitulation of the same mantra I'd had for the past year and a half.

Chapter 26

Al decided not to tell Pierce anything until he came home for Thanksgiving break. This wasn't the kind of news you want to give over the phone. Pierce likely would have a lot of questions and concerns that could only be addressed face-to-face. In addition Pierce and I still hadn't met. Of course he knew who I was, but only in the abstract. I doubt he knew, or even imagined, that his mom and I had an intimate relationship. No child ever suspects that his parents are sexually involved, let alone his mom with a stranger! Al and I both knew how delicate a situation this was, and delicacy and diplomacy were essential to give Pierce the time and space to accept another person into his and his mom's life. We expected that, despite everything he knew, Pierce still maintained an allegiance to his dad and his parental unit, and I certainly didn't want to threaten that in any way. Pierce had to come first, and the burden was on me to figure out how to be an added plus in his life, rather than an undesirable stranger infringing on his mom, his house, and the life he knew.

Of course I had kept tabs on Pierce from afar since the very beginning, albeit behind the scenes. When he applied to college I was the one who wrote his application essays. When he applied to business school, I drafted his petition. When he needed help as a freshman, I took time between patients to review and criticize his essays, we spoke on the phone a few times about his studies, and he was aware of my shadowy presence. He was smart and astute enough not to look this gift horse in the mouth. So I wasn't entirely a stranger or an unknown entity, though not yet an active player in his life.

This Thanksgiving was supposed to be the right time for an introduction. Of course I wouldn't sleep with Al, or even stay in the house. But I would be part of the Thanksgiving dinner. Al, being the excellent cook and hostess with the mostest (and the moistest!), always made Thanksgiving dinner for her relatives, and this year would be no different. But it would be very different with me there, and I hoped Pierce would be accepting. Since I didn't know Pierce at all except for what Alana told me, I was prepared for anything; I hoped for the best but expected the worst. I wanted so badly to make this work. Al knew how nervous I was, and told me just to be myself—the warm, friendly, loving guy I am—and Pierce would react in kind. Pierce was very perceptive, didn't suffer fools gladly, and had no appetite for being conned. He would have to draw his own conclusions, and all I could do was avoid kissing up to him, and just act naturally. Gladys' words from long ago echoed in my mind: Things usually have a way of working themselves out. So I came to the house on Thanksgiving morning feeling anything but comfortable but glad to be taking the next step, a necessary step if I wanted to be Al's partner.

Thanksgiving has always been my favorite holiday: food, family, and football. The very idea of Thanksgiving, taking time to recognize and be grateful for the blessings in our life, appealed to me as well. What could be better! Like Passover, with the added attraction of *football*!! I usually entered Al's house through the garage and back door; but that day I decided to ring the front doorbell, like any other guest, so Pierce wouldn't think I was too forward or familiar in his house. Of course Al had prepared him for my being there, and he didn't object. As I learned over time, Pierce is usually quite tight-lipped about things (very much like his mother!), and often keeps his feelings to himself. I thought he might answer the door, but it was Alana with a big smile, and hello, and I entered to the very familiar smells of turkey, stuffing, yams, etc. I knew there would be a culinary treat in store.

I looked around the front hall. Al read my mind and said, "The boy isn't home. He's at his friend Jack's house across the street, and will be back in a little while."

I came in and took off my coat. The dining room was set beautifully. None of the other guests had arrived—just me and Al, as usual.

"So how are you feeling?"

"Good. Busy."

"How's Pierce?"

"Fine."

"Did you talk to him about the surgery?"

"No, not yet. He just got home yesterday. I wanted to find the right moment, when we're alone and he can ask all his questions."

"Good idea. Would you like me to be there as well?"

"No, I don't think that's appropriate. He doesn't know you at all, and this is too personal a discussion for someone he doesn't know to be there."

"Okay. Whatever you want. You've got the best instinct as to how to tell him in a reassuring way. If he wants to ask me any questions privately, or pick my brain as a surgeon, tell him to feel free."

"Yes, I will."

Pierce came home shortly thereafter. He had run across the street barefoot and in his bathrobe (it was thirty-five degrees outside), and that's how we met. I was in the kitchen with Al trying to stay out of her way as she fixed the turkey and trimmings, and in through the garage burst Pierce. Of course I had seen pictures of him, and he had seen a video of me doing a commercial for a medical pharmaceutical company I worked with. Alana stopped what she was doing and introduced us (as if that were necessary!). Pierce walked right up to me, put out his hand, and looked me straight in the eye. "Hi. How's it going?" he asked. It must have been extremely awkward for him, but he didn't show it. I'm usually a pretty good judge of character, and sensed an outward, crusty machismo superimposed on a soft, inner filling—the proverbial riddle wrapped in a mystery within an enigma. He'd had to do a whole lot of growing up fast these past several years, and he did what he had to do. He wanted to like me for his mom's sake; she wanted him to like me, and I wanted him to like me. So we were all on the same page. I didn't expect any more than a brief handshake, but he gave me more. He started talking and engaging me. He knew I lived in Florida, and asked how my trip was, where I was staying, how long I'd be there. He asked a lot of appropriate questions, wanting to know more about this new person, clearly someone important in his mom's life, and likely in his as well. We only spoke for a few minutes but it was a good start, an ice-breaker that made the rest of the day much more comfortable. He went right into the TV room, and put on the first football game of the day. I stayed in the kitchen to help Al, but she silently motioned that I should join Pierce (I was always glad for any excuse to get out of the kitchen), so of course I did. We didn't have all that much to say to each other right then, but we talked about the Giants (both of us big fans), the NFL commissioner Roger Goodell (both of us big haters), college football (both of us big fans, although with different allegiances, he for IU, I for the Gators), and guy stuff like that. I was much more nervous than he, but it seemed like an auspicious beginning. I knew that if Pierce didn't accept (and hopefully eventually embrace) me, my future with Alana was doomed. And I also knew that there was only so much I could do. It was a fine line between extending the hand of friendship and appearing overly eager or obsequious (which would have been a disaster). I tried hard to put myself in his shoes and imagine how I would have wanted someone to be or behave had my parents gotten divorced and a new man started dating my mother. But I couldn't even imagine that. I had no experience with this, or guidance, or frame of reference. So I made a concerted effort to remain restrained, and somewhat peripheral, which seemed appropriate at the time. When we sat down for dinner I made sure not to sit at the head of the table. That was not my place, to sit in Martin's chair. The symbolism of my replacing his dad in his house and in his mother's life was too obvious and would have invited pushback and resentment, the last things I wanted. So Pierce took his dad's old seat as the new man of the house. That seemed right.

The rest of Alana's family arrived. Gladys came first, and I felt relieved to have another clear ally. Gladys kvelled over Pierce, very much as Alana did, and knew how important it was that Pierce accept, not resent me. Gladys and Pierce were very close, and always have been. He spent a lot of time growing up in her house across the street, when Alana and Martin were at work late or on weekends. Pierce, too, cared deeply about his grandma, and seeing her and me getting along so well and familiarly was important. Pierce knew something about my past history with his mom, but not too much. He wasn't ready to know our story then (or read this book) and he likely had some questions about how I seemed to know so much about his mom, her childhood, her parents, etc. With time, when he was ready, he would learn more. Alana and Gladys made sure to include me in all the conversations, to show Pierce I was friend not foe.

When everyone had left, Pierce took off to see his old high school friends. He made a point to say goodbye to me, and "nice to meet you." We shook hands again, this time a little longer and firmer than earlier (or maybe that was just my imagination and positive spin?). In any event, once he had left, Alana and Gladys both voiced their approval of this first meeting. I was happy, too, and invested my energy in cleaning up (one of my specialties). Not a word had been said about the upcoming surgery—a conversation for another day.

Chapter 27

I returned to the Melville Marriott (my home away from home) feeling very satisfied that the day had gone well—mission accomplished. I had met Pierce and I believed that his first impression of me had been favorable, a great start, something to build on. I knew I was in a tenuous position as far as he was concerned, and it would be natural for him to keep his distance. I was an outsider invading his space and his mom—what kid wants that? But, as I learned to know and appreciate increasingly over the years, Pierce was not just any kid; he was Alana's kid, a special kid, wise beyond his years and appearance. He loved his mom, was confused by his dad, and was just trying to figure it out. In the midst of my smugness I figuratively slapped myself and came down to earth: today wasn't about me, it was about Pierce, about introducing myself to someone who would become very important in my life, and to whom I hoped to one day be very important. I first met Jennifer when she was eighteen months old, and I adopted her (or she adopted me) when she was twenty-one. I didn't expect Pierce to adopt me (not literally, anyway), but I hoped we could be good friends, if not more. It was my job (with Alana's and Gladys' help) to make that happen, and I would do my darndest. I was impressed by Pierce's seeming acceptance of the new normal and my place in his life. I could only hope that when the time came Jennifer would be as accepting of Alana. But that too was out of my control.

The following day Alana spent with Pierce—Black Friday, time to shop and buy him Christmas gifts, new clothes, whatever he needed. I didn't see Al that day, but we spoke several times. She tried not to sneak behind Pierce's back, and she let him know when she was texting, emailing, or phoning me. She was attentive to his needs, and would not let anything interfere with their mommy-and-me time together. It was a day for quality time with her son, and Al intended to make the most of it.

That evening Al sat down with Pierce to talk brain tumor. He listened quietly, thoughtfully, seeming to appreciate the gravity of the situation. Al said she planned to have the surgery after New Year, before Pierce went back to school. Pierce had just one question: "What are you waiting for? You don't need me there. Have it done as soon as possible. I'd like to be there but it's more important to get it over with, get it out of your brain. Don't wait for me."

From the mouths of babes…Of course he was right. Al agreed, and that was that.

I came to the house again on Saturday. I wanted to give Al and Pierce uninterrupted quality time together, now more than ever. They both needed that. We went out for dinner on Saturday, just the three of us. Alana and Pierce are both foodies, and appreciate fine cuisine. We went to Piccolo, which has since become my favorite local Italian restaurant. Pierce seemed to be a regular, and knew the menu forwards and backwards before we even sat down. Italian food is comfort food, with the warm red sauces, meat dishes, and filling pasta. We broke (garlic) bread together, ate copious quantities, and drank. The undercurrent of tension (at my being there, at Al's impending surgery) gradually dissipated with each passing glass of wine. By the end of the meal we were laughing and sharing, like a family in gestation. There was a certain inexplicable ease with which Al and I related, borne of history, familiarity, and true caring for each other. I think Pierce appreciated that, something that had been absent from Al and Martin's relationship. After dinner we went back to the house, and I made an early exit to allow Al and Pierce as much time together as possible before Pierce left for school the following day.

Late that evening, as per our accustomed bedtime phone call, we talked about the day and the weekend. Alana didn't want to put Pierce on the spot and ask him how he felt about me, but he volunteered that I seemed like a good guy. Coming from Pierce that was high praise, and we left it at that. It was decided that the surgery would be as soon as possible, now that Pierce was on board. Al would call Dr. Trippi on Monday.

The next day I came over for breakfast before Al took Pierce to the airport. Before he left, I took Pierce aside, told him I understood how scary this must be for him, as it was for me, that I would stay on top of the situation every second and keep him in the loop...I would call him as soon as the operation was over, call him every day from the hospital, and he could and should call me with any questions or concerns. I knew that he would need caring and attention, and I would be his go-to person. It was the start of a beautiful friendship.

As planned, the surgery was scheduled for the following week. I took off the rest of the month from my practice, and returned to New York the day before the procedure. At 5 a.m. Al, Gladys, and I left for Columbia-Presbyterian. A calm descended on us as we drove towards we knew not what. There was no doubt this had to be done, and there was no doubt we were in the right place with the right surgeon. Despite the reassurances we had received that everything would be fine, we knew what lay ahead (generally speaking), and that anything can happen. As is my wont, I tried to find the silver lining: Al would not only fully recover but would be better than ever with the tumor out. Who knew what symptoms had gradually developed over the years as this tumor grew, symptoms she likely wasn't even aware of given the slow growth and long time span? The word-finding problems would be gone, her mind sharper than ever, her senses more acute than ever. Of course there were "no guarantees," and those words haunted me.

We checked in at the hospital, went to the pre-op holding area, and before I knew it Al was being led away. Gladys and I sat there, looking at the bay where the stretcher with our girl had just been, knowing that now it was in God's (and Dr. Trippi's) hands. We went to the chapel and asked God to watch over Alana and Dr. Trippi, then to the waiting area to begin the agonizing ordeal of waiting. I felt like I held my breath for hour after hour. Of course we weren't alone, everyone sharing the same agony. The orthodox Jews read from the Old Testament as they rhythmically rocked and swayed, calling upon their deep-rooted faith and generations of believers to get them through. The Catholics read from the New Testament and fingered their rosary beads. Gladys and I prayed silently, counting the minutes.

The woman sitting next to us spoke in Hebrew with her family. Hospital waiting rooms breed connections among strangers sharing the same overwhelming concerns. She told us her husband was having his fifth brain surgery for a malignant tumor that would never be cured, but at best be held in check for now, until the next time. She didn't use the words "no hope," although it was obvious she'd be back here again, praying again, if not for a cure but for a stay of execution. We felt uncomfortable sharing our "good" news that our loved one merely had a benign brain tumor that required cracking open her skull for removal—no big deal, right?

Al's friends and coworkers called repeatedly to check on her progress, and it was a relief to have some diversion from the eerie silence of the people in prayer. I texted Pierce every two hours to connect and advise him that his mom was still in surgery, and "no news is good news" in this situation. All we could do was sit and hope, just like everyone else there. The wait seemed endless. Finally we asked the nurse to check with the OR, and we were told that everything was as expected, although the surgery hadn't started until two hours after we thought. So the waiting game continued.

Every time the door opened we looked up, as did everyone else, hoping it was our surgeon with good news. One after another of our fellow congregants spoke to their doctors, and gradually the waiting room emptied. It was nearly 6 p.m. before Dr. Trippi arrived.

He seemed as cool, calm, and collected as one would want their surgeon to be. He already had his street clothes on, having changed out of his surgical scrubs, meaning to me that the surgery had been completed some time ago. Having met anxious family members thousands of times before, he understand our unasked questions and concerns, smiled, and said everything went well, as expected; there were no problems, no complications. Sweeter words were never spoken. "And the tumor?" I asked. Woody Allen famously said that in the past the most important words in the English language were "I love you," to be replaced in modern times with the words "It's benign." And those were the words we heard. He seemed unrushed (even though he had already spent ten hours in the operating room working on Al's brain!), and sat down next to Gladys. As he spoke in his usual steady, reassuring voice, he took her hands in his, and looked directly in her eyes. "Your daughter's fine. She's already in the Neurosurgical

ICU on the 9th floor, and you can go up to see her now." I wanted to kiss him, but settled for a handshake and a soft "Thank you."

I called Pierce and we spoke. He too had been waiting, wondering, worrying. I gave him the good news, and heard an audible sigh of relief. "I'll call again later after I've seen your mom," I told him.

And off we went to the Neurosurgical ICU. It's painful beyond words to see your loved one in distress. The surgery was done, and I suppose in the big picture the worst was over and we were out of the woods. But seeing Al in a hospital bed, a huge bandage covering her head, monitors beeping, surrounding patients moaning, nurses bustling, is shocking and sobering, even to someone who has seen the inside of ICUs a thousand times before. Al would sleep, then wake with a start, stir and moan, then drift off again. Clearly she was in big pain. As promised, the dressing was tight and painful. By history Al had a bad reaction to anesthesia, emerging with nausea and vomiting. This time was no different. But vomiting can increase blood pressure, which can increase post-op bleeding, so the agony was magnified. She was given Zofran, a standard post-op antiemetic but wretched anyway, with the pain etched on her face like I'd never seen before. I knew she would never remember this torture; I would never forget it.

I stood by her bedside for hours, stroking her arm, and whatever other skin was exposed (not much). I doubted she was aware I was there, but maybe. Gladys sat by the bedside, tortured in a way only a mother can suffer when she sees her child in agony. I spoke with Pierce. He asked if he could talk to his mom, but that was obviously impossible. I reassured him she was okay, and would likely be able to speak with him the next day (I made that up; I had no idea, but wanted to give him encouragement). Al kept asking that the headdress be removed, or at least loosened. Dr. Trippi had warned us in advance and insisted that the bandage applied in the OR be left untouched, and only he would remove it when the time was right. Al received pain medication, which made her more nauseated, and the cycle continued. But the nurses advised us over and over that this was normal, and there was nothing to be done but stay the course. It would be better in a few hours.

We stayed as long as they allowed us, and then had to leave. Gladys and I were staying in a nearby hotel. We went back to our rooms, and then met for dinner in the hotel restaurant. I'm not a big drinker, but I drank that night, as did Gladys. We kept telling each other and ourselves that at least the surgery was over and Al would be fine. But the vision of our girl lying on that bed, moaning, retching, and suffering was hard to dismiss. Even Dewar's only slightly numbed our pain. I checked in with Pierce before bedtime. Our community of three remained steadfastly focused on the person who meant the most to us.

Chapter 28

We returned to the hospital in the a.m. to resume our vigil, not sure what we would find. Amazingly, Al was awake and alert, sitting semi-upright in bed. Of course she still had pain, but the nausea had largely subsided, and she could talk. For the first time in weeks I finally fully exhaled and believed she would be okay. After a light, semi-soft breakfast, she was taken from the ICU to the floor, where things were much quieter and more pleasant. Yes, she had a room with a view, and the food (most of which I ate) was not bad, but the amenities were mostly for the guests, not the patient. Al went bed- to-chair for a few hours, and the following day we took a brief walk in the hallway. She seemed exhausted, more so than I'd ever seen. That's what happens when someone opens up your head to muck around. The good news was that she was oriented, knew who and where we were, and what she had been through. The neurosurgery residents made rounds every day, always assuring us how well she was doing. On the third post-operative day Dr. Trippi arrived, removed the dressing as promised, and seemed very pleased with his handiwork. Al couldn't bear to look in the mirror but she was feeling well enough to take a quick shower then get back in bed. On the fourth day we went home, the nightmare behind us.

I spoke with Pierce daily, as did Al, and did my best to fend off her well-meaning friends, who couldn't wait to see their person. Al did a lot of sleeping for the first few days, then gradually resumed limited activities in the house. Her healing really progressed once Pierce came home for Christmas break. His presence and love were the best possible medicine. After a quiet New Year's (and our forty-second anniversary!), I returned to south Florida to figure out my next move. I had already submitted my ninety-day letter of resignation to my partners and was counting the days to be free of encumbrances and move on with the next chapter of my life.

A month later I closed my last patient chart, packed up my office, and ended twenty-five years of active medical practice. I procured a job with the in-office pharmacy company I had worked with before, to act as a spokesperson and medical director. Their headquarters were in Miramar, Florida, and I would remain based there but with an agreement that I would transition to full-time residence in New York over the next six months. I had mixed feelings about giving up patient care, which I had done with such commitment for so many years. I really had no appetite for trying to start all over in medical practice in New York. The rebuilding process is too long, and meant for younger men just starting out, not for someone my age who had been so actively and successfully engaged for so long. But clearly I couldn't move forward with Alana if I remained in Florida. Long distance relationships may be okay for young folks for brief periods, but not for us. I had no choice but to retire and move north, which is exactly what I did, with no regrets. Once out the door, I never looked back.

Chapter 29

The ensuing months were busy with change. My new job was fine for the time being. I did a fair amount of traveling across the country to work with other medical practices and meet with legislators debating the pros and cons of physician dispensing. But at least my free time was largely my own to spend where I wanted. I rented a small furnished apartment in town ("the birth canal" as I affectionately referred to it), ten minutes away from Alana, and used it sparingly when Pierce was home rather than stay in a hotel. I kept my apartment in Miami Lakes, and stayed there when I needed to be at headquarters for one reason or another. It was a bit of a schizophrenic existence, but it worked for me, at least temporarily. Al and I spent as much time together as possible, and connected through the Internet and phone when we were apart. Not a day went by when we didn't speak at least once, and the dream became more and more of a reality with each passing day. I met more and more of Al's friends and colleagues, and gradually came out of the shadows. Everyone knew about Martin's bad acts and bad behavior, and few people took his side. Al and I began to socialize as a couple with her friends, and I too struck up relationships with the guys who had previously befriended Martin. He was gradually displaced from his home, his son, his neighbors, his friends, and his community.

Pierce was amazing. Disappointed in his dad's behavior, empathizing with his mom and what she had gone through, he was open to connecting with me, and I appreciated and was grateful for his availability. We continued to share our interest in sports, but soon we branched out and began discussing his academics, classes, major, goals, and dreams. Pierce had a difficult time his college freshman year and I hold his high school responsible. Very little was expected of high school students. As long as there were no mass murders *a la* Columbine, the principal and teachers were happy. School was almost like a detention center, where the kids had to survive during the day, and if that happened, then the school day was a success. Everything else, including academics, took a back seat. *Au contraire*! These kids were placed in AP and Honors classes, given high passing grades with little to no work or learning, and afforded the false expectation that they were prepared for college. In actual fact, none of them was ready for college-level work, and Pierce suffered because he was let down by his high school. He expected more of the same, and was surprised (and unprepared) when his college expected true academic achievement. So when Pierce was failing and needed help, I was there. I committed myself to giving him the guidance and mentoring that he had never received. I approached him gingerly and offered my assistance, in whatever capacity he felt comfortable with. Initially he was reluctant, too macho to need or accept help. But I made myself available until he trusted me enough to engage me and utilize the talents that my dad had fostered in me—a strong work ethic and understanding of how to succeed academically. So we started discussing classes, assignments, required reading, quizzes, tests, and papers. Together we approached each class the way he should have been taught in high school, but never was. At the end of his first year he was placed on academic probation, and Martin wanted to yank him out of school, stick him back in his bedroom at home, and enroll him at a local community college. In my opinion nothing could have been worse, and Alana would not let that happen. She was committed to making Pierce academically and professionally successful, and she insisted that he stay in school at Indiana (which he loved) and move on with his life. If he needed help he would get it. Failing out of school would have crushed him and made him feel like a loser. In Alana's mind her son was too big to fail, that was not an option, and would never happen.

Pierce and I worked together his sophomore year, and his grades improved. I studied the syllabus for each class, and made a "To-Do" list for every day, for every class, helping him focus on each assignment one day at a time. We spoke on the phone every night to review the day's classes, discuss upcoming quizzes, tests, papers, and be prepared for the next day. A big university tends to lose track of its students. Advisors are less than perfect; professors and TA's are less than accessible. But I made myself available 24/7. Al and I took a vacation in Barcelona (with a six-hour time difference from Indiana). One evening I received a call at 2 a.m. (Barcelona time) that Pierce needed some guidance on a paper due the next day. From 2 a.m. to 5 a.m. we worked on that paper together until it was done, and he handed it in on time and received an "A." I was always there for him, no matter what, no matter when. He knew he could count on me.

To Pierce's credit, he was very easy to mentor. He realized he needed help, was open to every suggestion I made, paid attention and wanted to learn, and was always appreciative. He never gave me pushback or attitude on anything, and was willing to put in the time and effort to become a better student. This wasn't the first time I had assumed the mantle of teacher. I worked with my daughter throughout grade school and college, reviewing her work, reading her textbooks, editing her papers, and teaching her in the same patient style my father had employed. He was a role model in every way, and I tried to live in his image. Some people (most in fact) criticized the fact that I worked so closely with Jennifer. "How will she ever learn if you do all the work for her?" they asked. But I didn't see it that way. She needed help, so of course I was there. I did the work with her, not for her, and at the end of the day we were both better for it. By the time she graduated from college she had become a legitimate student, who could attain a high level of achievement academically on her own. But, interestingly enough, she always kept me involved; even as she went through two Masters Programs and subsequent employment, she asked me to read over her papers and assignments. Eventually I had no further comments or corrections; she didn't need me anymore. It was gratifying to me how well she had learned my lessons, and heartwarming that she wanted to maintain that connection even when she had become a bona fide teacher in her own right.

Pierce followed the same path. The more we collaborated the better he became. We worked harder his junior year, and his grades improved again. His senior year he had learned the lessons that my dad had taught me when I was growing up, and Pierce, on his own, made the Executive Dean's list both semesters. He no longer needed me, and

I couldn't have been happier or more proud had he been my own son. I had taught a man to fish…

By the time Thanksgiving rolled around, Pierce and I had laid the groundwork for a long and beautiful friendship. I was spending more and more time in New York, traveling for work as necessary, staying with Alana whenever I could. Although we weren't obvious about it, and I never slept in her house when Pierce was home, Alana didn't raise a dummy, and he got the idea when I would call him late at night from Al's house phone to discuss academics of one sort or another. Although we never lied and didn't try to hide anything, we also didn't rub his face in it, and respected his place in the nuclear family as paramount and sacrosanct.

As another Thanksgiving approached, we planned a family get-together with me, Al, Pierce, Gladys, Ruth, Karen, Dale, and their children. Nat had passed away years earlier. We decided to rendezvous and spend the long weekend in a large house on the eastern shore of the Outer Banks of North Carolina. I looked forward to seeing the old gang again, for the first time since I was a teenager. No one can avoid growing older, but everyone looked surprisingly recognizable…the years had been good to all of them. Sitting together was like going back in time, or forward and closing one more big circle. Al and I were on the fence about the sleeping arrangements. Of course we should sleep together, or should we? Pierce had not been confronted thus far, and we were concerned about his reaction. So we asked him, straight up, if our sharing a bedroom would be a problem for him in any way. And like the mensch that he is (must have been inherited from Milton), he gave us his blessing. One small step for me; one giant leap for our relationship. Despite awful weather the weekend was terrific. Knowing everyone from years ago seemed to smooth out any awkwardness, and I felt right at home with my new (old) family. I was one step closer to Point B.

Chapter 30

Al's divorce crept along, derailed repeatedly by Martin's sleazy attorney and his client's passive-aggressive behavior. Add to the mix Alana's laid-back (nearly hands-off) council, and it was the perfect storm. It seemed that Martin and both attorneys were in no rush to reach the finish line, as Al stewed in the juices of anger and disgust. Multiple court dates were set for various motions, for which Al had to appear, to the detriment of her patients and herself. Time and again the proceedings would be stayed and delayed, with apparently no progress being made. The temperature was rising to the boiling point. I didn't know how much more of this Al could stand and maintain her equilibrium and sanity.

A Love Poem for my Girl

From A to B we move as one,
Our hearts in step from sun to sun;
Two lives apart, but just begun,
A love delayed but never done.

From A to B the plot plays out,
The players drive, resolve devout;
The road is steep with mines throughout,
The goal is clear without a doubt.

From A to B the days crawl by,
As *sturm und drang* intensify;
When calm and peace appear nearby,
Another storm descends to cry.

FIRST LOVES ARE FOREVER

From A to B the journey's long,
The pain is deep, the hurt is strong;
But through it all is heard the song,
Of passion, hope, and love lifelong.

From A to B we make our way,
Until we see the light of day;
We veered off course and went astray,
But now our love is here to stay!

The universal Law of Entropy was operative here as well: the system tended to default to absolute chaos and disorder without the constant input of energy to maintain structure, and Al was the one driving the process, albeit painstakingly. Finally, at her wit's end, Al sought a second opinion from another attorney. I went with her to their first consultation. Ron Dallah was an extremely unusual individual, worthy of joining the ranks of *Readers' Digest*'s "Most Interesting People I Ever Met." His office was in a large, old converted house, the waiting area being the old living room. When we were ushered into his office, we met a late middle-aged man, somewhat disheveled, whose wrinkled sports jacket was thrown over a chair. His tie was loosened, his collar unbuttoned and he was smoking a cigarette. Legal files were piled everywhere—on the desk, on the chairs, on the floor—with no apparent order to anything. He was a litigator, and we had been referred to him in the event that this case eventually went to trial. I couldn't imagine him appearing before a judge and being presentable and professional. But he was a genius in his own right. He shook our hands, gestured for us to find room on the two empty chairs, and immediately began discussing the case. He didn't need to ask Alana any questions or refer to his notes. Apparently he had discussed the case with Al's attorney, was already very familiar with her situation, and must have had a photographic memory because he had all the facts at his fingertips. He was a no-nonsense guy who made no small talk and didn't waste any time. "The way I see it, this case needs a kick in the ass to push it forward," he started. "Everyone is fiddling around while you're burning, and that will continue without a catalyst, which, fortunately, is at our disposal. Do you know what that is?" Al and I were taken aback by his forthrightness, but relieved at the same time that finally someone was going to take charge and be her advocate. We had no idea what he was talking about, and our blank expressions answered his question. "We're going to file a $2 million civil suit for damages consequent to Martin's assault and battery on you. Criminal charges can still be filed as well, as the statute of limitations hasn't expired. That should scare the pants off him. Whether or not we will actually proceed with the civil suit is beside the point. The threats, both civil and criminal, should be enough to leverage him to get off his ass and come to the table. What do you think about that?" We didn't know what to think, but we liked his approach and drive, so different from what we had become accustomed to thus far. "Look, I just want to get this done," Al said. "There are no custody issues, and I've already given up hope of getting any alimony or assets beyond what I've put into this marriage. I don't want to ruin Martin's life or career by filing criminal charges. I just want this to be over and done with, and sooner rather than later."

"Okay, then. I think we're done here. I'll draw up the papers and send them to you for review before I send them to Martin's attorney. I doubt we'll have to go to trial on this, but if we do we'll brainstorm about it later. For now let's put their feet to the fire. I think they'll come around." And with that it was done—no more than fifteen minutes, and it seemed like there was finally a light at the end of this long, dark tunnel. We left and drove home feeling more optimistic than we had in months. The papers were served, with the intended effect. Martin agreed to the same terms that had been proposed months before, and it was finally over. The papers were signed, the QDROs submitted, and the final Divorce Decree issued. Yes, it was a great relief. But, once the dust had settled, the anger dissipated, and the frustration put to bed, there was sadness, too...sadness at the end of a twenty-five-year marriage...sadness at the failures and disappointments of a once-promising union...sadness at the lost and wasted years...sadness at the collateral damage wrought on Pierce. Change is never easy, even after years of suffering. At least now Al could start healing.

Chapter 31

The last major stumbling block gone, there was nothing else in our way. It was a no-brainer that I would fully invest and commit myself to consummating my lifelong dream. Now, finally, it seemed within my grasp, more real and attainable than ever before.

I resigned from my job, left "the womb," and moved to New York. When Pierce returned home from school after his sophomore year, Al asked him about my moving in. He expected the conversation, and, even before she had finished, he voiced his consent, even approval. By then he and I had become good buds, and he trusted that I was good for his mom and for him as well. It was a surprisingly easy transition for all of us, likely because Pierce had had enough time to get to know me, and to understand that I was no threat to his nuclear family but instead brought my own gifts to the table. Pierce maintained his own relationship with Martin, and we all respected each other's needs. We didn't badmouth Martin, and started building our own new nuclear family. In truth I spent a lot more time with Pierce than Martin did, and he grew increasingly familiar with me around, and comfortable with including me in his life. I did my best to reconstitute my relationship with Jennifer. She had moved from New York to Steve's hometown of Baltimore, and I made the trip as often as I could, as well as calling, texting, emailing, and Face Timing regularly. I made a conscientious effort not to resent Jennifer's past coolness and rejections, and to remain involved in her life going forward. She became pregnant, and, of course, I was there for the delivery and her recuperation. Same thing again a year later. Al was anxious to blend our life with Jennifer's, and finally we visited in Baltimore with far less drama than I had anticipated. Al, I, Jenn, Steve, and the infants took a Disney cruise, Al's first time really spending time with the kids, and we all had a special and memorable week together. Jenn with her husband and the two babies visited and stayed in our house, quite a circus but another important first step in that arena. Gladys met Jenn again, nearly thirty years since their last meeting at my wedding, when Jenn was an infant, now with infants of her own: the closure of another big circle. Pierce did his part admirably, welcoming Jenn *et al.* into his new extended family. Seeing everyone around the table, comfortable as though we had been doing this forever, drove home to me how far we had come.

The following spring, when Pierce came home from school, the New York Rangers were in the Stanley Cup playoffs for the first time in many years. Neither Pierce nor I are avid hockey fans but this was an historic event, and I bought tickets for us at Madison Square Garden. Just he and I, like father and son, at a hockey game at the Garden. I hadn't been to a hockey game in forty-three years, and here I was, back at the Garden watching the New York Rangers, just as I had done so long ago on that fateful New Year's Eve. Then I was with a teenage girl, at the start of my lifelong romance. And now here I was with her twenty-year-old son, at the same venue watching the same team. Another great circle had closed for me. It was a very special night.

On April 26, the anniversary of Alana and Brett 2.0, I took Al to see a revival on Broadway of *Cabaret*. I had last seen *Cabaret* the day Al and I split up, and had conscientiously avoided that show like the plague. The memories of that day, sitting in the darkened movie theater, desperately, frantically, and futilely reaching out to Al, left me feeling ill even so many years later. But it was time to face my Waterloo and move on. So we went to Broadway, the curtain rose, and once again we sat in a darkened theater as the familiar overture began. Once again I put my hand on Al's thigh, tentatively, fully aware of the significance to me of this moment and this gesture. Al slipped her hand into mine with a familiar, natural gentle squeeze. I doubt she appreciated the symbolic importance of that moment, but it certainly wasn't lost on me. This time there would be no confusion, or emptiness, or goodbye. The past was past, and it was time to adapt to this new, beautiful, and remarkable reality. Another big circle completed.

Epilogue

There was one final circle to close, one that had started forty-five years before. I had dinner with Pierce, and told him how much I cared about him, like the son I never had, and how much I loved his mom, that I was committed deeply to both of them, and wanted his blessing to marry Alana. If he weren't on board, it wouldn't work for any of us. Without hesitation he offered his full support and encouragement. He would give his mom away and be my best man. We both loved his mom, and we bonded on that connection.

Father's Day came and I visited Jenn in Baltimore. She gave me a card that read as follows:

"Dear Dad,
"I am so lucky to have a dad like you! You have always been there for me, and I am so appreciative. You are the best! I hope and try to be as good a parent as you are. Thanks for being a great role model!
"Love,
Jennifer"

I flew back home that evening to find a card on my pillow from Pierce:

"Dear Brett,
"You've always given me everything I need in life...good examples, wise words, and advice from the heart. THANK YOU. Where can I begin? For the last few years you have been an integral part of my success. While you are not my birth father, I consider you almost a co-father or Dad as you have been nothing but loving and helpful to me. I want to wish you a very Happy Father's Day. I also want to say that I am happy about your upcoming marriage to my mother, and welcome to the family.
"Love,

Pierce"

A wedding ring…the eternal symbol of never-ending love, with no starting point or ending point…the last circle. First loves *are* forever, and our love made the circle of our lives complete. I have been in love with Alana my entire adult life and still feel the same puppy love I had as a teenager. How great is that!

On December 31, 1969, I was set up on a blind date by my best friend. And when I got to her house to pick her up, sight unseen, I came face to face with a breathtakingly beautiful young woman. I fell in love right then and there, and I've been crazy in love with Alana ever since. I'm sure that God danced the day Al was born. And I hope to have this dance with my partner for the rest of my life. We all know that a dream is a wish the heart makes, and I have been lucky enough to live this dream for nearly half a century. We all make mistakes in our lives, have triumphs and defeats, successes and failures; but if everything I've ever done, right or wrong, has led me to this moment and this place, then I have no regrets. Every guy, in his heart of hearts, holds a special place for the one that got away. Alana was my one that got away. Second chances in life are few and far between. How amazing to get that second chance and make it count! Happiness is mighty hard to come by in this world and in this life, but Al has given me more than my fair share. Thanks to her, my cup runneth over. Thornton Wilder noted, "We can only be said to be alive in those moments when our hearts are conscious of our treasures." I have never been as alive as during these past few special years, days, minutes when my heart has been full of Alana. I have loved Alana from the first moment I saw her, and will love her until my last breath. How lucky am I??!!!! And, God willing, we will live happily ever after…